PRAISE FOR
Faery Tale

"Pike's enchanting journey into the land of the faeries is more than a memoir; it's an earnest search for what is real in a world that is filled with illusion, and what is true in a world that is filled with falsehood. It makes you smile, and it makes you think."

—Marianne Williamson

"With a distinctive voice and elegant prose, *Faery Tale* captures the hopefulness of childhood and the magic of believing."

—HarpersBazaar.com

"Pike's wit, wisdom, and wide-eyed view of the world will help you develop your own sense of traveler's whimsy."

—*Women's Adventure Magazine*

"*Faery Tale* has given people so much—permission to explore, to question, and most of all to believe—not just in faeries, but in themselves, in each other, and the rest of the world, both seen and unseen. We absolutely love this book."

—Brian and Wendy Froud, conceptual designers of *The Dark Crystal* and *Labyrinth*, authors of *Faeries*, *The Heart of Faerie Oracle*, and many bestselling books

"I really didn't want to be entranced. I didn't want to be enticed into yet another world of strange fantasy beings. But with Signe Pike's *Faery Tale*—I was. Honestly."

—David Yeadon, author of *At the Edge of Ireland*

"A beautiful book, wide open and shimmering, full of enchantment, pain, and sweetness. Reading Signe Pike is like sitting over tea or around a fire with your best girlfriend, listening to her wildest tales."

—Carolyn Turgeon, author of *Godmother*

"There's passion, excitement, and playfulness in Signe Pike's adventures as she plays with time and space and people . . . and words. If you allow yourself to hear what she hears and see what she sees, some of that magic will seep into your today."

—Rita Golden Gelman, author of *Tales of a Female Nomad* and *Female Nomad and Friends*

continued . . .

"Faery Tale is more than just a refreshing romp among waterfalls, searching for that shining, hidden race of spirit people. It's Signe Pike's answer to a grief-sick heart. Whether you use the words faith or faeries, God or magic, Pike's thirst for belief is both moving and inspiring."

—Jeanine Cummins, bestselling author of
A Rip in Heaven and The Outside Boy

"Anyone who's ever seen something curious out of the corner of their eye, heard the million whispers of trees, or checked under their bed looking for more than dust bunnies will thrill to Signe Pike's Faery Tale."

—Cathy Alter, author of Up for Renewal

"Youthful and sparkling with lots of pizzazz sums up Signe Pike's book Faery Tale. For questers of faeries and just plain magic in the world, you will have a most enjoyable read."

—Tanis Helliwell, author of Pilgrimage with the Leprechauns
and Summer with the Leprechauns

"Magical and beguiling, tender and heartbreaking, Faery Tale is the work of a fiercely talented new writer."

—Michael Taeckens, author of
Love Is a Four-Letter Word

"Sweet, unsettling, and wise . . . Faery Tale is a book for anyone who yearns to understand the invisible, by which I mean everything that turns out to be right in front of our noses."

—Jennifer Finney Boylan, author of She's Not There
and Falcon Quinn and the Black Mirror

"Finding happiness is an adventure that everyone should take, and Faery Tale inspires you to go on that journey."

—Lucy Danziger, editor in chief of Self and
author of New York Times bestseller
The Nine Rooms of Happiness

"Do fairies exist? There is a certain innocence in the belief that they do, and a certain magic in that innocence. With considerable humor and flair, Signe Pike asks us to return to the awe and innocence we knew as children. It's a worthwhile journey."

—Sharman Apt Russell, author of Standing in the Light

"Faery Tale is enchanting. I don't believe in tiny magical creatures, but I do believe in a good story, and Signe Pike has given us one of those."

—A. J. Jacobs, New York Times bestselling author of
The Year of Living Biblically

Faery Tale

One Woman's Search
for Enchantment
in a Modern World

Signe Pike

A PERIGEE BOOK

A PERIGEE BOOK
Published by the Penguin Group
Penguin Group (USA) Inc.
375 Hudson Street, New York, New York 10014, USA
Penguin Group (Canada), 90 Eglinton Avenue East, Suite 700, Toronto, Ontario M4P 2Y3, Canada
(a division of Pearson Penguin Canada Inc.)
Penguin Books Ltd., 80 Strand, London WC2R 0RL, England
Penguin Group Ireland, 25 St. Stephen's Green, Dublin 2, Ireland (a division of Penguin Books Ltd.)
Penguin Group (Australia), 250 Camberwell Road, Camberwell, Victoria 3124, Australia
(a division of Pearson Australia Group Pty. Ltd.)
Penguin Books India Pvt. Ltd., 11 Community Centre, Panchsheel Park, New Delhi—110 017, India
Penguin Group (NZ), 67 Apollo Drive, Rosedale, Auckland 0632, New Zealand
(a division of Pearson New Zealand Ltd.)
Penguin Books (South Africa) (Pty.) Ltd., 24 Sturdee Avenue, Rosebank, Johannesburg 2196,
South Africa
Penguin Books Ltd., Registered Offices: 80 Strand, London WC2R 0RL, England

While the author has made every effort to provide accurate telephone numbers and Internet addresses at the time of publication, neither the publisher nor the author assumes any responsibility for errors or for changes that occur after publication. Further, the publisher does not have any control over and does not assume any responsibility for author or third-party websites or their content.

PRINTING HISTORY
Perigee hardcover edition / November 2010
Perigee trade paperback edition / November 2011

Perigee trade paperback ISBN: 978-0-399-53700-4

The Library of Congress has cataloged the Perigee hardcover edition as follows:

Pike, Signe.
    Faery tale : one woman's search for enchantment in a modern world / Signe Pike.— 1st ed.
        p.   cm.
    "A Perigee book."
    Includes bibliographical references.
    ISBN 978-0-399-53617-5
    1. Fairies.   2. Pike, Signe—Travel.   I. Title.
    BF1552.P55   2010
    133.1'4—dc22   2010023602

PRINTED IN THE UNITED STATES OF AMERICA

10   9   8   7   6   5   4   3   2   1

This book describes the real experiences of real people. The author has disguised the identities of some, and in some instances created composite characters, but none of these changes has affected the truthfulness and accuracy of her story. Penguin is committed to publishing works of quality and integrity. In that spirit, we are proud to offer this book to our readers; however, the story, the experiences, and the words are the author's alone.

Most Perigee books are available at special quantity discounts for bulk purchases for sales promotions, premiums, fund-raising, or educational use. Special books, or book excerpts, can also be created to fit specific needs. For details, write: Special Markets, Penguin Group (USA) Inc., 375 Hudson Street, New York, New York 10014.

This book is dedicated to my father, Alan S. Pike,
the greatest storyteller of them all. He walks the woods still,
in the memories of all who loved him.

And to my mother, Linda M. Johanson—for her wit, wisdom,
and unconditional love. Thank you for helping me believe.

AUTHOR'S NOTE

All experiences in this book are factual. In some cases, names have been changed to protect those who wished to obscure their identity, at their request. As with any memoir, dialogue and conversations have been re-created where required—if only I had known to carry a tape recorder on me at all times at age eight, my job would have been so much easier!—with the essence and authenticity being of paramount importance. In some places, time has been condensed in the interests of narrative length and pacing.

Throughout the ages there have been a variety of spellings for the word faery. For the sake of consistency, I've chosen to use the spelling seen in Edmund Spenser's sixteenth-century work *The Faerie Queene*. However, in this book, faery represents the singular use, while faeries refers to the collective or plural.

If you find yourself yearning to embark on your own adventure on the very same faery trail, and I truly hope you do, I'd only ask a few things.

Please tread lightly and with respect. Leave each place better, in some way, than when you came, and most important, be prepared to see everything—not just the faeries—with a grateful and open heart.

Your Fellow Adventurer,

Signe L. Pike

When my father is gone I will remember his voice
deep and charged with music
like falling water
my ear to his chest
each word a smoky pearl
his thick weathered fingers
would trace his progress across each page . . .

—SIGNE PIKE

CONTENTS

Faery Tale

Part One

I WAKE up every morning with a sense of purpose: I am a tastemaker. As a book editor in New York City, I think about it constantly: What do people want to read? What will they want to read in one year? What about two? Mostly I acquire books that entertain women, that engulf them. When I think about the reader, I think about you. I buy books that I hope will make you smile, make you believe in the magic of love at first sight—I buy books that I hope will heal your heartbreak. I read all the time, big, thick manuscripts. It's part of the job. Each night I take home chunks of pages in an extra shoulder bag. I read on the treadmill. I read while I'm eating my take-out dinner. I read before bed, propped up with a pillow, my glasses slipping down toward the tip of my nose. I'm beginning to wonder if carrying all the paper is the reason my right shoulder feels like it's filled with marbles.

In the morning I get up and I flip on the radio. NPR and a cup of coffee. I'm always running late—I can never figure out what to wear.

I'm almost twenty-eight years old and I'm always trying to look older. I hate blazers and button-up shirts. I hate walking the streets of New York in high heels; the men gawk and the concrete wears them down until the metal pokes out the bottom. I lock the door and say goodbye to the cat, hoping for her that today, there will be pigeons.

I read on the subway, pressed up against a big man whose breath smells like rotten eggs and stale coffee. Next to me is a fat, middle-aged stockbroker, staring over the top of his *Wall Street Journal* at the gap between the taught fabric of a blond woman's skirt. He has a slim gold wedding band on, and I wonder if the woman who gave it to him believed in love at first sight.

The train shoots underground and the faces around me look ashen in the yellow lights. I close my eyes for a moment, and everything, the lights, the people, the rapidly receding subway walls, slips away and I am rushing out into the bright sunshine. I walk up a long dune that leads to the beach, where I can hear the sound of the ocean. It sounds like a sigh. I open my eyes to see people looking back.

Has she fallen asleep?

I focus again on the pages in front of me. I tell myself, *All I want is to heal some heartbreak*. Upstairs in the glass-walled building, I flick on the desk lamp in my third-floor interior office. Without windows, the fluorescent lights give me a raucous headache, and I'm not usually a headache kind of girl. Glancing at my calendar, my eyes find the familiar photo pinned near the top of my bulletin board.

Have you ever looked at a photo so much that you can't even truly see it anymore? I examine it again, trying to break it down into pieces. I see a man who looks far older than his sixty years, walking down a winding set of stone stairs. At his feet, a small brown-and-white dog is captured mid-movement, and he has turned to face the camera above him, his eyes gazing back at mine. The expression he wears is one of faux surprise: he hardly ever plays it straight for the camera. I know this, because neither do I. In a moment he'll call out, *Hey, you coming?*

I see a flash of fabric breeze past my office door.

"Good morning, Signe," my boss says.

"Good morning to you," I say brightly. I flick on my computer and glance at the persistent blinking light on my phone.

You have five new messages.

I reach for the phone with one hand and my coffee with the other. Lately, I think, my face hurts from smiling.

"Hi, this is Signe Pike, returning a call . . ."

I am going to heal your heartbreak, because I have no idea how to heal my own.

1

Once Upon a Time

Come away O human child!
To the waters and the wild
With a faery hand in hand,
For the world's more full of weeping
than you can understand.

—WILLIAM BUTLER YEATS, "THE STOLEN CHILD"

WHEN I was a little girl I believed in faeries as a matter of course. To say that I was obsessed with faeries wouldn't be the truth—I simply believed in them is all. When my father took me and my sister walking, I imagined there were faeries everywhere: flitting through the bushes, underneath the toadstools, balancing on the petals of the wildflowers that forced their way through the snowy winter crust in spring.

When you're little, it's perfectly acceptable to believe in Santa Claus, the Easter Bunny, the Tooth Fairy. Do you remember the incredible beauty of those days? Lying awake listening for the faint jingle of a sleigh bell, or peeking through your eyelashes, determined to spot a magical creature with every creak on the stairs? But inevitably, reality comes crashing in.

We forget how devastating it was to learn that the magical creatures from stories aren't real. We come to understand that growing up means getting older. And getting older means facing up to a certain amount of loss. When I suffered my loss, I woke up one morning with the undeniable feeling that it was high time we sat down to discuss: We live in a world where 9/11 happened. We're involved in wars in both Afghanistan and Iraq. There's genocide in Darfur. There are murders, and suicide bombings, and newspaper descriptions of human scalps hanging off restaurant light fixtures. There's the melting of the polar ice caps, hunger, starvation, and the killing of precious endangered species. I wanted to say to everyone, I don't know about you, but this is not the happily ever after I was hoping for.

Worse, somewhere along the line I had lost my faith in humanity.

I began to wonder where all our innocence goes and why we let it slip away, when the thing to do at a time like now is to fight it. How might it change the world if we could reclaim some of our magic? How would we look at one another, treat one another, if each of us recognized that inside every man or woman is a little boy or girl who loves popcorn, is still afraid of monsters under the bed, or believes that fairy tales really do come true? Maybe we would treat each other with more kindness, more carefully, more respectfully.

I wanted to find something of the beauty of myth that we've left behind, carry its shreds before us all, so we could acknowledge it, somehow bring it back to life. I wanted to delve back into that world that cradled us when we were young enough to still touch it, when trolls lived under creek bridges, faeries fluttered under mushroom caps, and the Tooth Fairy only came once you were truly sleeping. I wanted to see if enchantment was somehow still there, simply waiting to be reached. When I felt my loss, I realized that if I could do anything in this life, I wanted to travel the world, searching for those who were still awake in that old dreamtime, and listen to their stories—because I had to know that there were grown-ups out there who still believed that life could be magical.

And in that moment, I decided, *I am going to find the goddamn faeries.*

Do you think that sounds silly?

A better question might be, do you think I'm kidding? I am deadly serious. If it makes you feel more comfortable, when someone asks you what you're reading, you can say, "Oh, this? It's . . . an examination of the loss of myth in modern culture."

And it wouldn't be a lie.

I really don't believe in faeries. But I really *want* to. Not just for me, but for all of us. Because we are battered by adulthood—by taxes, by loss, by laundry, by nine to five, by deceit and distrust, by the crushing desire to be thin, wealthy, successful, popular, happy, in love. All the while, we are walking on a planet that is disintegrating around us.

I would have thought this challenge insurmountable, had I not already encountered one such believer. And she just so happened to live in my building.

I first met Raven Keyes not long after I moved into my first apartment in New York City. She and her husband, Michael, lived down the hall, and it wasn't long before Raven and I were on a first-name basis. With her blond, curly hair and playful blue eyes, Raven exuded a warm effervescence that melted most people into a puddle of bashful smiles and adoration. I was no exception. She was a former actress turned Reiki Master, a tradition with which I was completely unfamiliar. Reiki, she explained, was an alternative form of healing where the practitioner moves their hands over your body without touching you. I was intrigued but had to admit at the time that for me, the best type of therapy was found either on the opulent sofa of an Upper West Side shrink, or the lavender-infused massage table at Bliss Spa on Lexington Avenue.

However, our perfunctory chats in the hallway evolved into glasses of wine, and before I knew it, a year or two passed and I was volunteering my apartment for use as her Reiki studio during the days, in exchange for a small monthly fee.

Raven's clients were aplenty, and due to long hours at work my apartment was typically empty, so it worked out perfectly. In any case, it was Raven who first let me know that my apartment was filled, very certainly, I mean chockablock, with faeries. She just came right out and said it.

You can imagine my surprise.

After two years of living in that apartment, not once had I been woken in the middle of the night by a tiny ring of creatures dancing merrily around my ficus tree. Nor had I been pricked, prodded, tripped, or poked, and no imaginary toddler had ever wandered off into the depths of my dark closet only to find its way home again days later with a frightening, changeling-like look on its face. In other words, I had no evidence of an alien occupation of my remarkably modest living space.

Not to mention, everybody knows that faeries don't exist.

At least not anymore, a small voice from the depths of my imagination said.

Shut up, I told it. Because they don't. Every adult learns this. Yet I found I was moved by Raven's innocence, and I suspected I was somehow mourning the loss of mine.

With my neighbor's startling declaration that there were, in fact, faeries in my apartment, it really got me thinking.

In the last few centuries, the archeological community has made some fairly astonishing discoveries, many of which point to the alarming number of myths and legends that possess at least a thread of historical basis. One great example is Troy, the legendary city at the center of Homer's *Iliad*—now thought to have been located near the coast of northwest Turkey. Everyone thought that German archeologist Heinrich Schliemann was completely out of his gourd when he began to dig on a hill in the Turkish countryside in search of the mythical city. But by following geographical descriptions from the text, Schliemann's obsession was rewarded when he found layers upon layers of a city that had been burned, pummeled to destruction, and rebuilt (about thirteen times). Among many other conclusive discoveries, archeologists have since unearthed shards of pottery that date to the time period that

Homer's epic work so definitively describes, as well as urns that stored grains and foodstuffs—in such great quantity that historians concluded the inhabitants were trying to store up for years while their walled city was under siege.

In the sixteenth century, Queen Elizabeth paid ten thousand pounds—about the cost of an entire castle—for a unicorn horn. I kid you not. Ancient Greek natural-history writers had begun describing the creature as early as the fifth century BC. Soon thereafter, writings chronicling the discovery of this mythical beast could be found across the world, from China and Japan to the streets of Israel in texts from the Old Testament. By the sixteenth century, the existence of unicorns was so generally accepted that the average medieval person would have been able to speculate on a unicorn's height, weight, and even their diet. It wasn't until later in human history that we discovered these sea creatures called narwhals with proboscises that look suspiciously similar to the horn of the fabled unicorn. But by then, the hunting and trading of the narwhal tusk had allowed the myth of the unicorn to thrive for centuries. Queen Elizabeth would have been none too pleased, I imagine, to learn she'd forked over the price of a castle for a mere whale tusk.

As time passes and we continue to find empirical evidence of the various truths that underlie myth, I continue to wonder if the whole idea of faeries couldn't somehow fit into a similar equation.

That faeries were a part of my imaginary world growing up was not surprising. As a professor at Cornell University, my father nourished me and my older sister with Tolkien, C. S. Lewis, Roald Dahl, Lewis Carroll, and pretty much any other magical, swashbuckling tale from his meticulously alphabetized library (or the depths of his fanciful imagination). There were make-believe games and long walks in the woods, where he'd tell us tales of trolls, giants, brave Native Americans, or the Greek gods with their water nymphs and torrid affairs. At playtime I'd imagine I could talk to the faeries, that I could see them flying around our vegetable garden on little transparent wings. The highlight of my elementary after-school career was playing Wendy in *Peter Pan*, sporting a bright blue flannel nightgown my mother bought me at Woolworths. I was devastated that Tinker Bell could despise me.

Our family wasn't particularly religious in any traditional sense, which is probably why, as an adult, I didn't feel so weird taking an interest in the truth behind the existence of magical beings. In fact, for me, "religion" boiled down to conversations with God in the bathroom.

It sounds bizarre, I'm sure, but I began to associate God and bathrooms when I was in third and fourth grades, in the years when my parents were constantly arguing, or when my father, beet red on a Tuesday morning, yelled at me for leaving my shoes in the middle of the living-room floor or for not drinking all of my orange juice. In those days, I was in tears most mornings before breakfast. I don't delight in describing my father this way; he was an exceptional man. He could quote Chaucer at length in Middle English. He taught us to swim, ski, hike, rock climb, survive in the wilderness. But my father possessed a deep-seated frustration that seemed to eat at him. Disappointment simmered in a vat somewhere beneath his skin until it erupted explosively in terrible bouts of anger. More than anything, Alan Pike wanted to be a great American novelist. Stories lived in him—hauntingly broken tales about Tibetan Longumpas and lone explorers, and he wove them aloud from time to time for friends over a glass of whiskey. But he never put a single word to paper. He couldn't.

When you have a gift and you stifle it, it will consume you. My father tried to force it down by smoking marijuana, by drinking double Gibsons with extra onions, you know, just enough to take the edge off. And at age forty-eight, he found himself with a wife who loved him but could no longer live with him and a family coming apart at the seams. While my sister gracefully tiptoed around his moods, I was too oblivious (or defiant) to take him seriously. As a result, I bore the brunt of his fury.

In third grade, during Mr. Yale's class, I would requisition the hall

pass and retreat to the bathrooms, which during class time, were blissful, spacious, private. There, I didn't have to pretend to be a happy,
normal kid. I could sit and, for just a few moments, allow myself to feel
the way I was feeling. It was there, next to the discarded paper towels
and bits of unused toilet paper, that I could ask for what I really wanted
and feel that someone, or *something*, might actually be able to hear me.
Since then, the bathroom has been my own personal church of sorts.
When most women retreat to the ladies' room to powder their nose, I
retreat for a spiritual tune-up.

When I began to look at my life in a different way, I wondered how
many people, like me, needed to seek God in the bathroom. The world
is falling apart, and outside the playground is splintered and dark.
Where can we go in our daily lives to feel the things we need to feel?
To feel the soothing balm of faith? To feel loved? Safe? Happy? What
about hopeful?

More important, what has happened to the magic we were surrounded by as children? The loss of our magic, our innocence, is the
worst sort of emotional deforestation. My biggest fear is that if we continue to stifle this loss, half the people on the planet will forget what
their forest even looked like in the first place.

The more I thought about it, the more I wondered where our modern culture had left faeries today. If they were ever "here," where did they
go, and why did they leave us? As I began looking closer, I found that
faeries still had a huge following—believers—all over the world. Perhaps these believers would be able to help *me* believe once more. Perhaps, with their help, I could even find a faery, sit it down for some
nectar or something, and ask, "Where did we all go wrong?" The heavi-
ness I'd felt on my heart began to lighten.

And my adventure was just about to begin.

2

Hunting Trolls in Paradise

Yes, faeries do still appear to humans—
often, in fact, especially if one learns the
best way to seek them out.
—EDAIN MCCOY, *A WITCH'S GUIDE TO FAERY FOLK*

I WAS sitting on a plane bound for Cancún, Mexico, my mind a fluttering mess.

Are the power outlets the same in Mexico? I don't speak enough Spanish. I really shouldn't have taken this time off from work. Does this seat recline? Ooh! My own little TV! Do the pilots for JetBlue receive the same training as the pilots for regular airlines? Or do the affordable prices signal some sort of half-baked pilot training?

Soon, I thought, *we could all be dead.*

If we all died, the chain of blame would regretfully run back to my poor friend Raven, who'd organized this trip. When she asked if I would be interested in going south of Playa del Carmen to participate in a week of yoga and meditation with a group of women, my sense of adventure kicked in and I couldn't say no.

But even more than time to bliss out on the beach, I had faeries on my mind. In doing some research I'd discovered there was a type of faery rumored to live in the ancient temples of Mexico—essentially "cousins" to the Celtic faeries—called Los Aluxes (pronounced *al-oosh-us*). I told myself this could be an interesting experiment. I'd do a little poking around while there, and if I found there was something to this faery nonsense, I'd go for it: try to make a formal, once-in-a-lifetime adventure of this faery search. Mexico could be a great place to begin. After all, if I could find evidence of faeries in Mexico, the least likely of places, couldn't I find them anywhere? I decided to leave the fate of my adventure up to the locals. Perhaps I'd find someone who could help lift the shroud of mystery that surrounded these strange little creatures.

I leaned back in my seat, hoping to relax, but the memory was too fresh. No sooner had I closed my eyes than I was transported back to the worst plane ride of my life. For one shockingly painful moment I was there all over again, on a flight from JFK in New York City to Ithaca, New York.

Outside it was dreary midwinter, and the tarmac was spotted with piles of black New York City slush. I had quietly asked the stewardess if I might move to sit by myself in an empty row. I couldn't stand to be near another human being, and despite how hard I was trying, I couldn't get my body to stop shaking—it was coming from the inside out. It was exactly one week before my father's sixty-sixth birthday, and instead of heading home to surprise him, I was going home to bury him.

I took a deep breath and managed to rein in the memory, along with the tears that threatened to slip out from underneath my dark sunglasses. Tilting my seat back and reclosing my eyes, I tried to get some rest.

~~~~~~

"Are we there yet!?" I yelled to be heard over the rushing air coming in from the windows. We'd been driving in the old Volvo for nearly seven hours. In the midsummer heat, my skinny eight-year-old legs were glued firmly to the vinyl seat. My bangs were sticking to my forehead. We had to be getting close. I could almost smell the salt air of the New Jersey shore.

"I swear to God. You girls ask me that one more time and we will pull. This. Car. Right. Over," my mother warned. My mom was suitably scary, but Kirsten and I shrugged. We were death-defying in our excitement.

"We'll be there soon enough, Sig," said my father. With one hairy, tanned hand guiding the wheel, he glanced at me in the rearview. Our eyes met and he flashed a grin, giving me a quick eyebrow raise above his aviators.

The moment we arrived at the rental house, we threw down our bags, changed into our swimsuits, and raced to the beach. Sleek in her black swimsuit, my mother settled onto the blanket as Kirsten, Dad, and I ran toward the water. In his navy blue Speedo my dad reminded me of James Bond, embarking on a secret mission into the midnight waters of the Caribbean. He used to be a frogman in the Navy, and even though he preferred to discuss books and philosophy, I guess they thought he was really good at what he did—the Navy SEALs tried to recruit him after he completed his officer certification training. He liked to tell Kirsten and me how it seemed like a great idea at the time. He was just about to accept, to become a real Navy SEAL, when he saw one of his buddies back from SEALs training. His nose was broken, Dad told us, spread all over his face. He said thanks, but no thanks.

I marveled at the look of my bare feet on real sand as we edged into the surf. Standing side by side with Kirsten, our toes greeted the water and it was freezing cold. I closed my eyes for a second to listen to the crashing of the waves against the shore, wanting this moment to last forever. I watched my father as he waded in, and in a moment he was gone, only to resurface several yards away with a loud "Whoop!" and a sputtering of water.

"Come on, girls! The water's beautiful!"

We glanced at each other warily, our arms and legs now covered with goose bumps in the cool afternoon breeze. Suddenly a swim didn't feel like the best idea.

"Dad! It's freezing!" Kirsten shouted.

"Yeah, it's too coooold!" I whined. He waded back over to us, taking a solid beating from a large wall of water in the process. As he leaned in close I could see his eyes were red from opening them underwater.

"You've just got to regulate the thermostat, girls. Take a little water, and get your wrists and the back of your neck wet . . ." He demonstrated, making splashing himself look like the most appealing endeavor in the world. "*Wooh!* Now you try it."

We squatted clumsily, sticking our wrists under the water. But it was no use. Surely this water was subzero. Eventually, after much deliberation, just as we sensed he was about to abandon us, his patience run dry, we decided to dunk under at the count of three. We dunked, and as I came up, I was hit full-force in the face by an incoming wave. Water rushed into my nose and mouth and I was swept off my feet. Tossed like a doll, I somersaulted over and over. I couldn't tell which way was up and my lungs were burning. I panicked. Soon my mouth would open without my permission, just to get some air. But as I began to spasm and choke, I felt a grip on my arm so tight it hurt, jerking me up through the water, and I surfaced, frantic and coughing. My eyes and nose were stinging. When I looked, I could see we were still out on the water, past the breaking point of the waves. My father's strong hands were buoying me, and Kirsten was looking on, wide-eyed.

"You're okay, huh, puppy?"

The water plastered his dark hair to his head, and he looked at me intently, assessing any potential damage—emotional or otherwise—brought by this, my first near-drowning experience. I could feel my face crumble. I burst into tears.

"I wanna go in! I wanna go to the blanket!" I wailed, snot bubbling from my nose.

"Okay, okay, okay," he sighed. I knew I had let him down. I knew he wanted me to be tough. It was our first swim of vacation and I ruined it. But I wanted my mom. My throat and nose burned from the salt water. I'd had enough.

He gestured and I climbed onto his back, wrapping my arms and legs around him like a petrified monkey. Kicking his legs smoothly, he reached the point where the waves were crashing and I reached around his neck to plug my nose, just in case. But we moved effortlessly through them, me hanging tight, his feet planting firmly in the sand. Up on the blanket my mother wrapped me in a towel and poured us ice-cold lemonade iced tea from a battered thermos. We sat quietly, the four of us. I wanted to tell my dad thank you, or I'm sorry. I turned, but his eyes were lost—he was seated, still as a Tibetan monk, gazing fixedly out over the ocean.

~~~~~~

"Ladies and gentlemen, we are now beginning our descent into Cancún." Jolted awake, I looked out the window to see crystal blue water dappled with the shadows cast from a few hovering clouds. As we moved inward over the continent, nothing but miles and miles of dark green jungle met the eye, cut here and there by stretches of sandy roads that dead-ended like an afterthought in the middle of the brush.

It was a straight shot down Highway 307 from the tourist trap that is Cancún to the New Age tourist trap that is Tulum. As we tumbled with our yoga mats and luggage into a waiting van, I felt a little nervous. Mexico had been the last place I'd expected to discover a cultural belief in faeries. But everything had seemed to come together with an odd synchronicity.

Out of curiosity I'd just begun reading up on faery lore from various countries. I was astonished to learn that from Japan to New Zealand, nearly every culture in the world believed in one type of faery or an-other. In Russia there were rumors of *Domoviyr*—male earth faeries that lived side by side with humans in their homes. Or the *Rusalki*—lovely female water faeries found in the shallow pools of Russia's forests. Polish folklore told of *Poleviks*, magical creatures that aided in the growing and harvesting of agriculture. Of course England, Scotland, and Ireland were just roiling in faery tales. The strongest lore came from Ireland and its famous ancient historical account, *The Book of Invasions*, which described a race of magical beings called the Tuatha Dé Danann, who legend told were among the original conquerors of Ireland. It struck me as inter-esting, because I'd read elsewhere that the phrase *Tuatha Dé Danann* was now synonymous with *faeries* in modern Ireland. And I found that in Mexico, there were stories of encounters with Los Aluxes, or "the little people."

The trouble was, searching for stories about Los Aluxes and actually encountering one were two very different things. How did one go about "finding" a faery anyway? Local wisdom dictated that Aluxes were tra-ditionally spotted in the temples of the ancient Mayans; and that if you encountered one, you'd recognize it because they look like small children, or sometimes like little gnomes. But let me just say: if I were to encounter a gnomelike "otherworldly being" while rooting around in an ancient Mexican temple, I would absolutely freak out and run screaming into the Mexican jungle, jaguars and poisonous snakes be damned.

This might be a good time to come clean: I am actually petrified of the paranormal. I'm convinced the second-floor hallway of my apart-ment building is haunted. Why else would I get a creepy, forbidding feeling when I round the second flight of stairs on my way to work *every single morning?* When my cat stares off into a corner of the bedroom I can instantly feel the hair on the back of my neck begin to rise. I don't like Ouija boards, séances, or cemeteries. I have no desire to see dead people, get touched by the hand of God, or attend a taped session of *Crossing Over* with *John Edward*. Yet here I was headed to Tulum, Mexico, to meditate—or *something*—in the ancient temples of the Mayans. I didn't have a plan. I just knew that I had to go.

Nearly three hours later the van reached the town's outer limits. I watched the road go quickly from paved to dirt as we passed a wild outcropping of rocks and open ocean, where dozens of brown-and-white pelicans were swooping at fish or waddling along the rocky shore. The first view of turquoise water was breathtaking, but I was anxious to arrive at Casa Violeta, where I could unload my bags and get a little downtime before dinner. At long last a purple picket fence came into view, and we pulled into the sandy driveway of our accommodation for the week. I felt my jaw slacken as I caught sight of the mistress of the inn, bounding gracefully toward the van as though she'd been awaiting our arrival all afternoon. Petite and darkly tanned, Karla had beautiful, large brown eyes and a pearly white, celebrity smile. Her long brown hair was touched with caramel highlights, and following close at her heel was a sandy Jack Russell terrier adorned with a collar of red Mexican beads.

"Welcome, welcome!" she cried. Karla caught each of us in her arms, giving us a warm embrace and a kiss on the cheek before leading us through a courtyard bursting with flowering bougainvillea and softly swaying palms. Stepping into my cabana, I let out a breath—draped in a cloud of gauzy white mosquito netting, my king-sized bed faced the ocean. The windows were cast open, and a gust of sea wind met my face. Breathing in the sweet salt off the water, I sank into my new surroundings. Paradise. I dropped my things and rushed out to the beach to relax on the sand and soak up some late afternoon sun.

Night greeted us with a million sparkling stars. The Milky Way arched like a midnight rainbow across the blue black sky—the Pleiades glittered, and the Big Dipper scooped down toward the water of a darkened ocean. There were clouds over the jungle, and toward the west, heat lightning flashed with a vengeance. The presence of the natural world in Tulum was so wild, you felt as though it could sweep you from your feet in a whisper of breath.

But later that night, as I squirmed under the mosquito netting in my muggy room, homesickness began to creep in. I couldn't open the windows because wind would blow the netting, the purpose of which was to protect me from the scorpions that nested in the thatched roof (it had looked so *quaint* in daylight) over my head, not to mention whatever creature was making that fluttering, squeaking noise. So I lay there sweltering, missing my boyfriend, Eric, horribly. He would investigate the squeaking. He would find some way to rig the netting so we could sleep in blissful, cool slumber. I was too petrified to move. Aside from being rescued, I wanted to share the experience of this place: the stars, the pelicans, the torrid tossing of the waves—because I knew he would instantly understand the natural "magic" of Tulum. I was dismayed by the fact that his absence made me feel like I was experiencing Mexico as half a person—which was perhaps why I was so adamant about coming here without him in the first place.

Without really noticing it, I had become used to waking up to find him there next to me. I was sure if I loved him too much, he'd stop loving me. In that way I am a consummate Scandinavian. *Why buy the cow when you can get the milk for free? Men like a challenge.* But sometimes, in those moments when he was sleeping and I was awake, I loved him so much that my chest clutched and I could hardly breathe.

One particular morning a few weeks ago, when the cat woke me up and sleep failed to find me again, I was content to admire his perfect triangle of a nose, his lips, his dark lashes against the flush of his sleeping face.

He must have felt my close scrutiny, somewhere in his depth of slumber, because he turned his face to the wall. It was then that I saw it. An unmistakably gray hair. I reached out and gently tugged it to make sure it was really attached to my twenty-eight-year-old boyfriend's head. It was. When it hit me, I couldn't help it—I started to cry.

I have come to a horrible realization since losing my father: we are here for however long our lives turn out to be. And in one lifetime, you will lose *every single person you love*. You will watch every single person you love die.

It is the saddest realization of life. I think about my mother; my sister, Kirsten; my aunt Micki; my uncle Ron; Eric. The incredible ache of it doesn't cease—not until you're gone, too. And maybe not then, either. Sometimes I wonder how we can have any happiness, with this huge elephant of loss lurking in the corner of the room. Eric and I were in love, and maybe someday we'd get married and have years and years of life together—the things we always talked about: growing our own tomatoes and sugar snap peas, grilling dinner outside, taking walks together on the beach, reading, writing, laughing, traveling, walking our dog, maybe raising some kids . . . and then one of us will pass away. And instead of those perfect Saturday mornings cuddling close, feet touching, curves snuggled in sleep, one of us will be sleeping alone. Feeling the never-ending burn of losing what we once had.

Am I the only person haunted by this? If other people recognize it, how can they bear to go on? How can they just walk down the street to buy bread or catch a movie? Maybe those people can say, you've only got this one chance, so forget about tomorrow and live life to the fullest!

Most of the time, I think that, too. I try to come to terms with the reality of it, push it away, and think, "Mmm . . . what should we have for breakfast?" And luckily, there are so many phenomenal distractions: the beauty of nature, good food, friends, family, great architecture, music, art, entertainment, animals, and twinkling white Christmas lights.

But I realized, when I saw that first errant gray hair, that my favorite distraction was there next to me, breathing softly, his feet twitching occasionally, and I was content to enjoy that soft limbo—snuggle myself against him, waiting for him to stir, for us to begin, for today. To move through our time with appreciation, with joy, with excitement, being close and loving, and falling into bed when it's all over, to dream our dreams and wake up again to mumble, "I had the craziest dream last night . . ."

The next morning I woke when sun struck my pillow. Outside the ocean was calling. I pulled on my swimsuit and waded in, letting the warm, salty water lap at my legs. I am used to the cool green, fish-filled waters of Ithaca. The ocean . . . ancient, powerful . . . well, it scared me. There were jellyfish to be considered. Stingrays with barbed tails. Sharks. Seaweed. Murderous currents. But I was so sick and tired of living in fear. I vowed that this trip would be a new beginning for me. No more would fear cripple me. I was here for seven days, staying in a picturesque cabana by the sea—a situation clearly requiring morning swims in the ocean. I sucked in my breath, mentally crossed my fingers, and plunged into the sandy-bottomed blue.

Over breakfast, I spoke with Karla about organizing a group trip to the Tulum ruins. When she suggested hiring a tour guide who could tell me more about the faery lore surrounding Los Aluxes, I cringed. I could just hear myself: "Hey, I've got a question: Ever spot any gnomelike creatures while you're touring people around? Are you *sure*? You'd recognize them because they're *very* little . . ." We spent the day doing meditation workshops and yoga, and I fell exhausted into bed that night, deep into the dreamless sleep of the well exercised.

The next morning there were three white taxis waiting for us in the driveway, each meticulously clean and equipped with black sunshades that pulled down over the back windows—presumably to keep the blazing sun off our already-burning white flesh.

The ruins were easy to find because after about a mile the road just ended. Outside insects hummed and a cacophony of birds called from the edges of the jungle. We purchased our tickets and commissioned the services of an Oakley-clad tour guide named Luis. He smelled clean and spicy, and his English was proficient but clipped. He had a rather endearing habit of pursing his lips and saying, "Mmm . . . uh-huh!" before or after he concluded any sentence. Like, "Mmm . . . Let's head this way now, mmm . . . uh-huh!" He'd clearly guided this tour about four thousand times too many. And Luis was obviously a man in demand because his mobile rang. Constantly. Let me tell you, there's nothing quite like salsa tones blasting from a cell phone to make you feel at home in an ancient wonder.

We left the pebbled trail, ducked through a portal in the stone wall, and emerged on what could only be described as the other side of the looking glass. In front of us lay a grassy expanse that sprouted with tall bursts of palm trees. Stunningly intact stone buildings lined the edge of a cliff, looking more like sun-bleached bone in the bright sun. Beyond the cliff's edge I could see the glittering of the ocean. We walked the grounds as Luis poured rich Mayan history and customs into our ears— things I hadn't read in books.

It was then that I learned with great dismay that visitors were no longer allowed inside the buildings, which of course ruined my plan.

How am I supposed to encounter Los Aluxes now, Luis?

As I felt the tour winding down, I forced myself to swallow my timidity and ask Luis straight up what he might know about the little people. My first attempt at faery journalism was feeble at best. But behind his Oakleys Luis looked momentarily surprised. He studied me a moment. "Mmm . . . Aluxes, uh-huh, yes, I know them." I couldn't believe my luck.

"I don't know where they came from," he continued, "but if locals want to live somewhere virgin, they have to leave an offering, because they're all over. They're everywhere. So if we don't do that, they're not going to let us build there. So it's like little persons, and yeah, they're very, very small. So yes. That's the, uh . . . details about them."

"And people still believe in them, to this day?"

"Oh, yes. They do." He nodded seriously.

"What about you?" I pressed. "Do you think they exist?"

He didn't miss a beat. "Oh, yes. They exist, for sure. You can buy them, actually. There are places, maybe at the market. Not here, you'd have to go more inland, where the Mayan places are. But there you can buy them and feed them."

My heart sank. "You can buy them and feed them?" *Luis, I may be a pasty tourist, but I will not be mocked!*

But Luis laughed. Reaching up to lower his sunglasses, I saw his brown eyes were puzzled and full of humor. "Uh-huh, it's kind of weird that you're asking, but yes! If you buy one, they can help you to take care of your home. But if you're not a good person, they're not going to be a good person to you. They'd always be bothering you, and if you sleep in a hammock, they'll always be poking you while you are trying to sleep."

"So . . ." I lowered my voice. "Have you ever seen one?"

"No, no, I've never seen one." He shook his head. "But I've heard lots of stories. People see them all the time."

"So, some people can see them, and others can't." I tried to make sense of this. "Do you think it'd be easier maybe for Mayans to see them?"

He thought on this. "Ah, yes. For Mayans it would be very easier, I think."

This was getting perplexing. "But if you can't see them, and you were to . . . purchase one, wouldn't you be buying it completely on faith?"

"Well," he considered this, lifting one finger as if to make a point. "Los Aluxes only come out at night. So if you bought one, it wouldn't be around in the daytime." He silenced his ringing cell phone and raised his eyebrows at me. "So no, you wouldn't see it."

Ah . . . I see?

My conversation with Luis left me befuddled. His answers seemed so casual, so authentic, and he'd had such an unexpected response. Tour over, I made my way down a steep set of stairs that led to the beach. Wouldn't it be crazy if this place was just crawling with these little invisible creatures? Smiling, I couldn't help but peek into the dark crags of the cliff as I made my descent. Could Aluxes be hiding in the cave's inky depths? Suddenly I saw a rustling in the blackness toward the back wall of the cave, and gasped. A pair of sinister, beady eyes were staring back at me. Squinting harder, I nearly doubled over with laughter as my faery waddled into daylight: it was an iguana. The other tourists spotted him, and in an instant fifty cameras were flashing as he beat a hasty retreat back to safety.

Grinning to myself, I made a mental note to move to Tulum immediately and begin selling Aluxes to tourists at exorbitant prices. *No, you see, they only come out at night! No, you have to be asleep. Like Santa Claus! Or the Tooth Fairy! And then they come out! Yup, you'll love it. You still can't see it? Just be patient. And, uh . . . try not to sleep in a hammock. That'll be six hundred pesos, please.*

That night I woke with my bladder near bursting. I knew a visit to the bathroom was unavoidable, but I was filled with dread. You see, Casa Violeta shut their generators off at eleven p.m., so you couldn't just flip on the light. Sure, I love the quasi-religious sanctity of bathrooms. I just *hate* going to the bathroom by myself at night. Especially in dark, foreign, spooky places. So much so that once, while camping, when I was beyond old enough to know better, I wet the bed because Kirsten wouldn't get up to go with me. Yes, I would rather *sleep in my own urine* than cross a scorpion-and-bat-infested cabana with no electricity at night to pee with the geckos in an open-air bathroom. But remembering my oath of courage, I reached for my penlight, pushed the mosquito netting aside, and scurried into the bathroom, repeating, *I'm not scared. I'm not scared. I am so not scared* . . . all the way to the toilet.

As I sat there in the dark, the palm fronds brushing the screen overhead, I got the strangest feeling that I wasn't alone.

I shone my penlight in the doorway, but there was nothing there. Still, every receptor in my body tingled. I could *feel* something. I looked away for a moment. When I looked back, it was there: a short, long-haired, troll-like man, with wild, brown, matted hair. His eyes were ovals of chocolate brown, his face was leathery and creased with wrinkles. His shoulders were hunched forward, his arms straight down at his sides, his chin thrust out, and he was staring at me.

I blinked hard. He was gone. Or had I even seen him in the first place? I weighed my options. I could grab my ladies' razor and face it head-on, just in case it had somehow scurried off into my bedroom. I could shatter the quiet Mexican night and yell for Karla or Raven, which was pretty tempting. Or I could realize that it was just my overactive imagination playing tricks on me. Bolstered by common sense, I washed my hands and, with a tight grip on my penlight, ran quickly back to bed, plunging my feet under the covers and tucking the mosquito netting tight under the mattress.

But no sooner had I closed my eyes than I saw it again. This time it was standing just inches from my face on the other side of the mosquito netting, staring. My eyes shot open. Nothing there. I closed my eyes, this time squeezing them tightly. Again, the image popped back into my head. *Okay, I can handle this.* I don't know what possessed me, but I knew that if I was serious about getting to the bottom of this question about faeries, I had better, imagination or not, try to talk to it.

Okay, little guy . . . I began. *Uh, I'm really glad that you're here! But* . . . *you know what? Tonight just isn't the best for me. 'Cause, God! I am so tired! And right now, I just really need to sleep. So* . . . *if you could just please leave me alone so I could go back to sleep, that would be great.* Then I added for good measure, *But, if you want to come back tomorrow, we can talk then, okay? Okay.* Now there was nothing to do but pull the covers over my head and wait for the sun to rise. I was certainly too shaken up to even fantasize about falling back asleep.

I did my best to push the events of the previous night from my mind as Karla and I discussed my search over a bowl of papaya the next morning. She recommended I visit a hotel up the beach, closer to the ruins, called the Diamante K.

"The Diamante K is full of Aluxes," Karla said, wide-eyed. "Just go there and ask the bartender. They speak English and they'll tell you—people see them there all the time." As up front as Karla assured me I could be, the amateur faery sleuth in me knew this was clearly an undercover job. I mean, really. You can't just show up at a hotel bar and start asking around about faeries. So I recruited my new friend Cheri from the group, and after our morning meditation let out, we hopped into a taxi to lunch at the Diamante K. As we made our way down the bumpy dirt road, I couldn't help but open up about my late night, possibly pee-induced hallucination.

"I don't know, Signe." Cheri frowned. "That completely gives me goose bumps . . . how do you know you weren't really seeing it? You know, these things, if they are real, maybe they don't exist in the same way we do, on this plane. Maybe the only way we can see them is by somehow using our imaginations. But that wouldn't make them any less real in their world."

"Okay," I conceded. "But if that were the case, then what's the difference between imagination and reality?"

"Perspective." She smiled.

Who knows, maybe she had a point.

We pulled up to the hotel and made our way down a sandy path to the open-air bar, where we settled in. *Dos Coronas, por favor.* The bartender gave us a once-over and nodded. The restaurant was open to the elements, and dozens of ornate mobiles—crafted from driftwood, shells, coral, and fishing wire—swayed in the wind. Also swinging were dozens of winged female figures, like those found on the prows of old whaling ships. Arrayed in hand-painted hues of purple, green, hibiscus, or sea-glass blue, they seemed to float in the ocean breeze. By the kitchen a waitress chatted with a line cook in Spanish, and behind us on the gently sloping beach, sedate hotel guests lounged in cushioned chairs or suspended hammocks. The atmosphere of the place was utterly tranquil. The bartender reappeared with two deliciously frosty beers.

"Here you go, guys," he said in flawless English.

Cheri and I exchanged a subtle look of surprise.

Not only was our bartender fluent in English but he sounded like a Californian surfer. His name was Rally, we learned over lunch, and he was born in Guadalajara, Mexico, but grew up in Santa Barbara. Now he was back in Mexico working the bar at the Diamante K while his girlfriend worked nights as an exotic dancer in a nearby city.

Three beers and a shot of tequila later, I decided to let Rally in on the real purpose of my visit to the Diamante K hotel. He nearly tripped over himself behind the bar.

"What?!" he exclaimed. "You heard about them? That is some crazy shit!" Recovering, he lowered his voice a bit and leaned in, excited.

"All right, here's the thing about them, the Alux."

I noticed that he called them simply "Aloosh"—rather than "Los Alooshus." A nickname for a faery?

"They're supposedly like trolls," he explained. "They're little, hairy, kinda ugly, and they're like . . . this tall." He raised his hand to the height of a three-year-old child.

"Have you ever seen one?" asked Cheri.

"Uh, I think so. See, that's the thing. They're . . . spirits."

"Really?" I asked.

"Yeah," he replied, getting more animated. "Some of them are nice, some are mean. But it all depends on you . . . and your vibe. If you have a good vibe, while you sleep, they'll sleep with you. But if you have a bad vibe, while you sleep, they'll do really bad things to you. Especially the female Aluxes." This was the first I'd heard about gender. The Mexicans believed there were male and female Alux?

"If you're a guy," Rally explained, "the females kind of . . . like you. They'll start doing mean things to you so you'll pay attention to them. But some of them, they seem to get jealous or something. If you have a girlfriend, or if you don't pay attention to them, you know, they might kill you."

"Kill you?!" Cheri and I exclaimed in unison.

"Yeah. But you won't believe it until you hear it from everybody else. There have been a few times where I thought I'd seen one, but I wasn't sure. I'd tell people here, and they'd be like, yeah, they're Aluxes."

"So," I asked, "do you think they might have some special tie to the Mayans?"

Rally leaned back on the counter thoughtfully. "Well, the Mayan people used to build little Aluxes out of rocks, sticks, whatever they could find. You understand? They were created to be like little scarecrows. It was just to scare off animals from their crops at first. But then, something happened: They started coming alive. They got little spirits.

"Out there in the Yucatán jungles, you'll still find them, little wooden or rock Aluxes, with their little hair. They say if you move one, the next day you'll see it standing over there," he said, gesturing out to the beach. "And then the next day you'll see it in a different position over there. They come out at night and start moving around. If they see people, they freeze, they stay still. If you steal one from the jungles out there, or if you find one, you have to take care of it. Put out a little water, a little tequila, and cigarettes, whatever . . . to please them. But you better be careful—if you stop paying attention to them, or if you start caring for someone or something else, they'll do bad things to that person, or animal."

I couldn't help but laugh. "So they're jealous little creatures, apparently?"

"Yeah, they're incredibly jealous." Rally looked at me for a moment, rather intently.

"That's so interesting, the whole idea that people can *obtain* them," I mused, sipping my beer. "Our tour guide was saying people could buy them. I don't get that. What are you buying? Are you buying a pile of rocks that you then put in your yard, and that would turn into an Alux? Like some sort of grow-your-own-faery Chia Pet? I mean, what are they selling really, to someone who doesn't even believe in it?"

Rally seemed disappointed in me.

"If you were in the right place you could see for yourself. Certain towns, they sell these little troll dolls made out of wood. The shopkeeper will tell you, you buy it, you better give it whatever it wants. *Every single day*. Because there's a spirit attached to that thing."

I told Rally that I'd heard the Diamante K was absolutely crawling with Aluxes. He hadn't seen any at the hotel himself, but he told me other staff members reported seeing them all the time.

"Out there by that last torch, they say they see them out there. They like to kick it around trees and stuff, and there's a little bit of jungle around here, so I'd imagine they come around. Little kids see them. They sometimes go play with them. But some of them, I tell you, they're not so nice. So they'll start hitting the little kids. You see the kids just wandering off and talking to no one . . . that's when you can tell they're talking to an Alux."

"So . . . do you believe that the Alux are real?" I asked directly. He squirmed in his seat uncomfortably and gave a little laugh.

"Uhhh . . . well, I've heard some crazy stuff. There's this good friend of mine, he's sort of a Rasta guy. He was digging a garden in his yard when he came across this little Alux, you know, the little wooden figure. It had been buried in the ground. He knew what it was, and he was psyched. He was like, 'I'm gonna keep this thing!' So he took it home and he took real good care of it. But he had this dog that he loved, though, and as soon as he brought the Alux home, he noticed that the dog started barking at night. Pretty soon, the dog started showing up with little cuts all over it in the mornings. He couldn't understand why. He wasn't letting the dog out or anything, so it didn't make sense."

Our beers were empty, and Rally reached swiftly into the fridge to grab us two more. "Pretty soon," he continued, "my friend figures out that there's no other way these little cuts could be showing up on his dog, and he gets so angry that the Alux might be hurting his dog that he kicks it across the room and starts cursing it out."

Rally paused for effect.

"He woke up the next morning and found his dog *dead*. It was hanging from the rafters."

"No way!" I whispered. The look of horror on my face was enough to lighten the mood, and Cheri and Rally both burst out laughing. "Yeah, they're scary," he agreed. "I tripped out!"

Since we were on the subject of Rally tripping out, I asked him to tell me about the time *he* saw an Alux. He nudged his chair in a little closer, looking slightly embarrassed.

"Well, here's what happened: I had just moved to a place out here in Tulum, just a little hut in the jungle. My neighbors had three dogs, and all of a sudden they would just bark and bark and bark. At nothing! Eventually, the neighbors told me, 'Seems like we might have an Alux in the backyard.'

"So one night, the dogs woke me up with their barking. I looked outside my door, and there was a little shadow right there. Some black thing standing in the doorway, looking at me. And then it just ran off."

He paused again for effect.

"I went back to sleep, but then I heard the barking outside again, and I started yelling at the Alux, like 'Get the hell out of here!' I went back to sleep, but the next thing I knew, I felt this, like, searing pain on my back—something was burning me! I look, and there's my lighter, lying there, right underneath my hammock."

The sun was setting and we knew we had to get back, but I couldn't help feeling a sense of foreboding about returning to my cabana. As we said our goodbyes, I saw two guys who looked like maintenance men carrying large metal pails through the restaurant. The billowy smoke was heavy with a spicy, earthy scent.

"What are they doing?" I asked.

"That's *copal*," Rally answered. "It's a special kind of incense. They burn it every day, about this time, for the Alux. It's like a tribute."

It was nearly dark as we made our way back up the sandy path, passing statues of Mayan demigods with their angry stone faces flashing at us in the torchlight. Back at Casa Violeta, Raven was concerned when I told her about the Rasta man and the bizarre death of his dog.

"Sigs, I really think you should sage your room before you go to sleep tonight. Light some sage and ask that the space be protected and cleared out. These things don't sound very nice, and I really don't think you want them hanging around."

I tried to laugh off my sense of unease . . . but I went straight to my room and burned the sage. As the pungent scent saturated every nook and cranny of my cabana, I felt my worry begin to subside. Glancing around at my newly sanctified abode, I thought, *This house is clear!* Stick that in your pipe and smoke it, little buddy.

Hours later, the sound of shattering glass shocked me awake. I bolted upright in bed, fumbling for the penlight on my key chain. Looking around in confusion, I saw that the glass candle, which I had blown out before falling asleep, had shattered into a hundred glittering pieces on the floor. Outside the cabana, the ocean wind was roaring. It must have somehow blown the candle clear across the nightstand. But it was so heavy, and it was right next to me—not near the edge. I suddenly felt the blood coursing harder through my veins. *It was the wind, it was the wind, it was the wind,* I told myself.

But, Signe, what if it wasn't the wind?

Don't be ridiculous! Listen to how windy it is outside . . .

What if it was the little—

La-la-la . . . I can't hear you . . .

—Troll-like creature . . .

La-laaaa-laaaaaa!

—with his dark, beady eyes, and his bizarre leathery skin and wild, matted hair—

Fabulous. Now my heart was racing. I was completely and hopelessly awake.

I searched the darkness for any movement, any shadow. But everything had gone eerily still. Suddenly, in a flash I saw the tanned, weathered face from the night before, now red with anger, lurch toward me in my head. But tonight, it pissed me off more than it frightened me.

I'm sorry, I told him, *But I won't be talking to you.* The image flashed at me with a renewed and more frightening veracity.

You must not have understood me. I am going to bed. And you are going to leave me alone!

(And I have *completely lost my mind!*)

I saw him one more time, and then he was gone.

I lay awake trying to make sense of my experience. I knew I had a vivid imagination, and that gave me pause. I read somewhere that when it comes to the human brain, we only truly understand how approximately six percent of it operates. To me, that means it's highly probable that the other ninety-four percent can be pretty darn tricky when it wants to be. But still, there was something so undeniably clear about that image I had seen. It was so incredibly vivid, and I *had* felt this big wave of anger, as though someone was standing there, flaming mad.

Regardless of whether there was any truth behind the stories I'd heard, or whether my ninety-four percent was playing some very frightening trick on me, after the night I'd just had, I could no longer play the part of the dispassionate observer. This trip to Mexico, my first real exploration into the world of faeries, had cemented something for me. I now felt that there *could* be something else out there, something unseen. And I wasn't satisfied.

I wanted to experience more.

3

Finding Faeries in Upstate New York

Every time a child says, "I don't believe in fairies,"
there is a fairy somewhere that falls down dead.
—JAMES MATTHEW BARRY, PETER PAN

A T the sound of the bell, I pushed my way downstairs and burst through the red double doors to find my dad parked out front in the rusted old Volvo.

"Hey, puppy! How was school?" He reached over to give my knee a solid pat as I buckled myself into the front seat. On Wednesdays, Dad had to teach, and I always loved the look of him in his beige suit, crisp white shirt, and paisley tie.

He flicked the volume back up on NPR, the theme song blasting. *"And now, this is the BBC World Service with News Hour . . ."*

"Siggie, I thought we'd take a walk, head over to Potter's Falls." He shifted into gear as we pulled away from the curb.

My heart sank. "Dad, if we go to Potter's Falls, will we *have* to walk all the way down to the falls?"

I looked at my brand-new, bright red Converse sneakers and silently cursed Potter's Falls for even existing, with its water-slogged and muddy trails that delighted in destroying all pretty red shoes that dared tread upon them.

"What's the point of going to Potter's Falls if we don't see the falls, Signifer? We'd be missing—"

"—the muddy part," I mumbled.

"Mmm-hmm," he said absentmindedly, tuned in to the broadcast now.

We drove out Route 79, listening to the radio as Dad tapped his finger on the console. The autumn sky was vibrant blue and shocks of red maple and burnt yellow oak leaves flashed past the dusty window until we turned into the gravel pull-off on the side of the road.

Despite my initial reluctance, the rocky, pine-shrouded path, with its shadowy greenness, always marked the beginning of some of my favorite, most magical woods. I shut the door with a heavy clunk and zipped up my jacket to my chin. The sun was still streaming, so while it was cold to the nose, it was still deliciously warm in the shafts of bright sunshine.

"Come on, *schlomo*. Let's get there before the sun goes down," Dad kidded, slinging his weathered blue JanSport over one shoulder.

As we moved down the hill, the tall pines on either side eased into a forest of maple, birch, and hickory. We dragged our feet, delighting in the crashing, swooshing noises it made as we shuffled through the bright carpet of fallen leaves. I caught up with him, slipping my hand into his, and he turned to me, his dark, crinkled eyes sparkling.

"You know, the Iroquois used to walk these same trails," he began, his deep voice hushed. "These were their hunting grounds. Close to water. Here they had everything they needed—deer, mushrooms, wild berries. We don't know *half* the edible things in this forest."

I could almost see the little girls wearing deerskin as they moved from bush to bush, collecting berries in a hand-stitched sack, and the men, creeping along the rim trail, bows taut, taking aim at a doe bent at the water's edge, peacefully drinking from the rushing stream.

"When they would hunt, or when they were patrolling in times of danger, they would slip on their hand-sewn moccasins, made out of the softest deerskin. And their feet would move over the ground like they were walking on a cloud of silence. They could move through this forest like a ghost."

"Whoa!" I whispered back.

Dad paused to look at me. "Do you think that you could do it, Signe, if your life depended on it? Do you think you could stalk deer in these woods like an Iroquois maiden?"

"Yes," I said, seriously. "I think I could."

He stood still then, a conspiring smile playing at his lips. The forest around us was silent except for the occasional twitter of a bird lodged high in the trees.

"First, you'd have to listen," he said. I stood stock-still, drinking in the quiet, the soft rush of the wind through the trees.

"Now," he said in a hushed voice. "Let's see if we can walk like an Indian."

~~~~~~~

"You're going to Cortland?" My mother chuckled on the other end of the line.

"Yes! Why is that so funny?"

"Honey, Cortland is the land God forgot." She paused a moment. "Well, God and Smith Corona."

I couldn't argue with that. Back when people still used typewriters, Smith Corona had a huge plant in Cortland, New York, only thirty minutes from Ithaca, where I'd grown up. Schools thrived and business boomed. But today Cortland is just another exit off the interstate, with a few car dealerships, fast-food joints, Blockbuster video stores, and a classic greasy spoon called Doug's Fish Fry.

Oh, yes: and a lady who makes faery houses in her basement.

Some months back, I'd spotted the odd little houses at a crafts store in Ithaca, and with some effort I'd managed to track down their creator who'd agreed to meet to answer a few questions.

"Let us never forget, Mom. Cortland is the Land of Our People!"

"Right." She laughed. "You have fun. And tell your cousin Stan I said hi."

Upstate New York was a wonderful excuse to spend time with Stan, who is eleven years my elder. He was there when our dad died, tirelessly helping Kirsten and me move our father's furniture into storage. He cleaned the layers of dirt, dust, and cobwebs that had accumulated in the last few years of my father's neglect, taking bag after bag of spoiled food from the fridge to the dump. He was one of the first people I called with news, and he seemed to understand me better than I understood myself. When I was growing up, Stan had his own TV segment on the *Rochester Morning News* called "Hey, Stan!" which made him a local celebrity. He would do things on camera like stay overnight in haunted places, impersonate a fifth-grader for a day, or get his back waxed. People loved him and were constantly coming up to him saying, "Hey, Stan! Get it?! 'Hey, Stan'?!"

No wonder he left.

Now he was married to a beautiful podiatrist named Suzi, and he made his living gluing together toothpick structures in his basement. He'd sold his latest creation, "Toothpick City," to an architectural museum in Majorca for a good heap of money. And now he'd agreed to take the weekend off from "Toothpick City II: Temples and Towers" to chauffeur me around upstate New York on this next step of my investigation into the world of faery.

The bus ride to the Land of My People was misery. By the time I reached Syracuse it was after midnight and my shoulder felt damp from my bus neighbor's drool. And of course it was raining. Cold, Land of My People rain. There are a few places in Syracuse you really don't want to be after midnight, and the bus depot is most certainly one of them. A presumably homeless man with his hand down his pants ogled me as I disembarked, and I felt his stare boring into the back of my head. Luckily, I quickly spotted Stan's hulky six-four frame in his battered orange Jeep.

"Hey, big cousin!" I said, relieved, as I hoisted myself into the Jeep and leaned over to give him a peck. "You look *great*. Did you lose some weight?"

"Suzi told me if I lost fifty pounds she would buy me a hot tub."

"God, your life is so *hard*."

"Hey, little cousin . . ." He grinned, looking me over. "You tired, or you think you can stay awake for a glass of wine?"

"I'm really tired. And I was counting on staying awake for a glass of wine."

"Perfect!" He patted me fondly on the shoulder.

The next morning was gorgeous and sunny as we took I-81 from Syracuse to Cortland. If you're just passing through, I guess you'd never imagine what it must have looked like four hundred years ago, before the first white people came, building houses that would grow into the squat towers of the city of Syracuse. This was the cradle of the ancient Iroquois Confederacy, the Six Nations. I knew all the tribes that came together to form the Confederacy, and my father would challenge us to list them on our fingers—Seneca, Cayuga, Onondaga, Oneida, Mohawk . . . Tuscarora. Thanks to my father, these woods were alive to me.

As we pulled up to faery artist Diana McClure's home, I noticed the houses were sprawling, with manicured lawns and picturesque views. I felt terribly judgmental, but somehow wealth and faery fascination hadn't seemed like an expected marriage to me. Grabbing my notebook, I turned to my partner.

"So, Stan, what did I say?"

"No talking, unless you give me the nod."

I waited, eyebrows raised expectantly.

"And no interrupting."

"And?"

He looked down at his sneakers.

"No making fun," he allowed, peering up at me.

"Good."

The Diana McClure who greeted us looked like she'd stepped from the pages of a Lands' End catalog—khaki pants, her hair softly graying, her light eyes shyly avoiding mine. It struck me that I was hoping she'd be . . . well . . . *weirder*.

"Thanks so much for having us," I began.

"Oh, well, I saw Stan's toothpick buildings online—and those are pretty darn amazing-looking!"

So there it was: my toothpicking cousin was my in.

Stan laughed, clearly tickled, and our carefully agreed-upon rules went swiftly out the window as he and Diana dove into an in-depth conversation about the virtues of toothpicking, the value of an excellent glue gun, and being someone who builds something in your basement. This gave me a moment to study the tableau that awaited our attention. In front of me an entire faery village was spread across the shiny dining-room table. It was like a Tolkien novel in miniature—little rounded stucco buildings six to eight inches high, painted in muted colors of green, pink, and violet, with tree bark or ceramic roofs. Each house was its own kind of child's wonderland, decorated with rough-hewn mica, quartz, agate, seeds, mushrooms, and miniature pinecones. On some of them, the tiny doors pushed open and you could see one or two items had been placed inside—a cloth carpet, a miniature wooden bed. It was simply amazing.

Peering over my shoulder, Stan pushed open one of the doors.

"Hey! There's a little flat-screen TV in there!" he exclaimed.

"Ha-ha-ha!" I laughed, shooting him a dirty look.

As we talked, I got the sense that the faery house business was booming. But I wondered if the people buying them were believers, or chintz collectors, like the people who collect shot glasses or spend their life savings on a mission to possess every known variety of Beanie Baby.

"So, Diana," I began, "do you think the people buying your homes believe that faeries really do exist?"

She considered this a moment. "Yes, I think so. I mean, if you buy a birdhouse, you're inviting the birds to come. It's the same thing with the faeries: if you buy a faery house, you're inviting the faeries to come."

"And what about you? Do you believe faeries are real?"

She avoided my eyes a moment, embarrassed. "I mean, I believe that all sorts of stuff we're not tuning in to exists. People always want to know where artists draw our inspiration. And I guess in this case, I'm going to have to blame it on the faeries. I think these houses incorporate their ideas as much as mine. I was a very limited artist before I began working on these. I'd worked with clay to produce functional pots, ones that would sell. These days when I'm working, the ideas just come. More ideas than I can really deal with!"

So it seemed that for Diana, the faery world was her muse. But I wondered, what inspired her—the *idea* of faeries, or the faeries themselves? As we trooped down the stairs Diana told me that she had never once heard little voices whispering in her ear. She'd never even seen a faery. And she wasn't sure she wanted to.

We spent the better part of an hour touring her basement workshop where she showed us drawers upon drawers of semiprecious gemstones meticulously organized by color and type. Plastic organizers filled with polyurethane-glazed mushrooms, pinecones, tree bark, and silk flowers stood stacked and ready for action.

Diana had mentioned over the phone that there was a psychic medium in Syracuse who I should really speak with while I was in town, a woman who, according to Diana, had an excellent rapport with the faery realm: Coleen Shaughnessy. Since I'd scheduled a meeting with Coleen right after my interview with Diana, time was running short. But as we said our goodbyes, I realized I had one final question to ask her.

"Sorry, Diana, I'm just wondering. Have you noticed anything in your life . . . *change* since you started working on these homes? You know, in trying to do something for the faeries?"

She considered this carefully. "Well, I guess it depends on what you believe. I mean, I'm not so good at the sales, and so I kept saying, 'Bring people to me that are interested in doing something with these.' And then . . . people came." Her gray eyes looked at me meaningfully. Did she mean me?

As we pulled away from the drive with a wave, I couldn't help but smile. I was inclined to disagree with Diana about not being so good with "the sales." Her houses start at thirty dollars apiece. She'd sold me two for eighty.

Coleen Shaughnessy looked like Joan of Arc.

"It's no wonder you're doing what you're doing!" she exclaimed, as she ushered me into her home. "You have *so* many little faery energies all around you!"

"Thank you!" I said, thankful I'd insisted Stan stay in the car for this one.

As I sat at her dining-room table I studied her small, roundish glasses and the etched lines around her eyes that suggested a lifetime of easy laughter. It was the bowl haircut that reminded me of the French saint. That, and the fact that Joan of Arc was known for her conversations with faeries.

At the mention of faeries, Coleen laughed girlishly, tossing her hands up in delight.

"I *love* the faeries!" she exclaimed. "I've known they existed ever since I was a child. At my family's lake house I could feel an energy between the water and the shore. It wasn't until later that I learned places like that—between the water and the land—are called 'tween places."

"'Tween places?" I asked.

"Yes. 'Tween places occur where two things overlap and become, for a moment, neither one thing nor the other," she explained. "Faeries love anything 'tween. There are 'tween times, too—between night and day, between morning and afternoon."

I nodded eagerly, waiting for Coleen to continue.

"As a little girl, I met flower faery friends, and there were little brownies that helped me clean. And then, of course, downstairs in the cellar, there were the dark elves under the stairs."

Oh, yes, of course. Dark elves. Who hasn't heard of them?

My look of fear must have betrayed me because, across the table, Coleen chuckled.

"No, no, don't worry, dark elves aren't *bad*," she reassured me. "But their eyes, their eyes do scare me."

"Why?" I asked hesitantly. "What do their eyes look like?"

She leaned in toward me. "When I saw them they were . . . bright. But the rest of them is inky black. And if they stepped out from the shadows they would be dressed from head to toe in dark clothing." I pictured an evil Legolas from *The Lord of the Rings*, jumping out from behind the washing machine. It was terrifying.

"But why are they there? I mean, why would they gravitate toward humans in a house? Wouldn't they rather be outdoors?"

"They don't gravitate toward houses. They gravitate toward *dark spaces*. There are dark elves outside, too. But in homes, *we're* the ones who stumble into their space."

She stopped and looked at me. "You could encounter them, too, you know! You've probably felt them, especially with your vibration. When you go down into the cellar and you think, 'Oohh.'" With a mock shiver she added, "'It feels like there's something down here.'"

Right. I wouldn't be trying to connect with dark elves anytime soon. Despite my new fear of dark elves (add that to the list), Coleen explained that making gestures of friendship is very important in the faery kingdom. Buying something like a faery house, for example, would be a good way to let them know you know they're there. Putting honey out, creating a little space for them in each room, talking to them, buying them shiny things—these were all good ways to open the lines of communication. As she described the various methods for building a relationship with the faery realm, it began to seem like an awful lot of work to me. They sounded just like . . . *women*.

"So is creating a bond with the faery world ultimately beneficial to people?" I asked.

"Oh, yes," she assured me. "Oh, the faeries can do *many* things. But unlike your angels and guides, the faery realm does not have to help you *a bit* if they don't want to, okay?" Her voice was stern.

"Okay . . ."

"So the fact that you already have a bunch in your aura, that told me right off the bat, 'Oh, okay, they already like *her*.' Believe me, that's a very good thing."

I found I was smiling at the thought that the faeries might *like* me, and were already hanging around me. Could it be true? And if it was, were they around *all* the time? Because that would be a little pervy.

"Some people have to earn their trust over and over again," Coleen continued. "But when they like you from the start, they can give you all kinds of gifts—health, wealth, prosperity, gifts of prophecy, clairvoyance, all those kinds of things. I'm very blessed. I get faery gifts all the time."

"So when you see a faery, what does it *look* like exactly?"

Coleen's face lit up. "Some of the time, I'll just see little lights. But sometimes, within the lights, I'll see their actual forms. There are also a number of things they can shape-shift into. They can become a dragonfly, a butterfly, a bird, or even a larger animal. You can tell the difference between a faery, or say, just a normal butterfly, because they'll do something unusual, out of character. You'll have it on your finger and try to fluff it off, and it'll hang on! And you go like this"—she shook her hand—"and he's still hanging on."

Thinking back to unusual encounters with nature in Manhattan, the only creatures I'd had regular contact with were cockroaches, and we met as mortal enemies engaged in combat. I refused to believe—no matter how fond of the natural world faeries were—that they would deign to shape-shift into the form of a New York City roach.

"So . . . sometimes faeries look like fireflies?" I interrupted.

"No," she insisted. "People always try to tell me that's what I'm seeing. But there is absolutely no mistaking it. It's bigger than a firefly or lightning bug, with a totally different color of light. And lightning bugs don't have little forms inside them at times. I mean, *hello?*"

I asked Coleen how someone like me might be able to see a faery, and she explained that anybody could learn to see beyond our physical world, see the faeries, if they wanted.

"If you develop a good relationship with the faeries—if they trust you and know you're an open person—you can't *not* connect," she explained. "But you must be a person pure of heart—a good, loving, kind heart. You must respect the earth and the faery realm, or they won't want anything to do with you." Thinking for a moment, she seemed to grow solemn and reached over to touch my hand.

"Signe, I want to tell you something."

"Of course."

"What you're attempting," she began, "this is a very important time to be doing it. Right now, the faeries are trying to reestablish contact, to get more information flowing back and forth between the human species and their world. If we work together, we can help to heal the planet. The planet is sick now, in a lot of ways. If we are going to survive, if the planet is going to survive, it needs a lot of healing. The faeries can help us to do that."

I felt as though I had been socked in the gut, and I couldn't help but wonder: Had my search for faeries begun with me turning off the radio when I'd had enough? Or was I really somehow responding to a larger call to action? Was I helping the faeries, or was it the other way around?

I snuck a peek at my watch and realized that Stan had been waiting in the Jeep for almost two hours. Yikes. Giving Coleen a hug goodbye, I made my way down the steps and opened the door to climb in.

"Sorry for the wait, big cousin, but I'm telling you—you would not have been able to handle it. You would have definitely had to crack a joke."

"Probably, but man. It would've been fun."

"Not for Coleen and me." I cleared my throat.

"Well, Siggie, I'm just glad you made it out in one piece," he said, glancing at his watch. "I was just hoping you weren't tied up somewhere in the basement. A captive of dark elves or something."

So even Stan knew about the dark elves?

I looked at him, then burst out laughing.

The bus ride back to New York City was long and quiet, with too much time to remember. I'd grown up breathing the air here, the particles of water that evaporated off the grass, the leaves of the trees. These hills were in me, my father, my mother, in Kirsten. I looked out the window past the fields and into the woods, trying to penetrate their greenness, somehow transport myself there from the confines of the mothball-scented bus seat. Under that wild canopy of green, with my feet planted on a winding trail or on the mossy carpet at the base of a rushing stream, I would be once more where the Indians walked.

As the Port Authority came into view, I wondered: What had happened to the girl within me, the one who was happy to take a walk in the woods, pretending to be an Iroquois hunter with her father? God, I missed those days. Coleen had told me I had faeries in my aura. If I did, I certainly wasn't deserving. Going back upstate made me realize that somewhere in my life in Manhattan I had become distracted by all the wrong things—the money, the clothes, the success, the shoes, the handbags . . . what had happened to the little girl who loved a good story and an apple on a log in the woods with her father? Every time I reached out and took a step toward the faery world, I felt closer to that little girl. With each small peek into the faery realm I felt as though I were somehow reclaiming a small piece of myself.

But coming back to Manhattan with faery dust between my toes came with its own price tag. The horns blared louder, the neon lights looked more garish, and I so missed seeing the great swaths of trees. Sighing, I tugged my duffel bag out from underneath the bus and headed out to the crowded New York City streets to fight my way into a cab.

4

A Faery Special Invitation

To see a faery one must learn to "see" with the heart
and mind as well as with the eyes.
—EDAIN MCCOY, *A WITCH'S GUIDE TO FAERY FOLK*

I AWOKE every morning to the sound of birds. Granted, they were pigeons on the fire escape battling over a discarded Frito Lay bag, but as far as I was concerned, they were bluebirds and I was a red-haired Cinderella, awakening in the soft light of dawn to begin the morning's duties. In April, Eric and I had packed up our respective apartments and moved in together to a newly renovated one bedroom on the seventh floor of my building. Our lives found a new energy: the house was filled with friends, great food, and music to fit every mood from Eric's collection of one billion CDs. We were madly and utterly in love.

My weekend trip upstate had been informative but the travel had been draining, and I soon realized that if Raven had seen faeries in my old apartment, perhaps it was possible to contact them from the comfort of my very own home.

There are, surprisingly, several books that teach everyday people how to contact, invite, and otherwise get in touch with the faery kingdom. Sadly, none of these books are written for people who live in New York City.

"Go into the forest at sunrise and gather the first dew from each blackberry bush that you see . . ."

Nope.

"You will need a small chime and a striker."

You want *how much* for that thing?

And then there was my all-time favorite: "On the first day after a full moon, bury six white rose petals under an apple tree."

Sure, I knew where to find white rose petals. But the last time I saw an apple tree in Central Park was . . . never. Other books included spells that called for such commonplace household items as red-tailed hawk feathers, six four-leaf clovers, hollyhock, or fresh—not bottled—spring water.

Poring over the books, I finally found some techniques that were a bit more city-friendly. With these in hand, my plan was to pull out all the stops for five New York days and nights; if there was any contact to be had with the faery realm in my apartment, contact there would be.

First of all, I wanted to know what faeries even *were*. Spirits? Pieces of our imagination? Living beings beyond our human field of vision? The word *faery* seemed somewhat limited as various creatures from the faery world came to light. Coleen had mentioned the dark elves. And the Mexicans considered the Alux to be faeries—but doesn't short, angry, deadly, and hairy bend your perception of the word a bit?

Every author presented a different theory on what faeries really were. The more I read, the more I realized I had no idea what exactly I was searching for in the first place. Worse, I began to realize that at the heart of a search for faeries lie important questions about reality, and the nature of our own existence, questions that are vital to uncovering any sort of truth relating to the existence or nonexistence of "faeries." Rally had believed the Alux to be "little spirits." As it turned out, other adults (and even scholars) had given the concept of faeries some thought, and over the past centuries had come up with some interesting theories.

There are five main theories I could find that attempted to explain faeries.

Theory one is the Pygmy Theory, which was presented by Scottish folklorist David MacRitchie in his book *The Testimony of Tradition* (1890). He asserted that faery belief stemmed from a folk memory of a prehistoric, possibly Mongolian race of people who inhabited the British Isles and many parts of Continental Europe in ages past. When the Celts encountered these people during their expansion, they drove them into the mountains and wilds, where MacRitchie believed a few of them may have survived until relatively recent times—therefore explaining the sightings of "faery folk" by the peasantry that were documented from the 1880s onward. But if a pygmy race of humans had survived even into the sixteenth century, wouldn't we have discovered some sort of empirical archeological evidence of these wee humans by now?

Theory two is the Naturalistic Theory. In prehistoric times, early man was bowled over by natural events: rain, thunder, lightning, the violent shaking and moving of the ground, mountains spewing deathly hot lava, the glow of the moon, the burning heat of the sun, the twinkling of the stars. Our human brain searched for an answer, and the conclusion was that it all must be caused by something greater than ourselves—this, of course, sprouted the earliest seeds of religion. This theory is certainly reflected in faery lore. In the beautiful sloping hills of Connemara in Ireland, for example, faeries were believed to have been just as beautiful, peaceful, and pleasant as the world around them. But in the Scottish Highlands, with their dark, brooding mountains and eerie highland lakes, villagers warned of deadly water-kelpies and spirit characters that packed a bit more punch.

Theory three is known as the Druid Theory, which states that faeries are a folk memory of the Druids and their mysterious magical practices. When the Druids were forgotten, legends of the faeries sprang up from underground. This postulation was put forth by two different men, both reverends, in the early 1800s. It was later expounded on by a Frenchman, Alfred Maury, who in 1843 took it one step further and wondered if the resurgence in art and literature depicting faery women during the Middle Ages may have stemmed from a folk memory of female Druidesses. However, the roots of the human belief in faeries can be traced much further back than the disappearance of the Druids: it seems to reach even further back in the timeline to ancient Britain and Ireland. To me, it seems far more likely that faeries, like shoulder pads, simply come into fashion from time to time. In medieval times, there was a big resurgence, but we would witness yet another faery resurgence during the Victorian era.

Theory four is the Mythological Theory, which many modern authorities on Celtic mythology and folklore embrace. The belief is that fairies, as they are remembered today, are actually diminished figures of the old pagan deities of the Celts, transformed over time into lesser beings through folklore as a result of Christianization. Of all the theories I found this one to be the most compelling and hoped to explore it moving forward.

Theory five is invented by a man of great importance—or perhaps he was a man of importance who would become of *great* importance to me later—named W. Y. Evans-Wentz. At first glance it was easy to dismiss Evans-Wentz as a bit of a quack. He believed quite earnestly that faeries were invisible "intelligences or entities able to influence both man and nature," according to his book *The Fairy-Faith in Celtic Countries*, published in 1911. However, the American-born author was a serious academic who'd earned both his bachelor's and master's degrees from Stanford, where he studied under William James and William Butler Yeats. He went on to study Celtic folklore and mythology at Oxford. While working on his dissertation, he became increasingly interested in, of all things, faeries. He began his exploration as a curious nonbeliever—not unlike myself.

"When I set out from Oxford in June," he wrote, "I had no certain or clear ideas as to what fairies are, nor why there should be belief in them. In less than a year afterwards I found myself committed to the Psychological Theory, which I am herein setting forth."

The Celtic belief in faeries, as Evans-Wentz described it, was quite simple. Faeries were spiritual beings who dwelled in a spiritual realm, which has existed from prehistoric times until today in Ireland, Scotland, the Isle of Man, Wales, Cornwall, Brittany, and other parts of the ancient empire of the Celts. Evans-Wentz believed that if fairies actually existed (and his investigation had led him to believe that they did), they weren't supernatural at all. "Nothing which exists through the natural world can be supernatural," he writes, "and, therefore, it is our duty to examine the Celtic Fairy Races just as we examine any fact in the visible realm wherein we now live, whether it be a fact of chemistry, of physics, or of biology."

That's a pretty explosive statement for a turn-of-the-century Oxford academic. If delving in had made a believer out of Evans-Wentz, perhaps it could make a believer out of skeptical ol' me. And where better to begin than my own home?

In D. J. Conway's *Ancient Art of Faery Magick*, I discovered a spell to welcome house faeries into your residence. In the countryside of Scotland, England, Ireland, and Wales, people used to set out libations of milk, honey, or freshwater to welcome house-dwelling faery folk. As recently as sixty years ago, locals believed that once a house faery had taken up residence in your home, it would look after the family, bringing luck, good health, and even helping to keep the place tidy. If treated with proper consideration and respect, it was said that a house faery could also act as guardian or gatekeeper, protecting the home and its human dwellers from outside faery mischief or even harm.

Trying to think "faery," I planned my Welcome Ceremony for midnight, a 'tween time. Conway suggested three different techniques:

- leaving freshwater out for the faeries to bathe in each night

- warming spices in the oven and performing an incantation

- conducting a ceremony to welcome a variety of faery species in from all four directions of the earth

I decided to do all three.

After work, I rushed to the supermarket to purchase the required items. And then, of course, I had to clean. Apparently there is nothing faeries detest more than a lazy, dirty housekeeper, so Conway advised that the first step to any invitation should be to clean your house. The danger being, a dirty home will not attract a high-quality house faery. But after giving this dilemma some thought, I decided to leave my relatively-tidy-just-don't-open-every-drawer apartment as it was. In my estimation, there couldn't be anything worse than tricking a lovely, neat, type-A sort of faery into living with the likes of me. I'd like a more tolerant faery, please.

At eleven thirty that night, I began my preparations. So far, I noted the cat was jumping at an invisible fly on the wall and tearing into the living room, only to tear back into the bedroom to claw at the mirror and make a terrible meowing sound. To be honest, as midnight approached, it was kind of freaking me out.

I stood in the kitchen, grating fresh ginger into a Pyrex bowl, then sprinkling ground cloves and cinnamon over the top as directed, mixing it together with my fingers. As I did, I began to feel oddly uncomfortable, as though someone or something was standing too close to me. I felt like I was being watched, and I began to get a bizarre case of the shivers. I've never really been a "shivers" kind of person, so the sensation was surprising. They ran from the base of my spine, up my neck, to the top of my head, and I experienced a series of five or six in a row. Often, I had read, when a faery is present, humans may experience something like this, but there was really no way to know whether I was in the presence of something paranormal, or whether this was simply a new manifestation of my (frequent) fear and neurosis. After all, wasn't every small noise making me jump?

I placed the dish in the oven, and as its scent began to waft throughout the house, I stood in the kitchen reading timidly:

"Nikka, nakka, kolba, min. You and I shall live as kin."

I could feel my cheeks heat with embarrassment. Yet, underneath, there was a push to make the words my own. I tried it again to see if my mouth could find a comfort with it.

"Nikka, nakka, kolba, min. You and I shall live as kin."

As I spoke, I imagined the scent traveling through the apartment as some kind of beacon, welcoming the entities into our home. The kitchen was quiet, save the hum from the cat's electric water fountain. What was I waiting for anyway? It wasn't like they were going to pop out of the elevator and ring the freaking doorbell, right? Moving into the living room, I checked the clock: 11:58. Lighting three candles on the coffee table, I set down an offering of ground ginger in one of my father's antique eggcups. Book in hand, I faced north—toward the new bagel place in my neighborhood, Fort Tryon Park, and the George Washington Bridge—and read:

> From the land of exotic snow crystals,
> From the dark green forests and the whitest of snow,
> I bid all faeries welcome here.

I went to each of the four directions in turn, summoning the creatures as the spell directed. Conway had suggested concluding with an ancient seers' method to catch a glimpse of any faeries that might have entered the room during the reading, so peeking to be sure Eric wasn't watching, I lifted my right leg off the floor and stood on my left, while holding my right arm out straight from my body, my left arm at my side. My right eye was supposed to be entirely closed, while my left was allowed to squint. I managed to get myself in position and stood there wobbling for a full minute, spying around the room with my squinting eye. I felt completely ridiculous. Faeries aren't stupid. I felt like a five-year-old who covers both eyes, shouting, "I'm invisible, I'm invisible!" Disappointed, I blew out the candles, placed an eggcup filled with fresh-water by each of our two faery homes, and crawled into bed.

The next morning I noticed a fruit fly in the bathroom, buzzing around my head. I usually only spotted them in the kitchen, or on rare occasions when they strayed as far as the living room. I'd read that faeries often shape-shift, and that one can differentiate faery from nonfaery by determining whether the animal or insect is behaving abnormally. But was this fruit fly behaving erratically? It kept dive-bombing my head, which was getting pretty annoying, but without an entomologist present, I was at a loss.

As I moved into the bedroom to get dressed, I was surprised to see a starling perched on the railing of the fire escape. Not a pigeon, a starling. I parted the sheer curtains, and it looked back at me until Willoughby the cat began to make her precursory chirping noises. At which point I burst into laughter and the bird flew away. Later, when I came home from work, I made sure to follow another piece of faery advice: don't acknowledge your house faeries directly. They don't like it. So I decided it would be best to check in with the cat.

"Hi, Willy girl! Were you a good girl today? Did you have fun hanging out with our new friends?" I looked at her expectantly. She had nothing to say for herself.

On Wednesday a heavy thermos fell from the top shelf of the cupboard when I opened it to grab a cereal bowl. As it came crashing down, just missing the cat's water, not to mention my toes, it made a real racket, and I let out a little scream of surprise.

Again I turned to my feline friend.

"Willy. Kitties are supposed to see these things. Tell Mommy if it was a faery."

She tilted her little black head at me, her green eyes questioning.

"Willy. Blink once if it was a faery," I commanded.

She looked at me another moment, as if to slowly shake her head in shame, then resumed eating her pureed turkey breakfast.

That night, I decided to try something different. Since peasants in the countryside would often leave fruit or vegetables for the faeries from the harvest, I sliced up some small pieces of watermelon and left them in an eggcup in front of each of the faery homes. *Remember this? This is for you.*

The watermelon was still there in the morning. Sure, I knew it wasn't going to disappear or anything. When it came to offerings, I'd read that faeries didn't literally *eat* the food—rather, they absorbed its energy or essence. Nonetheless, by day four I was getting discouraged. Despite all I'd read about faeries' reluctance to interact with humans, how one must be patient, how one must understand how horribly humans have damaged the relationship that existed between our two races in ancient times, after all I'd been told by Raven and Coleen about faeries being in my apartment and faeries hanging about in my aura, I had hoped we could cut through some of the usual formalities. If a human reached out in complete sincerity, shouldn't the faeries be *delighted* to make contact?

On this fourth day, I began to wonder, exactly how it is that organized religion gets *away* with this? I mean, how many people have actually seen God? We may see things that we believe *represent* God, like a beautiful sunset, a smile, a selfless or kind gesture. But those are all just things—we can ascribe any meaning to them. How many people have seen heaven, or hell, or demons, or angels appear right before them? Not very many, I tell you. And wasn't I trying to accomplish the same sort of thing? Billions of people believe God exists, angels exist. Millions don't even question. Wars are waged, causing tremendous human suffering, all in the name of something for which there is no empirical proof. And yet here I was, contemplating laying myself bare before so many disbelieving eyes, hoping to prove something that could very well be impossible. Why?

For the first time in months, I considered that I may never find proof to support what I so wanted to believe. I let out a long sigh. Maybe the real challenge was to acknowledge that there may simply be no way to prove such things. And to undertake to do it anyway.

When I woke up on Friday morning, the starling had returned, perched and gazing through our window. I crept closer and scrutinized it carefully. From its blue-black feathers to its iridescent green specks, I had to admit that this was a pretty convincing starling—there was nothing unusual about it. Nothing fell on top of me as I got ready for work, and nothing seemed out of place. I decided it was time to call in a very special reserve. Raven had a Reiki session in our apartment that day, and I asked her if she could tune in and tell me what she experienced, if anything. Upon my arrival home, I received the following note.

Hi, Sigs,

Arrived a bit early and the noises were there. I was leaning on the massage table, waiting for my client to arrive, when I heard them. I asked if "they" would give me a sign of their presence. The table began to tremble a bit under my elbows resting upon it. I went into meditation and asked who was there. I spoke to the energies in the room, telling them that I, too, serve the Great Mother and asked if I could see them. I saw shimmering around the plants and one of the plants started to move a bit. Then the noises went away and I didn't hear them anymore. That is my report for now.

I love you!
Raven

"The faeries came out for Raven, but they're boycotting me."

Eric and I sat over veggie pizza with half an eye on the Olympics.

"I'm sorry, honey, I don't know what to tell you. You've certainly been trying your best."

"They're hurting my feelings." I picked off a mushroom and contemplated it forlornly before popping it into my mouth.

"Hey, is it true what they say about cats being able to see them?" he asked.

"Yeah, that's what they say. In one of my books I read that the best way to chase away any uninvited faeries from your house is to get a cat. They see them and try to hunt them or something."

"Well, maybe that's why Willoughby's been acting so crazy lately. Just last night she was staring at the wall in the bedroom, like how she stares at a fly—she was trying to jump up and get something, but I looked and there was nothing there."

"Eric, are you telling me you think that Willy saw a faery?"

"Sure. I mean . . . maybe."

"How crazy is that? My boyfriend believes in faeries!"

"Well . . ."

"Shush, honey. Don't ruin it. As for you, Willoughby, you are no longer allowed to chase our new faery friends."

"*Mmmert?*" she responded.

"Nope. No more."

I put fresh honey out that night and changed the water in the eggcups.

This is for you.

The apartment was silent, though Willoughby had spent the evening tearing around the living room and jumping up so she could swipe at the walls.

"Good night," I whispered to the darkened room. "I do hope we can get to know each other soon."

With a small sigh, I turned and climbed into bed. I could give them the time they needed.

I hoped.

The experiment in my apartment might not have turned up any magical creatures, but it helped me realize that there was no more denying it—my quest had become an obsession, and a fun one at that. I made up my mind to plan a trip: one grand voyage to the home of the ancient Celts, to see what I could really discover about faeries. My only concern was how on earth I was going to juggle a grand voyage with work. I told myself that somehow I could find a way. Autumn came and the leaves began to turn, and Eric and I began talking about life somewhere else, but what a dream.

As the days grew shorter and fall decayed into winter, there were days when I felt the city was eating me alive. Every time I was pushed on the train it bothered me a little more. Every time I got stopped on the street by some spa promotion, I wanted my thirty seconds back. Every time a homeless man threw my money back at me because he wanted quarters instead of a stack of nickels, I got closer to saying, "See you later, Manhattan."

We each began to reach our own personal city limits. And the more we talked about the future, the more I started daydreaming about taking the time to really write this book. Eric had grown up in Charleston, South Carolina, and we fantasized about a house with a yard by the beach. His younger brother, Ben, still lived there and had a boat.

The next thing I knew it was December 15, and Eric was down on one knee, with a ridiculously sparkling diamond ring between his fingers.

"Signe, I want you to be my wife," he said, his soft brown eyes questioning. "Will you marry me?"

I'd been hoping, hoping so much, but trying not to expect. And now that it was happening . . . well, I didn't know I was a crier. Horrible, machine gun–like sounds issued from my mouth, and when I uncovered my eyes I whispered, "Ask me again."

I discovered in that moment, when you're going to be with somebody for the rest of your life, you get unlimited do-overs for embarrassing moments.

He laughed. "Will you marry me?"

"Yes!" I squealed.

That night we decided. So long as at least *one* of us could keep their job and work remotely, it was time for a change.

5

<hr>

Waking Up in the Kingdom by the Sea

I was a child and she was a child,
In this kingdom by the sea . . .
—EDGAR ALLAN POE, *ANNABEL LEE*

A WEEK before our move to Charleston, panic struck.

I had quit my job to search for faeries.

It was 11:24 a.m. on a Tuesday, which would typically find me in my office, fluttering frantically between emails and phone calls. Instead I was sitting barefoot in a Cornell T-shirt on the couch, with bile slowly rising in my stomach. What had I *done*?

Outside on Broadway I could hear the roar of traffic—my white noise. Looking around the room cluttered with half-packed cardboard boxes I couldn't help but feel I was being swallowed whole—everything in me and around me was under construction. And for what? I had quit my job and purchased myself a one-way ticket to utter obscurity. I pushed my breakfast away and ran into the bathroom, just in time to kneel and dry-heave into the toilet. I knew I should be welcoming this

change with optimistic excitement. But as I leaned my head against the
cold tile, I thought, *No*.

Periods of transition have never been my forte.

I sat on the long blue sofa, waiting. My mother looked tired sitting there
next to Kirsten, who was swinging her feet against the edge of the
couch. Out the big picture window I could see our birch tree, and a
gypsy moth caterpillar with long, spiky hairs, winding its way up the
trunk. I thought of the tin can filled with gasoline, the way my father
would pluck their writhing bodies from the papery bark, the way they
would twist and buck in the stinking liquid until they suffocated or
drowned. Either way was a terrible way to die.

Over on the love seat my father's fingers were interlaced in his lap.
He was letting Mom do this, this talk to us. *Trial separation* . . . I rolled
these foreign-sounding words around on my tongue, tasting them. They
were bitter and left a fluttering in my stomach. I glanced at him and his
face looked drawn and sad, like a quitter. He cleared his throat. "We're
going to fix up the house and sell it. So your mom and I can both get
new houses of our own."

"We're going to live apart." She paused. "And you two will live
with both of us . . . you'll spend time with both of us. What I mean is,
you'll have two homes soon, instead of just one."

My gut clenched.

"But I don't want to leave," I whispered.

"I know, sweetheart," Mom sighed.

There was a long moment of silence, as the weight of it settled in.

"But the most important thing for you both to know is that we love
you more than anything." Her voice caught in her throat.

"And that will never, never change. And we want you to know that
this has nothing to do with you girls—this is *not* your fault."

My fault? I hadn't considered this.

Later that week my fourth-grade teacher took me to the school library. Her hand felt cool and papery in mine, and it calmed me. We settled into a corner and she pulled books off the shelf. Inside I looked at pictures of children crying, all of them wanting to know, *Is it my fault?* My face flushed with anger. *They* were the ones quitting, pulling my home out from under me, making me leave the place where I knew every leaf and pinecone, every shortcut and mossy stone. *Trial separation, divorce.* They were the ones arguing all the time.

But if it didn't have something to do with us, then why did everyone keep bringing it up? Could it actually be our fault they couldn't stand to be together anymore? That we were going to leave our house on Woodcrest Avenue forever?

~~~~~

My New York friends couldn't really understand why we picked Charleston. But despite my anxiety, I knew we'd done the right thing. In moments when I least expected it, like a subversive magic, I could feel it calling. Locals called Charleston the little Kingdom by the Sea, and its majesty was undeniable. Its haunting echo felt ancient, dark, Gothic, and salty like the ocean. Some of our closest friends lived there—they were a built-in welcome wagon full of love. The city had done its part to lure me with palmetto trees, winding creeks, marshy wetlands, and the ghostly footprints history had left on its cobblestone streets. Now Eric and I were nothing more than hermit crabs, pulling our bodies blindly along the sand to the silty waters of the Lowcountry's Atlantic Ocean.

In my spare time I tried to learn everything I could about faery lore to create a foundation for my journey. I had purchased a round-trip ticket to England and once we got settled down South, I would be leaving for nearly three months. It was in the midst of all this mayhem and nausea that I made a very interesting discovery.

After reading volume after volume of folklore, I started to notice that all the stories were oddly similar. I'm not talking about fairy tales here, I'm talking about *faery* tales. And especially in British, Irish, and Scottish folklore, there were only a few variations on a very few themes.

Exhibit A: The Midwife. In this story, a midwife in a small town is awoken from sleep by a tall, well-dressed stranger, begging her to come help birth his wife's child. He promises a great reward, and she agrees. Once aboard his finely appointed carriage, she is asked to blindfold herself. Considering the heavy pouch of coins, she complies. They arrive at a great estate, and the woman wonders how such a grand building could be within traveling distance from her home without her knowing it. Inside she finds a beautiful woman in the throes of birthing, and all her concerns are put aside as she focuses on the task at hand. After the child is born, one of two things happen. There is either ointment that she is asked to put on the child's eyes (and some gets in her eyes as well), or all those present in the room pass around a bowl of water and are asked by the lord and lady to dot each eye—the midwife dots one eye, not two.

Thanked, paid, and delivered back home, she pretty much forgets about the whole thing, until one day she sees the beautiful woman walking through the crowded market. "Good day, my lady," she says, rushing over. "How is your beautiful child faring?" The woman seems surprised, but responds in kind, "He is quite well. And you can see I am quite well, too. You see me with both your eyes, do you not?"

At this, the midwife is confused. Of course she sees her with both eyes! But after a moment, she then realizes truly, she can only see the woman with one eye, her left.

"No, in actuality, my lady, I can see you only with my left," she responds, utterly befuddled. The woman leans in even more closely and softly blows on the woman's face.

"And now, you shall never see me again." With that, the woman disappears, and the poor midwife, it turns out, has gone instantly blind in both eyes, never to recover.

The same basic story is retold in England, the Isle of Man, Scotland, and Ireland, under various guises. Sometimes the victim is a poor woman in need of employment. Sometimes it is a blacksmith, even. But if the gender or type of employment varies, the result is always the same: when a human encountered the faery world, the results were never good. Blindness was a typical fallout from a faery encounter.

Then there are what I call the "Fall-Down-Dead Series," in which some poor sap is stupid enough to kick, taunt, or in some way try to trick or swindle a faery. Unfortunately, there is no mincing about in these cases—the person simply drops down dead. Regardless of country or narrative bent, the outcome is, quite predictably, the same. Humans who interact with the world of faery, whether knowingly or unknowingly, do so at great cost.

Leaving behind the stories of the midwives, faery servants, or blacksmiths, we come to the wonderfully woeful world of changelings. It's interesting to me that although the world of faeries in modern times has been so incredibly extinguished—I mean, who thinks about them, talks about them on a daily basis anymore—and yet your basic man on the street would at least know what a changeling was. Funny, isn't it? Yes, we've all heard about the practice of faeries stealing human babies, and leaving a sickly, or oddly "old"-looking child in its place. On the Isle of Man in the middle of the Irish Sea, mothers never left the nursery at night without placing a pair of iron tongs over the baby's crib, the fear of baby snatching was so prevalent. Apparently, the ancient word on the street was that faeries abhorred iron. It was the only weapon that worked against them. Growing up outside of Ithaca, we always had a horseshoe over our door for good luck, and it was a tradition I carried on as an adult. But as I did my due diligence in faery research, I learned to my surprise that the origin of horseshoe hanging, too, was connected to the faery world. Horseshoes were made of iron, and in days gone by, hanging one above your door was a signal to the faeries that they weren't welcome there. In fact, the belief was that if you had a horseshoe hanging above your door, a faery spirit couldn't even cross your threshold.

The day of the move came, and with the help of friends we managed to pack the truck in less than three hours. I carried boxes in and out of my familiar old building as though I were moving through water. It felt like some sort of space-time continuum had opened up and that every molecule of air was wavering like a desert mirage, breathing with uncertainty, with possibility. Before we knew it, we were driving away from New York City for the last time.

It rained our first week in Charleston. The water pelted down like silver bullets, its own type of confederate fury, as though the weather itself had sensed the presence of me, the carpetbagger. The house was empty, but it was ours, and for the first week while Eric worked furiously in his office to catch up from the move, I tried to settle into a rhythm that made me feel worthwhile. Boxes crowded every corner, and I worked on unearthing our belongings while Eric worked on earning us a living. I couldn't reconcile my place in the world—I had packed away for months saving for my trip into faery land. Now Eric was working and my job was to take care of the house—the unpacking, the estimate on the new roof, the putting together of furniture, the nesting, the arranging, the grocery shopping, the cooking, the cleaning. For that first rainy week, it devoured me. I felt like I had no control: I was there to open boxes and toast sandwiches.

Then, just as we were beginning to emerge into our new home, I woke up one morning and the sun had emerged as well. I picked up the cat and carried her with me into the sunroom, watched her pupils dilate as she took it all in—the sun shining through the river birch in the backyard, the male cardinal calling from beneath the waxy green leaves of the laurel bushes. I don't know how long we stood there, eyes darting from one thing to the next, two tame animals regarding the wild ones. But I can tell you one thing. For the first time in a long time, I felt like I was on my way to obtaining that elusive feeling of finding home.

At night I fell asleep to the persistent chirp of cicadas, and I woke to the singing of our backyard birds. Our Charleston friends opened their worlds, and in observing them, I was able to understand some of what my new life meant. I watched Eric's brother Ben balance barefoot on the edge of his flat-bottomed boat, arm arced smoothly as he cast his shrimp net into the muddy waters of the creek. I watched his girlfriend, Cameron, watering her sunflowers barefoot on Sullivan's Island. I watched Eric's intent brown eyes soften as he gazed out at the sea. It was in noticing these little things that I began to feel something stir within me. And I realized that somewhere along the line in life, I'd fallen asleep. Maybe this was why I'd had so little success thus far on my venture into the faery world. I'd been racing through my days with my eyes shut to the world around me, despite my best intentions. As I felt myself come awake, I wondered if I hadn't discovered the first real step to connecting with enchantment. How can we expect to see and experience the faery kingdom until we have come alive enough to notice and be grateful for the beauty of our own?

The night before I set off on my trip, we had out first party, both a housewarming and a goodbye, at least for me, for the rest of the summer. My heart was filled nearly to bursting. It felt so incredible to have the house filled with people, to hear the tinkling of glasses and the laughter bubbling from inside our new home, that in that moment, I deeply regretted my decision to leave this unbelievable life that had unfolded here in such a short time. My friend Laura made her way over to me from across the room, her green eyes not missing a thing. As we stood there she let out a little sigh. "You'll be back," she assured me, "but you know you've got to do this. You're embarking on an incredible adventure! And besides"—she leaned in with a smile—"if you're right about all this, you've got faeries waiting on you."

The next morning, Laura's words echoed in my head as I sat in the dim cabin lighting, the huge plane hurtling over the Atlantic Ocean.

In taking stock, I had come to a few realizations, if not rather belatedly:

1. I was unemployed. Yeah, I know, that was not news. But now, as the plane moved farther and farther from my creature comforts, the lack of financial inflow was seeming a bit more . . . realistic.

2. I was currently unemployed because I felt the need to fly to England in the hope of encountering invisible creatures of a nonhuman ilk.

3. Because encountering said invisible creatures seemed to require a single-mindedness and interior focus that I did not possess in my daily life, I had left an incredibly handsome and sexy fiancé behind.

It all seemed too immense. When the plane landed in London, my journey would truly begin. And I'd discovered an eerie coincidence. W. Y. Evans-Wentz had made this very journey—to many of the same places I hoped to visit—exactly one hundred years before. It was the summer of 1909 when Evans-Wentz began his exploration into the world of faeries, and something about the timing of it all sent a shiver down my spine. Either faeries were all around us, or they weren't. Either they existed, or they didn't. It was time for me to find out.

ENGLAND

6

An Enchanting Encounter in Hampstead Heath

As we humans moved away from our close
connection to the earth, we lost our link with
the wild folk. We forgot how to see them, how to
contact them, and how to treat them.

—ANNA FRANKLIN, *WORKING WITH FAIRIES*

WELCOME to Hampstead Heath: you are here."

When you're walking in the woods in the United Kingdom, you must be careful not to get "pixie led." The pixies, who are apparently a terribly tricksy bunch who delight in toying with mortals, will jumble your head, leading you this way and that, until you end up exactly where they want you to be—and exactly where you don't want to be. It seemed that, for reasons yet unknown, I was meant to be in the park, for the park certainly found me—despite my very best efforts. I turned and headed into the Heath, my feet following a thin dirt trail until the path exploded into a field of knee-high Queen Anne's lace and long, lush green grasses blowing softly in the breeze. It nearly took my breath away. But my fear of the unknown was palpable. Where did the path lead? If I got this lost attempting to follow simple directions, how on earth would I find my way back through an eight-hundred-acre park?

Breathing in the sweet smell, I found my way to a wooden bench under the shade of some tall trees at the edge of the field. I dug out my pen and a small notebook and began to write. I hadn't been writing more than a few minutes when I heard a snuffling sound coming up the path toward me and turned to find a floppy-eared black-and-white spaniel bounding toward me.

"Hi, puppy!" I crooned, massaging his velvety face in my hands. This dog belonged on calendars. I smiled at the woman following him.

"I love your dog," I murmured, as he jumped onto the bench next to me and proceeded to crawl into my lap.

"Oh, Harry, no!"

"It's okay, I don't mind," I reassured her. She looked to be in her late forties with dark brown hair and surprisingly warm brown eyes.

"You're American! How wonderful!" she exclaimed, setting me immediately at ease. As we began to talk, she not only gave me directions into town, but she told me about a stunning panorama of London that could be viewed from just across the road. "Actually," she said, glancing at her cell phone, "I've got a few minutes. Would you like me to take you over there and show you myself?"

"Wow, yes! That'd be incredible, thank you!" It was bound to be a little awkward, but I knew I was lucking out big time. Before I knew it, my new friend Alison, and her impossibly cute dog, Harry, had invited me to come along for their daily walk through the Heath. I wondered at my good fortune as we made our way down a shady path that led deep into a forest. Alison was fascinating. Five years earlier, she'd had a call to life when her husband of seventeen years came home and announced that he was leaving her. The next day she found out she had a life-threatening tumor that needed to be removed by surgery, which required her to be cut open from just below her breasts all the way down to her uterus. She vowed from that day on to live life to the fullest.

"Now I live for myself, and my kids," she said. "I do what I want, when I want to." She smiled. "So what brings you to England, Signe?"

I don't know what it was about Alison, but I found myself spilling my guts to her. I told her about my father passing away three years ago, about how hard it was to not know the hows or the whys, about how much I missed him. About meeting Eric, getting engaged, leaving New York together, and I told her about my desire to find out the truth behind the existence of faeries. "Because," I told her, "I find it really hard to believe in God. I mean, no one else in my family ever has. So in a roundabout way, if I can discover what else there is out there, maybe it will somehow make losing my father . . ." I trailed off, not really knowing how to finish.

She looked at me for a moment as if we were playing a game of chess and she was about to sweep in with one simple move that would change the game entirely.

"Well, really," she said simply, "It's entirely about trust." I waited for her to continue. "You're here searching, for what? I don't think you're really sure. But you're here, and I think that right now, you're having to teach yourself how to trust again. That's where the real magic lies. To find what you're looking for, you've got to learn to trust."

The second night in London I dreamed of my father. He was leaning against a column in my mother's living room, waiting for me to notice him. He looked just as he did before he died—some gray-white stubble beginning to show on his usually clean-shaven cheeks, his peppered hair thinning at the scalp. He didn't speak, but just looked at me, imploringly, sadly. He closed his eyes a moment, as if to show me how good it felt to rest. He looked tired. I understood what I was supposed to do—but all I could do was clutch him, lean my face into his as my stomach seized and I began to cry uncontrollably, tears streaming down my face. I could only say, *I miss you so much, Daddy, I just miss you so much that I just can't get over it,* as I wailed against him.

I knew he was asking me to let him go.

I just couldn't.

~~~~~

While in London, I was staying with Rebecca Campbell and her husband, Anthony McGowan, in their three-bedroom flat in West Hampstead. Becky now ran a fashion company full-time, but her novel had been one of the first I edited in my career, and over the years we had become closer to family than friends. Their home proved be the perfect nest from which to prepare my first steps into the world of faery.

Back in New York I had come across a documentary entitled *The Fairy Faith*, by John Walker. Walker's search felt very similar to my own, and we shared a similar sentiment, that the belief in faeries has been with humans for thousands of years. From the Greeks to the Romans, from the Japanese to the Celts, most cultures known to us believed in some sort of faeries. However, "in the past several generations," his resonant voice boomed, "we seem to have abandoned them, relegated them to the nursery. Science has turned an ancient belief into superstition."

In Devon, England, Walker had interviewed a man who explained that faeries can affect our minds as well as our imaginations. In other words, faeries can control what we see, and, therefore, they can control whether we see them or not. The idea that faeries could control or, in the very least, hold sway over our imaginations intrigued me—especially after my experience in Mexico. But what really blew me away was Walker's interview with Brian Froud. Together with a man named Alan Lee (now the Oscar-winning conceptual designer for the *Lord of the Rings* movie trilogy), Froud wrote and illustrated a book entitled *Faeries* in 1978. It was not only a *New York Times* bestseller, but it would become a classic that ultimately launched Froud's career. When Jim Henson discovered Brian Froud's work, he took a trip out to Devon to meet him. Before long, Froud was the conceptual designer for two of the most memorable cult classics for my generation: *Labyrinth* and *The Dark Crystal*. He was the mastermind behind the characters that had ignited my imagination as a child. Who doesn't remember the peaceful, humpbacked Mystics? I'd watched enraptured as they ceased their daily duties to raise their head and, each in their own tone, call out that long, deep note that summoned the One destined to find the missing crystal shard. Who doesn't remember the nasty, vulturelike Skeksis, with their Yoda-like "Mmmmhm! Gelfling, mmmmh!"

Brian Froud was the faery godfather of our imaginations. He was also the author and illustrator of nearly every faery book that had caught my eye in a Barnes & Noble long before I ever really gave faeries a second thought. *Lady Cottington's Pressed Fairy Book?* Brian Froud. *Good Faeries/Bad Faeries?* Brian Froud. His books have sold more than eight million copies worldwide, an impressive feat by any standard. But most alluring was one simple little fact: Brian Froud absolutely and unequivocally believed in the existence of faeries.

Thanks to John Walker, I had rediscovered the legendary Brian Froud. And by some miracle, after a brief introductory phone call, the quiet, magical man had invited me to come to Devon to meet and interview him and his wife, Wendy. Wendy Froud herself is an internationally re-nowned sculptor and puppetmaker. Known for her work on *The Dark Crystal*, *Labyrinth*, and the sculpting of a little character from *Star Wars* we like to call Yoda, she is no small potato in the fantasy world, either.

I would be traveling by train to Heathrow Airport, where I would pick up my rental car and make my way to Chagford, the nearest town to the Froud's home, a seventeenth-century thatched-roof cottage called Stinhall, located a mile or so from the village.

With Becky, Tony, and their two kids, I was properly marinated in a general feeling of safety, relaxation, and love, so the drive from Heath-row to Chagford was seeming somewhat less terrifying.

Sitting aboard the train, I was struck with a wave of gratitude for it all, and quite unexpectedly, I found myself suddenly close to tears. Twelve hundred thirty-three days ago I had lost my father. Twelve hundred twenty-four days ago I had gone back to work, walking the streets of New York City like a zombie for months on end. Seven hundred thirty-two days ago I met a man with a dimple in his left cheek named Eric at a party in Brooklyn. Thirty or so days after that, I decided I wanted to write a book about faeries. The weight of being here, on a train in England, settled in like ten pounds of gold, and my heart welled with it. I was alone, I was free, and I was here. I was living my dream.

And for the first time, it truly felt okay that I had no idea what would happen when I finally awoke. I only had to learn to trust.

7

Off to See the Wizard

At the edge of our dreams the faeries stand and
wait in reflective vigil. They have waited so long, and yet
so few of us have willingly crossed over the threshold.
—BRIAN FROUD'S WORLD OF FAERIE

THE moment I shut the car door and adjusted the mirror of my tiny rental car, my relative calm went right out the window. My budget had forced me into a manual transmission, and the stick shift was on the left. I am miserable at doing *anything* with my left hand. Toss into the mix driving on the "wrong" side of the road, the twisty English roadways, my debilitating lack of a sense of direction, and little gifts from Satan called roundabouts, and you've got one hell of a recipe for disaster.

I arrived at my first British roundabout to discover that all common sense had left me. I knew I had to drive on the left, but should I go *clockwise* or *counterclockwise* around the circle? Lord help us all, I was un-knowingly ill-prepared for roundabouts! Taking a deep breath I pulled out on the left-hand side of the road, heading counterclockwise. Directly into oncoming traffic. I must have screamed. What had been an empty roundabout a split second before was now a major thoroughfare of flashing metal and blaring horns. Terror struck, and I did what any sensible person would do. I froze. And the car stalled. *Shit, shit, shit!* What would Lynda Carter do? Starting the engine again, I worked my foot on the clutch as I struggled to find first gear. And instead shot backward at top speed. I slammed on the brakes and finally managed to pull over. How on this sweet earth was I going to drive the three hours to Chagford? I was going to kill half the population of England.

I'm going to go to England and prove the existence of faeries! La-la-la! Rainbows and butterflies! Teach me, faeries, and I shall live as you do, on nectar alone!

I wanted, so badly, just to smack myself, really, really hard.

I must have sat there on the side of the road for ten minutes as the cars whizzed by, just thinking about life, and my father, and what a good driver he used to be, before he had trouble driving, and faeries, and wondering why, if I had come all this way, the freaking faeries couldn't just flit out from behind a tree or something and take care of this whole driving thing. Meet me halfway here, faery folk. Finally, I took a deep breath, and gathering every ounce of courage within me, I waited for a break in the traffic and swung the car around.

Chagford, here I come. Just please let me make it there in one piece.

British people drive fast, very fast. Of course, I wasn't expecting this. After all, the Brits are such an incredibly buttoned-up and well-mannered folk. But their blinding fury of flashing lights, horn leaning, and zooming past me at nearly one hundred miles per hour sent me a helpful message about the rules of the road, and after a few close calls I was getting the hang of things.

Before I knew it my lovely electronic navigator was announcing, "Please take the next exit, off the motorway. Take the exit, now."

The scenery had surely sprung from the pages of a picture book. As I wound my way toward Chagford, I could hardly believe my eyes. The verdant green fields were dotted with butter-colored wildflowers, and tall, ancient oaks towered, casting shadows on the asphalt in the late afternoon sun. The road slimmed, as if to be less intrusive, from two lanes down into one. Now high boxwood hedges and stone walls lined the narrow lane, and when a sign for the village led me to its center, I delighted in seeing a beautiful old church, a stone-walled graveyard, a dairy shop, cheery pubs, and a few small shops.

Finally arrived, I parked and lifted the heavy iron knocker on the door marked "Cyprian's Cot" and was met by the proprietress, Shelagh Weeden, who instructed me to wait in the back garden for tea after I got settled in my room. My home for the next few days was perched at the top of a narrow flight of stairs where two twin beds with flowered comforters were nestled between two large windows and a sloping roof. I had my own private bathroom with an electric shower, small sink, and toilet. It was simple, clean, perfect. Downstairs I stepped over the terrier gate propped up in the hallway, through a small covered courtyard, and out an open door to the back garden.

"You've got to be kidding me," I murmured. Before me was a series of gentle hills that rolled into the distance as far as the eye could see. Beyond Shelagh's fence more than fifty sheep were grazing, and I could hear the long, plaintive calls of a lamb, his mother drifting too far in her search for tender spring nibbles.

The sun warmed me, but there was a soft breeze blowing the flowers about on their stalks in Shelagh's garden, tumbling swaths of purple, pink, white, and green. I moved toward a picnic table and sat, as Shelagh's two terriers, Nutmeg and Spice, wiggled their Tootsie Roll bodies around my legs. Every stress, every doubt, every minor trial and tribulation from the day melted away as I sat and stared out into the beautiful countryside of Devon. A shuffle of feet announced Shelagh, who came bearing a tray of hot tea and freshly baked brownies. I gave her a grateful smile—I couldn't imagine a more beautiful place to begin.

That night after dinner at the pub, two patrons perched at the bar asked me what brought me to Chagford.

As I sat talking with Ed and his friend Jo, both locals, I told them about the book. Ed looked amused; Jo looked somewhat consternated.

"If you're interested in faeries," she began, "have you been out to the stone circle in Scorhill?" Of course I hadn't. I'd been hoping to see a circle or two in England because they fascinated me, though I had to admit that despite my love of history, I didn't have much of an understanding as to what exactly they were. But to my delight, Jo offered to give me a personal tour.

"If there are faeries anywhere"—she smiled—"you'll find them on Dartmoor."

We swapped numbers, and I agreed to call her to set up a meeting for my last full day in Chagford.

Leaving the pub that night, I could hardly wait to do some reading up on the area. What exactly *was* a stone circle, and what did we know about the people who had made them? Hill forts, passage graves, stone circles, barrows, and henges. I let the new vocabulary flood me as I read through a stack of books that Shelagh had left on the living-room table. Dartmoor was really just a large, open plain in Devon, a "moor," in addition to being a national park. What I hadn't realized was that the Dartmoor area was known to be one of the richest prehistoric areas in all of Britain. Evidence of human habitation there dated back as far as 8000 BC, and I got the impression you couldn't walk very far in Dartmoor without tripping over an ancient stone site. The majority of the sites were Bronze Age burials (2000–500 BC), passage graves, which were essentially large tombs made from huge blocks of rough stone. The tombs themselves were buried after construction, and marked with giant stacked stone markers aboveground. Aside from the gravesites, there were, I learned, *twelve* stone circles on the moor. One of the most impressive, interestingly, was at Scorhill, where I would be visiting Jo in two days.

The atmosphere at these sites was said to be both moving and mysterious. It was interesting to me that Jo linked the world of faeries with these ancient sites. I'd read a fair amount on ancient burial sites in Ireland, and for the rural Irish, these burial sites were always known as "faery haunts." Now I'd learned, at least from one local woman's perspective, that this connection between ancient gravesites, stone circles, and faeries seemed to exist in England, too. But *why*? Nothing I read gave me any clue. Researchers suspected that the standing stones were built as early as 3300 BC. At least nine hundred stone circles were known to still exist, though it was thought that many more would have once decorated the landscape. They were destroyed throughout the centuries—farming, war, increases in settlement.

I had also thought that the stone circles were somehow connected to the Druids. But hard facts pointed out that this was an impossibility— stone circles predated Druids by thousands of years. And why did I have the impression that Druids and faeries might be connected anyway? Maybe because if faeries weren't a Christian convention, they had to be a pagan one. And Druids were pagans. But then again, wasn't everyone back then who wasn't a Christian considered a pagan?

More mysterious was the purpose of the standing stones. A lot of outrageous claims had been made regarding the function of the circles. Some thought they were UFO landing pads, while others contested they were astronomical observatories for a highly evolved class of pagan priests. Historians and researchers suspected they were more likely used as multipurpose tribal gathering places, where people would come to conduct rituals having to do with the seasons and the fertility of the earth. I looked at the clock on the dresser. It was two thirty a.m., my head was filled with questions, but I was wonderfully exhausted. I stacked the books in the windowsill and reached over to switch off the light.

I headed out for the Frouds' house on foot. It was a beautiful sunny morning, and I walked out of town on the narrow road, past a gathering of local townspeople preparing for an annual race up the steep hillside known as Meldon Hill. The morning was bursting with activity, and I couldn't help but get swept up in the utter charm of the bustling village—the combination of sweet early summer air, sheep grazing on dew-wet grass, and the shouts from the bottom of the hill below gave me a surge of happiness as I continued out of town on the narrow little lane.

As I approached the tiny hamlet of Stiniel, the leaves from the towering oaks overhead dappled the road with patterns that danced in the sunshine. A tall hedge ran, ten feet if not taller, on both sides of me, and I couldn't help but feel as though I was walking a lordly green corridor that led all the way to the ancient "Stone Hall." At last the hedges ended and I came to a rusted fence that ran alongside a field of tall grass and wildflowers. Beyond, the cluster of cottages that made up Stiniel came into view. A two-story house had been clipped from the pages of a Grimms' fairy tale and duly pasted onto the horizon. Tall and hewn out of hefty stone, a thatched-straw roof arched across it from which two chubby stone chimneys protruded. Just gazing at it made me . . . hopeful. Who knew places like this could really exist?

Turning down the dirt road I came at last to the Frouds' gate. Their drive was lined with wild bluebells that gave off a delicate, heady scent like hyacinth, and their house, like the one I'd seen from the road, was a marvelous thatched-roof beauty. Taking a deep breath, I found my way to the sturdy oak door and lifted the knocker.

A moment later I was standing face-to-face with Wendy Froud.

8

Down the Rabbit Hole

Where I live, I am surrounded by a landscape of wild beauty.
When I touch a rock or stand under a tree, I am in the presence
of sentient beings. What do they feel or look like on the
inside? What they look like are trolls, gnomes, and faeries . . .
I look at the land, I listen for the story it wants to tell.
—BRIAN FROUD'S WORLD OF FAERIE

WENDY was a red-haired beauty with gorgeous blue eyes and a wide, warm smile. As she ushered me inside and called to Brian that I'd arrived, I noticed that everywhere around this airy, enchanting space were little creatures. (Aside from their little terrier, aptly named Elfie, that is.) Wendy's creature creations, some beauteous, some wizened and gnarled-looking, decked tables here and there. Brian's paintings hung from the walls, the very paintings I'd seen as simple pages in his books. I heard a shuffling coming down the hallway and a moment later Brian appeared, leaning a bit on a wooden walking stick.

"I seem to have wrenched my back," he explained, giving my hand a hearty shake as we moved over to the big kitchen table.

I thanked him for seeing me, especially given his injury, and as I settled in, taking out my notebook and recorder, I couldn't help but marvel at the two of them.

Their clothes were simple, ordinary—but there was something about the way they looked that made them seem somehow timeless. Maybe it was Wendy's long, wavy red hair, or Brian's mustache, glasses, and rosy cheeks. But something told me I had stumbled into faery land. A rather complicated woman once asked me, "What are we here for, if not to live our own fairy tales?" Sitting at the table with Brian and Wendy Froud, I knew I'd been led to exactly the right place.

I told them a little more about the book I was working on, even sharing my bizarre experience in the cabana in Mexico. Then, clicking on the recorder, I settled in with my tea, and began.

"So," I said with a smile. "Tell me about the faeries."

Brian chuckled. He told me his interest in the faery world had first been piqued by the art of Arthur Rackham. The trees that Rackham painted had faces, and Brian realized quite suddenly that was precisely how he felt about nature. As a little boy he'd spent his free time playing in woods: climbing up trees, crawling through secret places in the undergrowth. Even then, although he didn't know how to explain it, he believed there was an inner life to trees, that trees had soul, personality.

"It was when I began to wonder what was going on behind the drawings that I began to reexamine fairy tales. I wanted to understand the reality of faeries. I started doing some exploration, reading other people's theories on the faery world. At first I thought, I don't know . . . all this sounds a bit weird." He laughed. "And at the same time, a lot of it sounded like common sense. It's very typical of faery, actually. In one way it simplified everything for me, and at the same time, it suddenly made everything very complicated."

I asked what he meant.

"Well, the most basic belief is that there is spirit behind everything. Everything has life and soul. And the complication is, of course, is that if everything has life and soul, then everything is very individual. It meant I had to have a relationship with everything now, in a very precise, individual way. If you start to believe in faeries, it's a reengagement with the world. It's a reengagement with the minutia of this world."

"Okay, I can understand that," I replied. "But what do you mean when you say there's spirit behind everything?"

Brian sat back in his chair a moment and then explained that the Mystics from *The Dark Crystal* are derived from the spirits of the trolls he felt on Dartmoor. When Jim Henson had seen Brian's first painting of a troll, he wanted some of that feeling in the movie. The Mystics were the spirits of rock and earth all around him, which Brian began to recognize when his eyes were opened to the world of faery.

As for Wendy, faeries were always a part of her life. As a child her mother read her Tolkien and the Chronicles of Narnia and Wendy believed in them so much it never occurred to her that there *wasn't* another world. After all, her parents *had* named her Wendy after the Wendy in *Peter Pan*.

"I was devastated when I got old enough to realize that Peter was never going to come and take me away to Never Never Land." She smiled. "But as I got older, I realized that through my work, I had actually helped to *create* the world I myself wanted to escape to. Now I'm one of those people that helps other people get there."

"Yes, it's very sad," Brian agreed. "As children, we're very involved with the faeries. But there comes a time when adults say, 'Don't be silly, dear.' And so our belief is eroded. When we rediscover our belief, it results in a reawakening. At my readings and signings, people express it to me by saying they feel they are coming home. They tell me they want to go away and write, or make something, or they want to write a letter to somebody. They wanted to reengage with friends, or family, or themselves. It reminded them of connection . . . to everything."

"So often people have a creative response to our work," Wendy added. "And what could be better than that? In my puppet-making workshops, we begin by doing a meditation, where my students see something that comes from their own creative mind. Then we work to take that image and make it three-dimensional. It's a bit of the faeries, a bit of magic, that they've created and can take away with them. And of course, now they can have a relationship with that being."

"What do you mean by 'a relationship'?" I asked. "With a puppet?"

"It's beyond what they create," Brian explained. "Within the meditation, you do actually genuinely touch faery land—you're in it, whether you realize it or not. So when you come back, and make a figure, it's imbued with its own personality. After all, the being itself has helped you to make it. It wants to be brought into our very human world. And very often, this is because there is some interaction or relationship that needs to take place between the human that is making the figure and the being that wants to inhabit it."

"You are essentially imbuing those figures with spirit. Not unlike," Wendy mentioned, "the stick figures you mentioned from Mexico. People were creating those figures and bringing them into our physical human world, and in doing so, they were imbuing them with spirit."

My mind flicked back to the stories about the Alux. The Mayans created the scarecrow-like figures, gave them offerings, prayed to them, honored them. But really, who was the creator and who was the doll? Perhaps humans become the conduit that the faery world can orchestrate in order to create something . . . or get what they need or want. Wasn't that what I was doing in putting my entire life on hold to come halfway around the world, searching for answers, searching for this elusive thing called magic . . . on what level was I also doing their bidding?

"Sure, it's just . . . sticks and stones or, in our case, material stuff," Brian continued. "But somehow, it contains the magic. It contains spirit. They've essentially gone into faery, and what they're bringing back . . . well, it's not just a puppet, not just a toy."

"Ha!" I exclaimed. "I wonder if the word hasn't gotten out . . . the faeries know they can come to Brian to get their portraits painted, or they can come to Wendy to be given a portal into our world."

Brian and Wendy seemed to think this was one of the funniest things they'd ever heard. I found I delighted in making them laugh.

"I suppose there is some truth to that." Brian chuckled. "In my work, there is typically a central figure . . . and round the edges of the picture come crowding all of these faces. It's like they all want to be in the painting. They don't jostle, because the way that I paint, each thing has a relationship to the thing close to it, but they all sort of . . . *get in.*"

In *Brian Froud's World of Faerie*, Brian wrote he truly felt the beings that visited him came to impart a message to the human world. He was, in a way, only their bridge. But what I hadn't expected was to be so taken in by the book. I mean, sure, it's beautiful. It's a large, glossy coffee-table book, filled with shimmering paintings of a fantasy realm. But as I turned, gazing deeply, page after page, something struck me. It was their eyes. Something about their eyes alone grabbed hold of me, and drew me in. There was something about those eyes that was so incredibly individual, so incredibly real, so incredibly wise. It was as though for a moment, in returning their gaze, I was almost able to recapture something long forgotten. I remember thinking, so this is what it might be like to be gazing into the eyes of a real, live faery.

When I shared my impressions of his work with Brian, he smiled and bowed his head a moment. "It's important that I talk about this," he began, his voice soft. "I'm an artist. And I use any trick I can possibly use to make you believe. In reality, there's no such thing as painting faeries as precisely as they look, because they are changeable, mutable, and often you're trying to paint impressions. My experience with faeries is that you can feel their presence very strongly, you understand that they're there, you understand what they look like, but pinning it down to a precision is impossible."

He explained that when he painted, he tried to do it intuitively—trying a series of lines until one felt right. Eventually he'd notice something emerge; a face that now had its own personality.

"I really don't have an imagination." He smiled. "I don't picture things in my head and then paint them. I paint what it *feels* like. Hopefully I'm getting it right. When you're looking into the eyes of the faeries I paint, you are, in fact, looking into the soul of faeries, the soul of the world and beyond, into the very cosmos itself. Because faeries, like the cosmos, are infinite. Faeries possess an unimaginable depth."

I nodded, taking a sip of the sweet homemade elderflower liquor that Wendy had placed before me.

"Traditionally in folklore, when you enter into the faery world, you get trapped, lost. You lose sense of time, or you go mad. So my paintings, actually, are very akin to maps. They are flat, they are meant to be read in a linear way, there's geometry going on underneath, and so the eye travels along a flat plane. When people look at the paintings, it allows them back into faery land on a *safe* journey. They're a way to take you where I've been, and safely back again."

"How do people get lost in that world?" I wondered.

Brian thought a moment. "Truly I think it's the faery glamour . . . people think that it's pretty and lovely, and safe, but it's *not*. It's dangerous. You don't realize it, but when you're in a faery place, or you're meditating, visualizing a journey into the faery realm, it's bringing you into contact with real things, with reality. What I'm doing is not fantasy, it's reality. I'm trying to reengage you on a deep level, to what that world is really like. And then, when you 'come back,' you're experiencing the world in a much more open and connective way."

Brian believed the trouble is that most of us walk around completely deaf and blind to the world around us. To begin to really engage with the faery world, we had to understand that we are all connected through our very own essence.

"We all have souls," he explained. "And for thousands of years the earth itself was seen to have a soul, you know. If you can understand this, that we're all just made of this 'soul stuff,' then you begin to see faeries are just made of soul stuff, the trees are made of soul stuff—

you begin to understand how we, as humans, are connected to the faeries."

I nodded, waiting for him to continue.

"Nature is wonderful, beautiful, mysterious," Brian went on. "But people forget that nature is dangerous. They forget that you have to treat it with respect. You can't condemn a river, saying it's *bad* because it drowns people. But the fact of the matter is that a dangerous river can kill you. It's the same thing with the faery realm. There are energies out in nature that you just really have to respect."

As I asked Brian more about the process of actually seeing a faery, he was able to shed some profound light on the subject.

"It's often thought that faeries use our own thought patterns to manifest themselves. For example, when a faery appears to a person, it will typically look quite similar to the creatures we see in storybooks. This is because if you were to see a ball of energy, would you really know it was a faery? No. So they try to 'speak' our visual language. We see wings, and flowing dresses, and heads and eyes. The problem is, we think we're just making it all up."

It was a tricky bridge the faeries must maneuver, in using our imaginations. It struck me that in Mexico, I might have succeeded in "seeing" a faery. It just wasn't a type of faery I found very desirable.

"Everybody thinks that faeries are on the margins," Brian continued. "They talk about how faeries live in the 'tween places, between light and dark, et cetera. They're right, in a sense. Faeries are on the edge of everything. What they don't understand is that faeries are on the edge of the *beginning* of everything else that exists."

Brian and Wendy assured me that something *does* change when you begin to acknowledge faeries, and they encouraged me to try it for myself. They might begin to give me gifts, Wendy explained, little things that I could come across that most people might just walk by but that meant something to me. I promised to keep my eyes open.

"So, given all your experience with the faery world," I ventured, "do you think there could be a way for me to prove the existence of faeries?"

"No," Brian replied. "But on the contrary, perhaps there's no way to disprove them, either. Just be aware of everything when you're trying to interact with them. You'll find it's often the most seemingly insignificant things that turn out to be the most important. And that's what fairy tales tell us all the time."

"Look." He softened, as though encouraging me to take heart. "There is no conclusion. Every ending is merely a beginning. Once you step onto the faery path, and you have, there is no way off. You can't go back, and you can't step off. Because they won't let you. So you have to keep going. You just have to stay open."

As I headed back down the road toward Chagford, Brian and Wendy waved from the front of the house. Looking back at them against the stone wall, I felt like I could've been Mandy Patinkin or Andre the Giant in The Princess Bride, you know, in that classic scene where they get the miracle pill coated in chocolate and set off to rescue Princess Buttercup. Brian and Wendy, standing there side by side, were perfectly suited for a much younger (and far more attractive!) Carol Kane and Billy Crystal as they waved, wishing me luck on my journey.

"Bye-bye, Signe!" I imagined Wendy calling.

"Have fun meeting the faeries!" Brian chimed in.

(Under her breath to Brian.) "Think it'll work?"

"Her? It would take a miracle."

I smiled to myself. This would take a miracle indeed.

Back at Cyprian's Cot, Shelagh served tea and we chatted about the history of the house. To my amazement, she told me it was built in the sixteenth century.

"Wow. That's incredible," I mused. "With so much history under its belt, do you think this place could be haunted?" I asked, half joking.

"Actually, it's funny you should ask," she said. "I've been at the house by myself at night, and walked past the living room and smelled the very distinct smell of pipe smoke. With no reason as to why I should be smelling it. But it's so strong, it's almost undeniable. And"—she glanced at me—"I've had guests tell me they feel like they're being watched, at night, in your room."

Well, that was enough to freak me out.

"I did have a woman who came to stay here once, who claimed she could see and communicate with spirits. She told me there was definitely a presence in your room, and in the living room." She must have seen the look on my face, because she quipped, "But she said it really seemed to be a calm, protective presence, more than anything. Not harmful at all. Really."

That night I slept with the radio and the bedside lamp on. Faeries, I was getting a little more comfortable with. Faeries, I might be able to take on. Ghosts, no way. Not in this lifetime.

The next morning I nervously set out to drive the heinously narrow Devon roads to Scorhill where I would meet Jo, the woman I'd met in the pub my first night in Chagford.

Of course, en route to the stone circle I got into a car accident. Someone came around a bend on the single-lane road going about fifty miles per hour. Realizing in a panic that he wasn't going to slow down or even acknowledge my presence, I jerked the wheel as far left as I could to avoid the head-on collision—slamming my precious rental directly into a stone wall. He kept on driving. Hands still shaking, I arrived at Jo's to find her waiting near the road and made myself, for the time being, ignore the fact that the driver's-side mirror was now dangling from a wire. *And on the second day, God created car insurance.* Summoning a smile, I let Jo take the lead as we made our way up the lane toward the entrance to Scorhill moor.

Jo was an energy healer, which meant, like Raven, she worked to heal people's ailments through the practice of Reiki. She believed that our world was filled with energies that existed beyond normal human perception, and that everyone could interact with this energy, if they wanted to. Jo first became aware of energies—which she broke down further into faeries, stone circle guardians, and the like—by spending time on the moor while she was first studying Reiki. At first she was only aware of energy she could feel coming from rocks, and she noticed that when the wild Dartmoor ponies were pregnant, the expectant mothers would often sit in the ancient circle of stones just before giving birth. Eventually it evolved into what she said was an ability to discern different types of energies—and on Scorhill she believed she often felt the energy of faeries.

The wind whipped across the broad moor. Covered in tall yellow grasses, the gently rolling landscape was scattered with ancient thorn trees with dark, gnarled trunks, each one framed against the spring blue sky like its own private Rackham painting. As we neared the crest of a small hill, I spotted my first ancient stone circle. It wasn't hard to see why Jo felt this was a magical place. If I closed out everything else—the rushing of the chilly wind, every errant thought spinning around in my head—and took it in like a piece of art, the circle—with its jagged stones still thrusting up from the earth in irregular fits and starts—was telling a story about relationship to the land. The moor felt vast, haunted, desolate. The sky composed the rest of the world, nearly crushing itself down upon the grasses. Whatever had drawn the ancients to this site still seemed to linger, despite the tremendous passage of forgetfulness and time. The rocks tied heaven to earth, cradling the power of the universe within their thick, stony fingers, if only for a moment before it dispersed wildly, out across the massive moor.

What I imagined were once towering stones had been worn down by wind, water, and time to leave what stood before me that day—twenty-three standing granite stones and several fallen ones formed a circle about ninety feet across. It almost seemed to be built into a dip in the land that physically drew me in as I approached. I looked at Jo, who was standing at the edge of the circle, as if waiting to go through. As I approached she turned to me. "I like to ask permission before I enter."

"Permission?"

"Yes. From the guardians of the circle. I feel like there's a male and a female spirit, somehow still here—I don't know . . . perhaps they were invoked during the time this circle was in use, or invoked in the building of it. They were probably made offerings when ceremonies took place here. I can still feel their presence." I hadn't considered this before, but regardless of whether the idea seemed far-fetched, there was something beautiful about it, something respectful, and I preferred it to tramping clumsily into an ancient wonder unannounced.

"But how will I know when it's all right to enter?" I asked.

"You'll just get a feeling. Something inside you will say yes. Sometimes you might almost feel there's a hand at the small of your back, gently pushing you in."

"What if I get a no?" I wondered.

"Trust me. You'll know if it's a no." Closing her eyes a moment, she entered. I stood at the edge and gave it a try.

May I have permission to enter? I waited, trying to quiet my mind, but felt nothing aside from my own impatience. Still I waited a moment longer before stepping gingerly inside.

It's believed that Scorhill Circle was originally made up of seventy standing stones, which would have made it the densest stone circle on Dartmoor. Now that I was standing in the midst of the circle I felt something very distinctly. It was almost like a slight drop in pressure. I also felt sad, curious and sad. I sat down in the grass, along a furrow in the ground. I wanted so badly to be able to imagine what this monument would have looked like, to see the people who'd used it, to know what they used it for. Artifacts gathered from the vicinity of the circle dated anywhere from 8500 to 700 BC. That was simply too much history for me to wrap my head around, and I felt lost in it. We sat there, each in our own space within the stone for what must have been several minutes before quietly rising and continuing along the moor.

"The interesting thing is that this stone circle seems to align with that huge granite rock." Jo pointed to a faraway hill. "So you can imagine that you could always use those rocks as a guide to find the circle." She pointed to another far hill where a similar huge stone was perched. "I think that rock acts as a sort of energetic battery pack for this stone circle. It sits up there in the sun, and this circle is tucked away on the moor. Of course, the stones were taller before the stone cutters got to them."

"Stone cutters?" I was astonished. "But who would touch those? I mean, how could they?"

She gestured to a number of damaged stones that lay in the vicinity. "It was easier to harvest these rocks when people needed stones to build their houses. Also, the circles were considered to be pagan places—so there were some who wanted to destroy them. There were men who went around hauling up the rocks and inserting them back in the ground upside down. I've been to some of those circles, and I can't stand to be in them. The energy feels completely wrong, like there's just pools of chaos now."

We made our way out over the moor where we came to a slender, rushing river, which Jo told me was the River Teign—it ran from the moor all the way down to the English Channel. Jo pointed out the remnants of ancient stone hut circles, occupied during the Bronze Age, most likely. I'd never in my life witnessed human habitation this old. Down the river, we came to a huge boulder with a perfectly concentric hole that ran through it, down into the water. "This," she explained, "is the Tolmen Stone. It's believed that if you drop through it, it cures arthritis, but it's been used by people here going back centuries. In ancient times it was most likely involved in cleansing rituals of some sort, as the hole could represent coming through the mother's womb and a rebirth of sorts could take place."

"It's incredible!" I breathed, climbing out onto the rock and lowering myself facedown, so my dangling hair was inches from the cold, rushing river.

Jo laughed. "Fancy a swim?"

"I wish," I breathed. The water was so clear and cold it was all I could do to stop myself from putting my lips to it and drinking. But the freezing-cold gorge waters of upstate New York, I had a feeling, couldn't hold a candle to how much I'd suffer from a dip in this river. I sat for a few minutes at the edge of the Tolmen Stone, listening to the soft rushing of the water. *Pillow your head on a rock and wash your ears with the sound of a stream*, my father used to say. A line from a famous poet, I'm sure, but when he said it, with his deep voice as we stood, arms linked, by a shady gorge back home, it became his own. We moved back out to the moor in silence, until we approached a grove of ancient-looking trees that looked out over the hills of Devon. I sat under a twisted old tree with spongy green moss mounded at its feet and aligned my spine with its trunk. Jo smiled.

"They're curious about you," she said.

I understood her. "Who, the faeries?"

"Yes. They're kind of wondering why you want to know about them. Maybe you should explain why you're here."

I thought for a moment. "I want to know about them because they're magical. And if magical beings exist, there's hope for us all."

"Well, they think that's pretty funny."

I didn't see what was so funny about that. In fact, I was beginning to glower at the fact that perhaps these English faeries weren't taking me very seriously. We walked on and out of the moor, and even as we did I could feel its immensity at my back, as though it stood there witnessing, as time moved through the rest of the world.

I liked Jo. She was kind, quiet, earnest, and honest. Back at her house Jo snipped fresh herbs to make us tea, and we arranged to meet back up at dinnertime.

My curiosity had been piqued and not satisfied by my visit to the moor. Some digging uncovered a few more interesting facts about the legends surrounding Scorhill and the vicinity. One notable thing pertained to domesticated horses. Dating back as far as local memory ran, riders on horseback could not get their horses to enter the circle or pass through it at all. And yet there was also a written account of someone in the nineteenth century who had witnessed a line of wild Dartmoor ponies approach the circle, and enter it one at a time, each waiting for the one before it to linger and then exit before entering themselves, just as Jo had told me. Perhaps the wild ponies knew more about its original purposes than we could ever hope to.

The Tolmen Stone had derived its name from the Celts, *tol* meaning hole and *maen* meaning stone. Naturally formed from thousands of years of water erosion, there was speculation from an early Dartmoor writer that, during Celtic times, Druids used the stone to purify people who had been accused of some wrongdoing within the tribe. Holed stones like the Tolmen were sometimes found as entrances into burial chambers or ancient tombs, like portals into another world. In addition to the supposed cures from arthritis, the Tolmen Stone had been used to cure children of whooping cough and tuberculosis. Some believed that passing through the hole could enable you to see the future. It was believed that looking through a holed stone could give a person "second sight"—the ability to see into the land of the supernatural, making faeries and other spirits visible.

That night was my last in Chagford, and Ed joined us for dinner. As Jo, Ed, and I sat outside in the cool May evening we talked about life and the meaning of magic, until it was time for them to head home and for me to walk the deserted streets of the tiny village, alone but not unsafe, to Shelagh's door. It opened with a creak, and I made my way swiftly down the hall, ignoring my intoxicated notion that there was someone in the living room who must be responsible for that waft of sweet-scented tobacco, and someone moving behind me up the stairs like a mother shooing her child into the nursery, hours past their bedtime.

9

Morgan le Fay and the Isle of Apples

*In the olde days of the king Arthur, of which Britons speak
of in great honor, all this land was filled with faery. The
elf-queen, with her jolly companions, danced full often in
many a green meadow; this was the olde opinion, as I
read it . . . I speak of many hundred years ago.*

—CHAUCER

THE next morning I said farewell to Shelagh and set out on another dreaded drive, this time to Oxshott, where I was picking up Raven for our journey to Glastonbury. Glastonbury had captivated my imagination since I'd read *The Mists of Avalon*, by Marion Zimmer Bradley, as a teenager. I was utterly enthralled by Bradley's gorgeous turns of phrase, rich with the hues she lent a legend I thought I knew. She wrote of the mythic Isle of Avalon, which legend says was a holy pagan island. In her epic, Avalon was home to the great Priestesses of the Old Religion, and the book bears witness to the clashing of the Old World with that of the new, as Christianity became popularized in Britain. Avalon was an island shrouded in mist not just in legend, but in literature as well. People have translated the name to mean "Isle of Apples," and it had been linked time and again to the Arthurian legends through an enigmatic heroine: Morgan le Fay. She was often spoken of as a priestess, but in earlier stories (namely Geoffrey of Monmouth's *Vita Merlini*, circa 1150) she was called a faery, a healer, and a shape-shifter. Some claim, or perhaps even Monmouth himself claimed, that he was working from genuine Celtic material when he created the poetic work that first truly popularized the Arthurian legend for greater Europe. According to that legend, Arthur was brought to Avalon to be healed by Morgan le Fay of his fatal wounds from the battle at Camlan. Some believe that, to this day, Arthur and his knights yet lie sleeping in the hollow hill of Avalon until such a time that Britain needs its legendary hero once more. Each year thousands of people come to walk the steep slopes of Glastonbury Tor, where many believe that Arthur still lies in magical slumber. And still others believe the tor is the domain of Gwyn ap Nudd, a faery king and lord of the underworld in ancient Welsh mythology.

But at the heart of Glastonbury is the Chalice Well, one of the best-known holy wells in Britain. For nearly two thousand years, people have visited to drink the waters, thought to have healing properties. The water flows at the same rate and temperature regardless of draught or other climate-related conditions—miraculously it has never, at least not in recorded history, run dry. In the late 1950s, the Chalice Well Trust was established to protect the well and surrounding area. "The ancient people saw wells as gateways where the veils between human existence, the world soul and the spirit realms became thinner, and beside them they established shrines and conducted ceremonies," according to the trust's website. Because the well waters are rich in iron, they turn the rock they flow over a brilliant red color, which at first glance is a little alarming. Today people come from all over the world to meditate near the well, walk in the healing pool, or to simply sit and enjoy the beauty of the extensive gardens.

Glastonbury and the Chalice Well aren't home to King Arthur and the faery folk alone, however. Legend has it that Joseph of Arimathea, who some say was great-uncle to Jesus, spent time in Glastonbury with Jesus as a very young man, and that upon Jesus' death, Joseph traveled to Glastonbury with the cup from the Last Supper, hiding it in the depths of the well. While Jerusalem to England would have been a long journey, it was certainly possible—England was a part of the Roman Empire during Jesus' time. And thus there are those who believe the well represents the blood of Christ: to drink its waters is an ultimate communion with the son of God.

Raven had visited Glastonbury back when we were first becoming friends, long before chasing around after faeries was even a pixie-sized thought in my mind. When she first mentioned finding faeries in my apartment, she'd also cited two unusual experiences that she'd had with faeries there. She'd been staying at the Inn at Little St. Michael, owned by the Chalice Well Trust. She was so taken with the beauty of the gardens that she would often wander through them at night. One evening she had a strange feeling that she wasn't alone and turned just in time to see a small silhouette with a rounded hat move across a shaft of light from the garden lamp. She had also seen strange lights in the bushes and trees, on various occasions. Now, Raven is a very close friend, and I trusted her inherently, but believing or not believing in something is not a leap I take lightly—I need proof. Raven was so "in touch" that often she didn't question things, and that I couldn't trust. But her experiences were intriguing enough to make me want to see if there was something in Glastonbury that I could experience for myself.

I invited her to come with me, but just before we left for Charleston, she'd broken some bad news.

"Signe, there's nothing I would love more than to come with you—believe me. Glastonbury is like *heaven* to me." She looked at me intently over her wineglass. "But I'm just not sure I'm meant to be there with you. You need to be the one reaching out to them. Not me."

My face fell. "But, Raven, I need you!" I begged. "I have no idea what I'm doing. I'll have no idea what to do!"

Panic began to rise in my chest. I only had nine weeks in Ireland and the United Kingdom in which time I desperately needed to get in touch with something—nine weeks in which I desperately needed to rediscover a sense of enchantment. And the one woman who had opened the door for me in the first place, who I'd traveled with to Mexico, who had become like a second mother to me in New York, was trying to bump me out of the nest. She was my Gandalf and I was a lost and bewildered Frodo, now being sent off to the ends of the earth completely alone. Now I knew the fear and the braveness required to bear the terrible weight of the hero's journey. *There can be only one.* No, wait. That was *Highlander*. But nonetheless! It wasn't that I needed her to prove to me that faeries were real—I knew that was something only I could do for myself. But Raven was my interpreter. She was versed in the world of faeries; she spoke their language. She'd seen them, she could sense their energy, and she knew what to do to get in touch. And I wanted her with me because she has a talent for making life magical. Even though she is a grown woman, she can see the world through the eyes of a child. Raven never doubts herself. Her life experiences have given her a purity of belief. And she is open to a magic that I don't think the rest of us understand.

I had steeled myself to journey through England alone, when a month and a half shy of my departure she called with good news—she would come after all. She told me that something interesting had happened: she'd received a message that there was something in Glastonbury waiting for her.

In case it's not already self-evident, I should state for the record that Raven is a bit . . . magical. To be perfectly blunt, she's a goddess-worshipping ordained priestess, Reiki Master, hypnotherapist who is trained in shamanic journeying. I mean all that in the nicest way. She's both enlightened and incredibly down-to-earth. The perfect copilot for my quest, if only for one leg of my travels.

What made Raven change her mind was a "message" she received while in a shamanic state, or "journey"—a dreamlike, out-of-body experience (are you still with me?) that offers a bridge to the spirit world. The "message" she received was that if she chose to accompany me, there was something she would experience that could change her life forever.

At long last I arrived at a stately home in Oxshott, in the fashionable county of Surrey. It was the home of Jill Schmidt, a friend of Raven's. At the sound of the car Raven appeared at the door, her blond hair wild with curls against a dark green cloak, the likes of which only she could pull off. I extracted myself from the car and nearly ran into her arms. It was so good to see such a warm, familiar face that I couldn't keep my eyes from welling up.

"I'm so glad you're here," I sighed.

"Not any gladder than me, darling." She smiled.

After a quick lunch, we set off together to Somerset. Now that Raven was in the car with me, everything felt safer, calmer. I told her about Ed, Jo, the Frouds, my time in London, as we wound our way through roundabouts and finally onto Route 303, a two-lane road that twisted through the English countryside.

A wreck on 303 caused us to creep the majority of the way—not a problem when you get to pass Stonehenge at three miles per hour, but it meant we didn't arrive until after nine o'clock. At last we pulled into the parking lot of the Inn at Little St. Michael. Raven had told me that if we wanted to double our chances of catching any faery activity, we needed to have access to the Chalice Well Garden at night. During the day, the gated gardens were open to visitors for a fee, but those staying at the inn had the benefit of twenty-four-hour access.

We rang the bell and were given the grand tour by a member of the Chalice Well Trust who told us the house rules (no cell phones, no electronics, no shoes, no kidding) and finally showed us to our bedroom. A serene and airy room with three twin beds, sturdy wooden rafters, and a cavernous fireplace, the house was clearly several hundred years old, but its condition was excellent.

We took a few minutes to get settled, before Raven looked at me, wild with anticipation. "Want to go out to the garden?"

Mmm . . . not especially, is what I longed to say. But how could I? This was what I was here for, and night frights or not, I instructed my head to nod. An auto-light went on as we exited, illuminating a paved path that led from the back door up a set of stairs. In the darkness beyond, I could make out a picnic table and an arching trellis. All around us were the shadowy outlines of hedges. As I squinted toward some large trees up ahead, something caught my eye. It almost seemed like the foliage of the tree, maybe two hundred feet away, was sparkling ever so faintly with tiny pinpricks of light. But no sooner had I registered it than it was gone, leaving me wondering if it hadn't been fireflies. I took a deep breath to relax and found the air was thick with the scent of honeysuckle and rose. As we climbed the stairs, the motion-sensitive light shut off and the only sound was the soft rustling of the wind through the garden foliage.

"Isn't it beautiful?" Raven whispered.

"Very," I whispered back, noticing the walkway ahead ended in a T.

"If you go to the right," she explained, her voice low, "that's the way to the Chalice Well. The well is just above a small waterfall. Heading left just goes to the fence at the edge of the property."

I studied the path to the well. It was pitch-black and completely enclosed among tall bushes and hedges. There were tall coniferous trees, and I could hear the sound of running water. It almost seemed to beckon. And yet the air around me felt . . . aware somehow. I had the oddest feeling that I was trespassing, unwanted.

"Want to go?" Raven whispered excitedly.

"Uhhh . . . maybe not tonight . . ." *Have I mentioned I'm afraid of the dark?* Think of an excuse, damn it! "It's so late already," I finished lamely. "But tomorrow for sure."

I could tell Raven was disappointed, so I suggested that we stay out for a few more minutes just to get acquainted with where we were, and that seemed to satiate her need for adventure.

Luckily for me, it seemed the garden of the inn had conspired to break me in slowly. After a moment I could tell that this part of the garden was spacious, open, not at all like I'd feared. I'd been picturing Raven, blithely trying to lead me through Sherwood Forest in the middle of the night—where baaaad things could happen! But as I sank into the grass, I discovered this was the perfect way to unwind. Before us was a small, grassy slope that harbored the trees I'd noticed from the door. Their old branches swept out, the delicate twigs etching themselves against the indigo sky. Were they thorn? Apple? I couldn't tell. But they seemed to give the back garden its presence. For a few minutes I sat, my head tilted back to take in the night sky, the stars beaming back at me from so many light-years away. Eventually, my exhaustion got the better of me. The morning had structure and excitement—we were meeting with Peter Knight, an author and sacred-sights tour guide, who was going to take us around Glastonbury and hopefully give us some insight into its incredible history. That night we slept with the window open; the breeze off the garden tickling my cheek, I fell utterly and blissfully asleep.

The next morning found us in the garden, eager to see it in broad daylight. I was stunned by the incredible bloom of flowers—a dozen shades each of pinks, purples, reds, blues—and the lush green grass that begged for bare feet. We followed the path uphill where we came to the small waterfall, clear water running over bloodred rock that opened up into a pool marked the Healing Pool. I dipped my fingers in to discover it was freezing! *You call it healing; back home we'd call it bracing . . .*

The waterfall, dubbed King Arthur's Court, had a thick foliage of trees above it, and it was cool in the shade. Though there were visitors milling about, people kept their voices hushed in reverence—the well emanated a sense of majesty. The well head, encircled on a raised stone platform, had its ornate wooden cover lifted so visitors could glimpse into the cool dark of the underworld. Peering down, the stones seemed a gateway into the very depths of the earth. People had been drinking these waters for two thousand years? It made me feel, for a moment, entirely insignificant. Lifetime after lifetime, from one religion to the next, this well was a constant, revered by all. I left Raven beside the well and went to explore the nearby Sanctuary—a rounded rock wall with built-in benches. Small tea lights had been lit on shelves hewn in the rock, and I sat down for a moment to let the serenity of the whole place sink in. I was feeling deeply relaxed when I heard a soft fluttering of wings and opened my eyes to see a little robin had landed near my feet. It was far smaller than the robins I'd seen in the States. It looked at me inquisitively and hopped closer to my toes.

"Hello . . ." I said softly. It seemed so tame. The bird came within a few centimeters of my toes and then, cocking its head, flew away.

Traveling up the path past the well head we came to the Lion's Head Fountain, where spring water spouted from the lion's mouth into a glass cup. I watched a woman take off her jewelry and dip it into the cup, running it under the water, and recognized that she was cleansing it, charging it with the supposed magic of the water from the spring. From the fountain, the path curved gently uphill until it passed under an arbor covered in masses of green, opening to reveal an expansive meadow. I wanted nothing more than to linger, but our bellies were grumbling, so we reluctantly retreated to the room to prepare for the day.

From the inn, we headed to High Street, Glastonbury's main shopping area, to rustle up some breakfast and see the town. What an eclectic mix—ancient-looking buildings, animated by the sparkles and organic-dyed hemp of a new generation. The shops of Glastonbury were outrageous. We strolled past store windows with mannequins decked in gauzy fabric complete with huge faery wings of green, red, orange, and gold. Inside nearly every shop were faery figures, wings, wands, wreaths made of silk flowers, ribbon, and fake ivy, and faery oracle cards. In another store, there was an entire rack of Brian Froud's art printed on every type of T-shirt imaginable. It seemed, judging by retail representation alone, I had hit the faery mother lode.

We met Peter Knight outside St. John's, a stately twelfth-century church with a massive bell tower on High Street. He was tall and slender, with bookish looks, and yet he radiated a warmth that made me feel instantly at ease.

Inside the church, Peter elaborated on the story of Joseph of Arimathea and Jesus. He emphasized that Jesus, of course, during his time, wasn't a Christian as of yet. Rather, he was a man (son of God aside) who found the religious practices of his time to be outmoded. He was searching to find something he could subscribe to, and being a free thinker, he began to devise his own practice based on love, kindness, and compassion. It was beautifully expansive—I'd never really thought about Christianity in this light. From the church we walked to Glastonbury Abbey as Peter detailed Glastonbury and the abbey's connection to the rest of the world, through a series of ley lines.

"If you think of planet Earth as one big, round body," he explained, "the ley lines would be like the veins. They carry the lifeblood or energy that radiates from within the earth, from one place to another." People called dowsers could trace these lines using their dowsing rods— L-shaped rods, made of simple metal—which have been used since ancient times for various purposes: to find sources of water, metal ore in the mountains, or even to sort out someone's guilt or innocence in a trial (yikes!). Dowsing rods were even used in Vietnam by marines in an effort to locate underground tunnels that concealed stores of enemy weapons. The Earth's electromagnetic energy runs through these veins, and Peter whipped out a map to show us the grid of lines that has been constructed through the cooperation of many dowsers over many years. Dowsers in Britain had discovered that ancient sites oddly seemed to be in line with one another. Ancient churches, holy wells (like the Chalice Well), ancient burial sites, and stone circles appear along the same line that can be traced for miles on end. Stonehenge was in line with Avebury, and Glastonbury, Peter pointed out, was a convergence point for ley lines from all over the world. I looked at the map and saw various colored lines drawn from the pyramids in Egypt, from Jerusalem—a dozen or more lines converged in Glastonbury.

"This makes sense to me," Peter offered. "Here in Glastonbury we have centers for people of every religion: Christians, pagans, Muslims, Jews . . . and somehow they all coexist. Everyone seems to want to claim a part of this place, and it continues to draw people from all over the world."

Glastonbury Abbey is the site of the first and oldest church in all of England. As I was to learn on my trip across Europe, if I wanted to find an ancient site to conduct field research on faeries, all I had to do was look for the foundations of the oldest church. Ninety percent of the time, churches were built directly on top of sacred pre-Christian sites. The ruins of the old abbey were haunting in their decay, and the grounds were meticulously kept, save the huge, old trees with tall rings of grass around them. Whether it was for lack of a weed whacker or some older, more forgotten reason, the circumferences of grass surrounding the massive trunks had been left wild, and it looked like the perfect habitat for faeries. This was a custom I would notice across much of England.

As we made our way through the Lady Chapel, Peter explained that there was a ley line flowing directly through the space. Ley lines actually move at a rate of a few miles per hour, Peter estimated, so there was, he claimed, an actual current of energy flowing beneath us that radiated up through the ground. When I asked him which direction it was moving, he stepped to the side of the chapel and smiled. "You tell me."

Out of his bag he pulled a set of dowsing rods, which he placed in my hands.

"State your intention, 'I'd like to find the Mary line, please,' and hold them gently, loosely in your fists in front of you." He demonstrated. "When you hit the Mary line, the rods will move on their own; you don't have to do a thing."

I took the rods gently in my hands and walked slowly across the church from west to east, as Peter had indicated. I saw a slight movement, like they really *wanted* to move, and then they died.

"The trick is you don't want to exert any pressure on them," he coached me. "You just need to let them move of their own accord. Try again."

I did. Nothing.

"Hey, why don't you give the rods to Raven, and she'll have a go," he suggested, giving me a look that radiated pity.

"Oooh, dowsing rods!" she exclaimed. "I've never had the chance to try *these* before." Grasping them gingerly in her hands, she walked across the church and midway across, the rods swung violently to the left. As she continued on, they obediently swung back to their original state.

"Wonderful!" Peter beamed. "You've found it!" Taking the rods in his own hands again, he walked through the current and the rods swung swiftly in the same direction. "The rods are pointing in the direction the current of the ley line is flowing. If we stand right here"—he guided us to the center of the Lady Chapel—"you're standing right in the middle of the flow. This energy represents the divine feminine, and you can feel it flowing through you if you try." I stood still, trying to see if I could feel anything. After a moment we walked the length of the chapel to a mortared wall at the north end of the chapel. "This," he said, "is the reason the Mary line runs through the chapel. Behind this wall—they've since closed it off—was where Joseph of Arimathea's body was enshrined for a time. It's believed Joseph, along with members of his family and a small contingency of followers, sought refuge here in Britain after the crucifixion of Jesus. In any case, if you ask me, he must have been a very spiritually powerful man."

I was trying to pay attention, but since we'd arrived at the chapel, my lower stomach was really hurting. Something occurred to me.

"Uh, Peter," I asked. "When you say people can feel the energy of the Mary line, what does it feel like?"

"Well, it feels like a gentle sort of pulsing to me, and it makes me feel a little woozy. Women, however, say they feel it pulsing right through their gut, you know, right through their *womb*."

Yup. That's what it was, there was no mistaking it. Talk about feminine energy—believe it or not, I had just gotten my long-awaited, um, monthly, that very minute while standing in the Mary line. And, man, was I cramping.

We spent a few hours exploring the abbey grounds before taking Peter to lunch at an organic café, where I finally had the opportunity to quiz him about his views regarding the world of faeries.

"Faeries, I think, are creatures of another world," he said thoughtfully, putting down his fork. "I think there are unseen realms that occasionally flicker into our reality. Some people say faeries are winged creatures; some people say they are more like some sort of orb. But I think perhaps there are different types of faeries, like there are different types of people and different types of animals here on earth." He echoed the sentiment that people on virtually every continent have seen them, drawn them, for ages, so in his mind, that indicated that there was something to it.

"I believe as humans," he concluded, "we're only seeing a very small part of what actually exists in the universe."

"But why aren't we able to see them?" I asked.

"Well, you might as well ask, why can't we see X-rays? Why can't we hear a dog whistle? Why can't we see the rays coming out of our mobile phone? There are lots of things that we know exist in our world, and we can't see them. Why should faeries be any different?" He smiled.

"So that's it then? There's no hope that I'll ever be able to actually see a faery?"

"I think you can," he said. "I think if we can change our consciousness, change our state of being, we can catch glimpses of them. I think that's what people experience. You know, people tend to see bizarre things like UFOs and faeries when they're not looking for them. It's times when people are kind of chilled out, drifting off into a bit of an altered state. In other words, is there a faery sitting beside us right now?"

I glanced to my right somewhat hopefully. Nope. Peter laughed.

"The truth is, we wouldn't know, because we're focused on having our lunch, aren't we? Imagine that outside of what we can see, there is a door, and beyond that door exists everything else. Some people say that the faeries have retreated, into the deeper realms, because of what we're doing to the planet. But perhaps it's us who have separated *ourselves* from the faeries. We just don't *see* the earth anymore. I think we need to look at the earth again through the eyes of a child if we want to communicate once more with these beings."

Being awake, seeing the world with the eyes of a child, these were themes that kept recurring. I couldn't help but bring up some of the darker things I'd read about the faery world, the trickery, death, blindness, the baby snatching. But Peter shrugged off my neurosis.

"Don't forget that a lot of that is just Christian propaganda. 'Now the devil lives here . . .' or 'the faeries and the witches are carrying your kids off . . .' It could have all just been Christian propaganda that then worked its way into fiction. But then again, who knows? Could you blame the faery worlds for being upset with humans, what we're doing to the planet? They had every right to fight back, I suppose. I think there's a darker side to everything, but that doesn't mean that it's bad. You have to have a balance. I don't think nature sees good and bad, positive and negative. I think it just does what it does, for the good of the whole."

Near the end of our tour we ended up in a bookstore on High Street where Peter suggested I buy *The Traveller's Guide to Fairy Sites*, by Janet Bord.

I could hardly believe my luck—you mean they actually made travel guides for people who were looking for faeries? On the front it said, "A guide to 500 places that fairies have actually been seen." *Cha-ching!*

"And, Signe, there's someone else I think you should talk to while you're here," he said in parting. He gave me the name and number of a woman who worked and lived in Glastonbury. "She might be a better person to speak with if you want to get behind some of the mystery of the faeries." I slipped the number into my wallet and we said our goodbyes.

10

Into the Night Garden

If we are to relearn the ways of working with the faeries . . .
we must follow the ancient pathways through the forest, where
it is sometimes dark, frightening, and perilous . . .
—ANNA FRANKLIN, *WORKING WITH FAIRIES*

OVER fish and chips that night, Raven described the ceremony she'd devised for us to conduct in the Chalice Well Garden.

"If you want to see the faeries," she said, "I would be very surprised if this doesn't do the trick." The students from her Mystery School, a weekly class that she teaches, had undertaken shamanic journeys on our behalf and created a ceremony for us, for which I was completely game. She and I were to sit back-to-back somewhere outside, bring candles to light, chocolate to leave as a gesture of friendship, and mirrors to lay in the grass so that the faeries could see themselves sparkling in the night. Raven had brought with her only the best chocolate for our soon-to-be faery friends—bars upon bars of Toblerone. And we'd already been partaking, I had to admit. It was all, you know, just practice for the big night. We split a bottle of chardonnay and lin-

gered over our dinner, knowing that the sun wouldn't set until nine or
later that night.

Hunger satisfied, we returned to the inn to freshen up for our
nighttime sojourn into the Chalice Well Garden. I sat on the edge of the
bed as Raven packed her supplies into a small satchel, adding her iPod
so that she could record the whole evening, just in case anything unusual occurred. We dressed up in our finery—Raven in a white dress she
wears for all her ceremonies, and I with my red hair twisted and pinned
at the nape of my neck, a nod to the Raphaelite paintings that felt oh so
faery to me.

My heart was beating in my throat as we stepped into the night.
Raven took my hand, and we made our way up the path and through
the gate toward King Arthur's Court—the waterfall of the Chalice Well
that fed into the Healing Pool. We passed the garden lamp where Raven
had seen the short figure flash by years ago, and continued up the path
into the dark, following the sound of the clear running water. Maybe
normal people would have thought wandering through a deserted garden in the middle of the night was awesome. Me? Not so much. I felt
like there was someone behind me, breathing down my neck in the
dark. I felt like there were a thousand eyes in the trees. I felt like we were
intruders, out of our element and unwelcome. But Raven, oblivious to it
all, carried on blithely. The waterfall, which had seemed so tame during
the day when I'd encountered that friendly little bird, now felt wild and
dangerous. I kept my gaze fixed on the back of Raven's head as we hiked
uphill, past the gently trickling Lion's Head Fountain, under the long
tunnel of the arbor. The breeze played with my hair as we emerged on
the meadow, and it was a relief to see the open evening sky.

"Where should we go?" Raven whispered.

"How about we sit under that old tree?" I gestured. It had caught
my attention earlier that day because it looked just as one would imagine a faery tree should look—ancient and gnarled . . . rather like the trees

I'd seen near the Scorhill Circle. Close to a thick row of hedges that marked the edge of the garden, a thick, low branch jutted out from the trunk at waist level, barring access in a way, keeping it secret, untrodden, if only visually. We went around the back of the tree and thought it would be polite, since the area felt so secluded, to ask permission to enter. We lit the candles and set them out in a circle around us, placed the mirrors on the grass, and put one near the trunk of the tree. I stood next to Raven as she lifted her arms and began speaking, calling in the directions, her voice resonating in the quiet night.

"Spirit of the East, spirit of air, we come before you with empty hands and open hearts, teach us, show us how to live . . ."

As she went through each of the directions, she softly explained that this would cast a protective circle around us, one that would also help us tune in with the energies of the earth. When the circle was complete, we sank down in the grass back-to-back. I felt safer this way, even though the darkness was thick all around us. Raven said aloud that we were there to connect with the faeries, in whatever way they saw fit. More than a few of her students had come out of their journeys to advise that we should be very clear about our intentions. In light of this fact, I decided perhaps I would write the faeries a letter. I pulled it from my pocket now and began to read aloud. I told them how I wanted so badly to know if there was magic, still, in the world, and that to me, they represented everything magical there is. I told them I believed as a little girl, that I'd loved them, that I hoped I'd been loved by them, and that if we could make this connection, maybe through sharing any experiences I was granted, I could help others believe once more.

We were quiet for a moment then, not quite knowing what to expect. My eyes searched the bushes and trees all around us, watching, waiting. Mentally I willed something to happen. *Okay . . . here I am! Sitting in the dark . . .*

Suddenly, something began to move in the bushes at the edge of the clearing. Raven was facing the open slope of the meadow, but I was facing a dense, tall crop of grasses with thick hedges beyond. I froze. I could hear the rustling—*shuffle, shuffle.* (Pause.) *Shuffle, shuffle.* It couldn't be more than ten feet away from me, by the sound of it. It seemed to move matter-of-factly, and I could hear it getting closer. I tried to keep calm, but I felt my chest tightening. I reached back and clutched Raven's arms, linking them in mine. I could tell her ears were keenly perked as well, but she was radiating excitement. *Shuffle, shuffle* . . . I couldn't see what it was, but *something* was coming toward me. My legs felt vulnerable, my bare feet so close to the edge of the circle, to the edge of the grass. Any moment it was going to appear—was it some kind of animal? I really didn't want to freak out; this was where it counted.

But some sort of Homer Simpson–like noise issued itself from my mouth.

"Neeeaaahhhhhhhhhh . . ." I said, pulling my legs into my chest. Just as I thought I was going to have to shout "Stop!" as soon as it had come, it was gone. My heart was clamoring inside my chest.

"Raven, I did *not* like that. I did *not* like that at all."

She patted my arm, completely unfazed. "Do you want to go in?"

God, I was such a sissy! "No," I said, reluctantly. "But can we switch places?"

I mean, come on! It was only natural that the brazen sorceress with the magical powers should be facing the *scary* part of the hill, right?

"Maybe we should sing," Raven suggested. So we sang . . . and it was truly challenging to come up with songs that a faery might like. According to legend, faeries possess the most beautiful voices and create the most unearthly enchanted music imaginable. Uh, what have we got that compares?

I heard Raven shuffling through her bag as I was winding up with my contribution—an off-key rendition of "Dream a Little Dream of Me," and she picked up her iPod to see the time.

"Well, Sigs, we've been at it for fifty minutes," she said. "But we can obviously stay out here as long as you'd like . . ."

"Let's stay out a little longer," I said, wanting to be patient. We decided to sit in silence for a while, taking in the night.

We'd been sitting quietly for a few minutes when I was startled by Raven letting out a loud gasp.

It scared the living hell out of me.

"What? What is it?" I whispered urgently.

"Oh my God!" she said, her voice filled with wonder. "Signe! Do you see it?"

"No! See what?"

"Oh my God, they're everywhere!" She sounded shocked, almost beyond words.

"*What?* What are you seeing?"

"I—I'm seeing little lights everywhere. You're not seeing this?" I could feel her moving her head from side to side in disbelief.

"No," I whispered fiercely. "I'm not seeing anything." My eyes strained in the darkness. I turned to look over her shoulder and saw nothing but black.

"Signe," she said seriously, "they are definitely here. I cannot believe you're not seeing this! They're zooming right over your head!"

Of course they were. They were probably thumbing their noses at me while they performed the opener from Riverdance on my forehead. But I thought a moment. What if this was really happening for her? Why couldn't I see it?

"Tell me what you're seeing," I whispered, my brow knit in concentration. "No, wait, don't tell me. I don't want to have any impressions for my mind to work with . . ."

But Raven wasn't listening. She was laughing, laughing in delight, and looking around her in utter amazement.

"Oh," she whispered reverently, "thank you . . . thank you . . ."

I rolled my eyes. I didn't want to accuse her of making this up, and I certainly didn't want to disrespect her, but how could I know if what she was claiming to experience was real?

"Signe, seriously, they keep just zipping right over your head. I can't believe you're not seeing this."

I felt my frustration flare, but I made myself sit quietly, squinting around me, hoping to see something, until she let out a long sigh that signaled the event, such as it was, was over. If there was nothing there, it meant I couldn't trust my friend's accounts. Every instinct in me, since I first met her, had told me that Raven was the real deal. But if there *was* something there, why wasn't I able to see it? I was, once again, being snubbed by the faeries.

That night we unwound by nibbling on some Toblerone and reading in our respective beds. Raven was knee-deep in *The Teachings of Don Juan*, by Carlos Castaneda, and I had flipped open Janet Bord's book on faery sites to a section on the Isle of Man. As I thumbed through, I was astounded—the author had devoted nearly ten pages to this place that I'd barely even heard of, and there were no fewer than sixteen well-known sites on the tiny island! Then again, Wales, where the author had lived for the past thirty years, had an astonishing sixty pages. It would be far better to head there next—and I was far closer to Wales than to the Isle of Man. On the other hand, I would be driving Raven back across the country to Oxshott at the end of our trip, so I'd be equally far from both places, it seemed. How to decide, how to decide . . .

The next morning we went to check our email at an Internet café in town, where I discovered, with nausea-inducing shock, that my car accident in Chagford would *not* be covered by my insurance, as I'd been led to believe.

I began to panic. This could cost me thousands of dollars. That was my budget for the whole summer. I would be stuck in the United Kingdom, starving and alone, with no way to get home, no way to pay my bills that were accumulating there in my absence.

Slowly it dawned on me that this had faery mischief written all over it. I seethed with anger. How *dare* they? I had given up *everything* to come here for them. I'd left everything behind in this stupid effort to believe. And what *was* this, some kind of test? I had tried to be forthright in my skepticism, but always respectful, and I considered myself a hopeful skeptic at that. How could they have let this happen to the one woman who was trying to revive them, trying to champion them?

After I'd exhausted myself venting to Raven, I decided to switch gears and call Peter's acquaintance. Anything to set aside the growing knot in my stomach.

I flipped open my UK cell and dialed the number I had jotted down. When a woman answered, I explained why I wanted to speak with her, but she seemed very reluctant to meet me.

"Please," I begged, "it would mean so much for the book. I can respect whatever terms you'd like . . . I'd just really like to talk with you."

She let out a long sigh on the other end of the line, but agreed somewhat warily. "All right then. Give me your number, let me check in with them"—I assumed she meant the faeries—"and see what I can tell you. I'll call you back and let you know what I hear. But I can't make you any promises," she warned.

Wow, I hadn't come across this yet. Her secrecy made me all the more eager to meet her. And her tone made me feel like a scolded child.

"Okay, I understand. I'll . . . just look forward to hearing from you then." Hanging up the phone, I tried not to chew my fingernails as I waited. I wasn't sure when she would call back, so I was surprised when about half an hour passed and my phone rang, startling me from my reverie.

"Thank you for understanding," she said, her tone completely different than before. "I'm allowed to speak with you, about everything.

Some of it for the book, and some of it just for you. And you're not to use my real name, or write about where we meet. If you can agree to this, I can meet you now."

"Okay," I said quickly. "Um, when would you be free to meet?"

"Now."

"Oh, right! Now." I raised my brows at Raven as I snapped my laptop closed. "Okay, no problem, just tell me where."

The directions were easy to follow and as I entered the building, I was met by a middle-aged woman with sparkling eyes and curly, dark hair peppered with white.

"You can call me Ninefh," she said, slipping me a card with her contact information and proper spelling of the pseudonym printed in capital lettering on the back. Gesturing for me to make myself comfortable, she didn't waste any time.

"Well, so, you're looking for the faeries. You'll be going to the Isle of Man next, I suppose?"

I couldn't help but laugh. "I am now," I murmured.

Earlier that day I'd noticed an advertisement for the Isle of Man in the window of a travel office near High Street. Now this was the third time since arriving in Glastonbury that I'd come across it. This time it was a sign I couldn't ignore.

"Good," she said. "When you get there, there's a special place I need to tell you about. Have you heard of the Fairy Bridge?"

"Only in passing," I admitted. The bridge, she explained, was significant because in forgotten times, it marked the boundary between the elves' land and the land of men. Legend had it that a great battle had been fought at that site, between human and faery, and the faeries won. Now as long as anyone could remember, it was an island tradition: those who crossed or even passed by the bridge must salute the faeries—a gesture of acknowledgment and respect that would ensure safe travels on the island.

"Otherwise the islanders are absolutely terrified something awful will happen to them," she said. "And this includes really wild bikers . . . they will all do it, because they are afraid they won't get off the island in one piece otherwise."

She looked at me intently. "In a country where the belief in faeries is endemic, there's always a fear of offending. And you do have to be careful. Because there's just no restraint." She paused for a moment, then repeated, "There's just no restraint. That's the simplest way to put it. If they're enjoying themselves, there's no restraint; if they are going to have it in for you, there's no restraint. They just don't have the same moral code that we've got, so . . . you offend them at your peril."

As I listened to her talk, it seemed that the Isle of Man faeries worked on a tit-for-tat basis. To have a favor granted, or to contact them, for example, one must sacrifice something in exchange. Ninefh went on to describe a visit to a place called Elfin Glen with her husband, who had been having problems with balance. She made an offering—a pink quartz heart—and it immediately began to snow. Her husband's balance problem disappeared. But on the way down, she fell and sprained her knee.

"You see, it was my knee in exchange for his healed sense of balance. But don't worry," she went on. "If you cross the Fairy Bridge, and you stop and acknowledge them, they will guide you from there."

I couldn't understand why the faeries would want to help me. "But why would they want to guide me?"

"Ah," she said with a laugh, "because they'll use you. It's as simple as that. They won't do it unless it's beneficial for them, don't you worry about that. And they're not to be treated as lovely little New Age angels," she added. "'Cause they're not."

I laughed. "That's something I learned pretty early on," I agreed, telling her the story about the Alux showing up past midnight in the cabana bathroom in Tulum. It seemed to be true that, as Peter Knight said, the world of faery was populated by many different creatures, spirits, if you will, and in fact very few of them might have "wings" in the way we imagined.

But it was hard to understand this new world I had encountered. And the question "What is a faery?" still loomed large in my mind. Ninefh was happy to be plied with questions, and there was something about her that made me trust in her experience, so I let fly.

"Maybe you could tell me," I ventured, "what is the difference between faeries and, say, angels?"

"Well, angels have to do as they are told." She flashed a wicked grin. "Faeries . . . don't." Ninefh believed that faeries are only partially incarnated, or physically present, on the earth. They were lacking one element, unlike us who have access to all four elements. The faeries, she explained, use us as a go-between, to do things for them in our world that they cannot do.

And according to Ninefh, there was a specific reason that twilight and nighttime were the best times to encounter the faery realm. In a wood at twilight, trees, which are always "breathing" in and out, breathe "out." Their respiration cycle reverses as the light fades, and suddenly, carbon dioxide is released. Ninefh believed that due to their biological composition, certain beings are able to "hide" easily in air saturated with oxygen. However, their biological composition makes it more difficult to mask themselves as the night air becomes more saturated with carbon dioxide. It was enough to send my head spinning, and I took a moment to gather my thoughts.

"I've read a lot of folklore that describes kings and queens of faery land," I mentioned. "Where do they fit in all of this?"

"Ah, the gentry," she mused fondly. "Well, as far as I understand it, you've got a level of tiny faeries, like worker bees. They're the ones that go out and do things, and they behave in one mind—they have one sort of collective mind. Then you have the royal court, the Shining Ones, or sometimes they're called the lordly race. They oversee and direct the rest of them. They're tall and beautiful to look at. There's a lot of ancestral ties going on, and the races of faeries change depending on where you are geographically. It's not dissimilar to what you find with people, really."

It was beginning to feel like the more I learned about the faery world, the more I didn't understand. And now here I was on this journey, with the feeling that I was expected to do something for the faeries, but what? The words of Brian Froud echoed in my head: *Once you begin walking the faery path, you don't need to worry about straying . . . they won't let you off.* As we moved toward the door, I looked at Ninefh, searching for the right question. Her warm eyes sparkled at me, and she gave me a reassuring pat.

"You know," she said, "there's always an element of choice: you can make it difficult for yourself, or you can make it easy." With that, she burst into laughter, as though this were the most amusing thing. I couldn't help but feel a sense of dread creeping in.

"I see . . ." I began tentatively. "You're saying they'll have me either way."

"Yes!"

"But . . . they would also protect me, right? Because I do feel a little frightened . . ."

"Oh yes," she reassured me. "If you do as you're told."

Somehow that was less reassuring than I think she intended. How on earth was I supposed to know whether or not I was doing as I was told? And what if I did something offensive, or wrong, and they . . . killed me or something?!

When I posed my quandary to Ninefh, she recommended I try asking for a faery advocate—someone in the faery realm who might agree to "sponsor" me, for all intents and purposes—protect me, guide me this summer, perhaps grant me experiences with the faery realm. "I can't guarantee you'll get one," she said, "but it couldn't hurt to ask.

Look," she continued, growing more serious. "It's a narrow line, you see. It's very much like the old country, where you do them a favor, and they'll do you a favor. And their favors can be great indeed. But that isn't why you do it. It can't be your motive."

I thought a moment. "My motive is . . . I suppose . . . to help people believe in magic again."

At this, she beamed.

"That's it." She smiled at me. "That's exactly it."

"You know, Signe," she said after a moment, "you've got to find your own way. But to be fearful is not being respectful. You can respect them . . . it's their territory, you don't want to tread on their toes, but you needn't fear them. If you're just doing as you're asked, and doing things intuitively, through your feelings, you don't need to be frightened of it. Not of any of it."

The night after meeting Ninefh I couldn't fall asleep. The room was alive with energy, and I had the weirdest feeling, as though there were someone, or *something*, reclining on the empty bed next to mine, watching me intently.

I tossed and turned, but sometime in the early morning hours, I must have fallen into a dream. I found myself in my father's house on Bundy Road in Ithaca, in my old room. I wandered around, my fingers exploring the things that were familiar—sheet music that had been torn from one of my piano books, my old school things, my father's writing pens. Suddenly I realized with excitement that if I was in my father's home, with all our old things, he must be there, too! I rushed to the kitchen vibrating with anticipation—I could *always* find my dad in the kitchen. But when I got there, his chair at the cracked tile table was empty.

The whole house was empty. I wandered, desolate, into his bedroom and looked out the large picture window, studying the trees that had greeted him each morning of his life there. It was then that the emptiness hit me like a river. And I couldn't stand any more pain, my body just couldn't hold it all. I collapsed onto the carpet, breathing in the familiar smell, and sobbing, absolutely sobbing for him. I was alone. He was dead. My heart broke all over again.

A wail escaped my throat, and I woke to remember I was in Glastonbury. I turned my face into my pillow to find it was soaked with tears. Why was this happening now, here, on this trip? I'd dreamed of my father and his death, twice now in two weeks. Why did I have to feel all this pain now, when all I wanted to do was heal? For the moment, I felt exhausted, wrung clean, but I knew it was only for the moment—I had reservoirs of pain inside me, spilling over, and I just didn't know how to make them recede.

I turned toward Raven to find her lounging under the covers, her glasses perched on the tip of her nose.

"Hello, beauty," she said. "I was just doing a little journeying. And I have some messages for you." I waited, wondering what to expect.

"First of all, you've been assigned what's called an advocate. A faery man has volunteered. He wears silvery clothing, and he is a very 'big deal' in the faery world. This advocate is going to assist you on getting through your fear, and your sadness, because you are a brilliant being and you should be radiating joy. There is room for nothing less in the faery kingdom."

A faery advocate, just like Ninefh had suggested? But I hadn't even asked. I didn't know what to make of it. Later that morning I went to do laundry and check my email. Noticing my cell phone had several unchecked messages, I dialed in. The first message stopped me cold. It was Ninefh, calling to follow up. "I checked in with the faeries, and although they were a bit concerned at first, everything I shared with you is okay. Oh, and I wanted to let you know—you've been assigned a faery advocate, so you needn't worry about anything anymore. Just thought you'd like to know."

In less than three hours, she and Raven had given me the same message.

What if I *hadn't* been imagining the feeling of that presence, studying me last night as I tried to fall asleep? If Raven and Ninefh were right, there was an advocate, a faery teacher and protector, somewhere out there, waiting for me on the other side.

Part Two

11

Beyond the Veil: Entering Avalon

WHEN the veil begins to draw back, it changes everything. Will you step across the threshold with me? Here, in Glastonbury, where the veil between the worlds is thin. From here, everything will change, and me, I will change with it. If you want to believe, I will tell you everything, just how it happened to me.

My feet wound their way through the garden, up the path, through the arbor, the sunlight playing patterns on my skin. I felt pulled like a magnet to the gnarled tree, which stood at the top of the hill as majestic as it'd been the night before, and I found an odd comfort sitting at the base of its trunk, sheltered under its boughs. Closing my eyes, I let my mind go blank.

I still felt emotionally exhausted from the gut-wrenching power of my dream, and I tried to shut everything up, all the jumbles of thoughts, doubts, and criticisms. *Don't let your imagination take you anywhere!* it said. *You'll be making it all up . . .*

But I was too worked over to fight it; I let my imagination take me where it wanted to lead. This, Raven had told me, was the first step in taking my own journey. Within our imagination, she believes, lies the key to accessing even the most distant of worlds. As I lay on my back in the grass, my mind and body completely at rest, I concentrated on being open, being present. Mentally, I sent out a wish: If I did truly have a faery advocate, could they give me a sign? I lay there, healing, relaxing, recovering. After a few minutes, I opened my eyes and sat up—I had the most distinct feeling that I was to wait for something.

I heard a soft flutter of wings, and the next moment a little robin, looking much the same as the one I'd seen the day before, landed on a branch close to me. Delicate and brownish gray, with a burnt orangey-red breast, its eyes were filled with a curiosity, a remarkable intelligence. I gazed back, and it fluttered closer, as if trying to capture my attention. Now it was within ten inches of my face, so close I could see the layers of feathers that made up its breast. But a moment later, it flew off.

That was weird, I thought. *The birds here are so uncannily friendly!* Not knowing what I was supposed to do to get in touch with my advocate, I picked up my pen and journal to do some writing while I waited for this mythical faery man to appear. A moment later I was startled by the reappearance of what looked like the same bird, as close as it had been before. I noticed with surprise that this time it held something in its beak—a large ant. With the ant in its beak, it cocked its head at me.

"Mmmm, yummy," I joked. The bird flitted from the branch onto the grass at my feet, looking at me rather expectantly before flying off again. I glanced over at Raven, who had made her way to a shady spot nearby, and saw she had an inquisitive look on her face.

"It's a flirty little thing, isn't it?" I called to her. "Not at all like the robins back home!"

"Mmmm." She nodded, gazing at the tree intently.

I had just put pen to paper when I heard a soft noise and glanced up to see the robin had come back—this time with some sort of wasp in its mouth. I dropped my pen in my lap and watched, completely puzzled.

"Signe," Raven called in a loud whisper, pointing, "I think that bird is trying to tell you something."

I considered this and gazed back into its deep black eyes. It was just standing there, regarding me. And I never knew robins were such efficient hunters—it was a matter of less than a minute between the two insect captures.

Is that true? I thought. *Are you trying to tell me something?*

The odd thing was, the bird wasn't eating the insects. It was just holding them, *showing* them to me. It took a few hops toward me and then took off—to finish its meal, no doubt. But I couldn't help but feel for a moment like Snow White—why, I bet if I had stretched out my hand that little robin would have alighted right on my fingers!

Gathering my things, I ambled over to Raven.

"What do you think that bird was trying to tell me?"

"Signe," she said, shaking her head, "I have no idea."

I thought for a moment, then smiled. "Maybe he was saying it's time for dinner." I laughed it off, but secretly, I was flustered—I had just been visited by the same bird, three times in a matter of minutes. What was it trying to say? Having spent the whole day in the gardens, it was now late afternoon. Gathering our things we retreated inside to freshen up for dinner.

Sitting outside over a glass of wine, we savored our last night in Glastonbury. I remembered Coleen Shaughnessy saying that faeries would often come to people in the form of insects, even birds. Birds I love; anything furry or with feathers could perch on my face for all I cared—after all, I was known to crawl around on the carpet with other people's dogs. But something of a disenchantment had happened between me and insects, I realized, as I looked down at my arm and noticed, for the third time that day, there was a tiny green insect with transparent wings that had perched itself on my forearm.

Since it was our last night, we decided to enjoy the sunset on Glastonbury Tor. I figured there wasn't a better place to be than on the top of the faery king's hill as twilight emerged, and I was determined that tonight I would not be afraid. To burn through my fear (quite literally), Raven had suggested that I write a promise to the faeries and, at sunset, set the paper on fire at the top of the tor. Perhaps I needed to cement my goodwill, to let them know that I would do whatever it takes to complete my journey.

As we climbed the series of steps that led up the steep slope of the tor, the sun lit the grasses in gold. There was a nunnery on top of the hill at one point, which some say is the reason for the bizarre-looking terracing along the hillsides. Others said the terracing was caused by the trail wound by the pagan worshippers in the thousands of years they made their pilgrimage up it. Our breath grew short, and I thought of Gywn ap Nudd. In 1275, an earthquake brought down that nunnery, leaving only the tower. It had been rebuilt, dated to the 1500s, and now, once more, all that remained was the tower, stuck on the top of the hill. As we climbed, it seemed the great faery king had certainly had the last laugh. What it really had become was one large standing stone, I supposed, channeling the energy between heaven and earth, just like the stones at Dartmoor.

We reached the top of the tor as the sun was a few degrees shy of setting to find more than a dozen people gathered, transfixed by the splendid coming of twilight. The sun burned its way down toward the ocean, dark pink and magnificent in its enormity, and the hills of Wales were shimmering in the blue distance. A woman with a camera and boom mike was questioning a group of teens who were sitting with their backs to the tower. "But you're up here this evening," I heard her say, "so wouldn't that put you into the group of people who want to believe magic still exists?" I smiled inwardly. It was comforting to know I wasn't alone.

I drank in the beauty of the countryside, letting it fill me completely. I remembered something Peter Knight had said yesterday, and I tried the words on for size: *Fear is an illusion. Fear is an illusion. I choose love . . . I choose love.* Everything in my life had funneled down into me sitting at the top of that hill, looking out to Wales, with Raven leaving the next day, leaving me to pursue this quest alone. What was I so afraid of? Trees? Hills? *Nature?* My father would be so disappointed.

As the sun sank, I felt something lift from the center of me—not completely, but noticeably. I could feel my fear, for the first time in years, beginning to dissipate. I had the most powerful sense that I'd felt this freedom from it before. I felt like I could soar from the top of the tor, hollow-boned like a bird.

All this time, Raven and I were silent, feeling. A pearly crescent moon rose above the tor, and from inside the tower, I heard the low rumble of a didgeridoo. The long notes buzzed deep into the coming night, vibrating through everything in their path, vibrating through me. I wondered what it would be like to be the man who made a nightly pilgrimage up the tor to blast the evening with ancient song. We saw him as we made our way to the wind-shielded side of the tower, walking with the massive instrument balanced nimbly between his fingers. Under the shelter of the tower we knelt, and I pulled out my promise, holding the thin slip of paper between my cold fingers as they fumbled against the wind to light a match. The paper caught and burned, and I watched as the fire ate it up, taking my words with it, into another form. Raven's hair glowed in the light of the flame, and I thought of the other priestesses who had walked this hill before, thousands of years ago when this place was known as Avalon.

We stayed until the wind whipped up and the stars multiplied, carpeting the sky. As we descended down the steep stairs I wasn't worried about tripping or falling. I wasn't frightened of the enveloping blackness around me. I wasn't worried that we were trespassing on the sacred mound of an ancient faery king. As the wind blew, the trees at the bottom of the hill bent toward me as if they were bowing, their leaves shimmying in the moonlight. We made our way through the gate, across the road, and back into the Chalice Well Garden. After the vast expanse of the tor and the countryside around it, the garden felt cozy, secure. Raven had given me her cloak, and I walked through the night garden barefoot and hooded in green, a woman not completely myself, yet more myself than I'd ever been.

As we reached the tree, we sat once more, back-to-back. I gazed out at the night around me, but there was no more fear, just curiosity. *Fear is an illusion, I choose love.* It radiated from me, from the very center of my chest, and I felt timeless. Last night, when I heard the shuffling noise, I'd been afraid—and my fear had broken the moment. Was it a test? If so, I'd failed. Tonight I could feel the land singing to the stars, feel the trees gently twisting in the wind, the bushes rustling as though they were papered silver in the moonlight. Behind me, Raven was humming something soft and delicate.

It was then that I began to notice tiny pinpoints of lights from town, blinking in the bushes. I watched them as they twinkled in and out, in and out. But after a moment, it dawned on me—I couldn't be seeing lights from town. I gently shook my head in confusion. I was looking at a thick hedgerow, with an orchard on the other side. We were sitting at the top of a hill, but I knew that banking the hedges on the other side was only another hill—the orchard itself. Meaning, beyond the hedge was nothing but the slope of earth and grass.

If I were seeing lights from Glastonbury, I reasoned, I would be able to move my head, and the light would stay fixed, possibly be blocked by leaves when gazing from another perspective. Then again, Glastonbury was hardly a glittering metropolis. Even as I reasoned, even as I puzzled, I watched a blue pinpoint of light move slowly at first, then zip into the tree above us. There were dozens of them now, delicate dots of light glowing within the dense blackness, one deep blue, another orange like fire, many in bright white. They began to move, to come alive it seemed, and I let out a small gasp in disbelief. These were not man-made.

"Are you seeing them?" Raven whispered.

I hardly wanted to move my lips, afraid my voice would put a stop to whatever was happening around us.

"Yes," I managed. "Yes, I'm seeing . . ."

I understood now what Coleen Shaughnessy had meant. This phenomenon was vastly different from any fireflies I'd seen. Fireflies are a flash, a burst of light, and compared to these, fireflies were too large, fuzzier and clumsier somehow. As I marveled, the lights moved around us, glittering and dancing in the night. And as I sat there, beneath that ancient tree, my spine resting against the spine of the priestess, I began to cry.

All I could do was sit there and acknowledge that the implications of this moment could change the course of my life forever. I shook my head in amazement, and leaning back into the cool night grass, I gave myself over to it.

12

Knock Nine Times
on the Faery Door

As much as I wanted whatever was happening to continue forever, to keep twinkling until the sun rose over the hills of Somerset, whatever we were seeing was certainly not at our beck and call. I had the distinct feeling that we had been granted something, and then it was over. Had it been minutes or hours? We lost track of time. I said thank you, and we made our way back through the night garden. My head was reeling, my body electrified.

By the next morning the human brain had recovered itself and began the process of doing what it does best—denying. I had known, even as I slept snug under my blankets, that this would come, that it was an inevitable part of the process. *I know what I saw*, I thought as I drifted off to sleep. *Nothing will change in the morning.* Morning had me back at faery hill examining the hedges, the bushes. I had no explanation. There was, indeed, just a hill on the other side of the hedge where I'd first seen the blue light, and the bushes were so incredibly thick, it seemed doubtful that light could penetrate them at all. And yet still, the more time that passed, the more I wondered—had I really seen it? Couldn't my eyes, in concert with my imagination, have been playing tricks on me?

Soon it was checkout time, and Raven was in tears at the thought of leaving. Bags packed and in the car, we sat at the well head, each mourning our departure in our own way, and I realized that there was indeed something waiting for Raven in Glastonbury. Here, she could be herself. People walked the streets in cloaks, they sprinkled faery dust in stores, they walked around wearing ribbons and elf ears. Here people conducted ceremonies at any time of day or night, or played the did-geridoo on top of the ancient tor. She had fallen utterly and irrevocably in love with Glastonbury. And her heart was absolutely breaking for it.

"I just want to be here, I just want to stay," she said softly, brushing tears from her eyes. I hugged her close, and said, "You can always come back. Someday, maybe you can buy a house here, your very own house where you can live with Michael, and you can walk down the street in your faery ears, and you can do so many ceremonies in your very own backyard."

I gave her hand a squeeze and left her to say her goodbyes in pri-vacy. I wandered back over to the stone wall, the Sanctuary, and sat down on the bench. It seemed like weeks, not days ago, that I had first arrived. I thought about last night, about the bird, and about the ques-tion of a faery advocate. I wanted so badly to know if it had all been real. If there was truly some spirit that would be accompanying me, to guide me, protect me. At the Chalice Well gift shop, I'd purchased a necklace with the symbol that represented Glastonbury to wear on my journey. I felt it was important to honor this place, where I broke through my fear for the first time, where I saw the tiny lights glittering back at me in the darkness. It was the oddest thing, but I *missed* that little bird. A thought flashed into my mind then, a gentle chiding. One that didn't feel like my own.

You know I'm not the bird.

I brushed the thought aside. I was so fond of that little bird, I wanted so badly to see it again, to say goodbye before I had to leave.

My breath caught when, a moment later, the robin landed beside me on the bench. Who was I, Sheena, calling to the animals of the garden by pressing my fingers to my freaking temples? As the bird hopped down to my feet, I shook my head in disbelief. In its beak, it was holding an insect. I didn't know what any of this meant, but nothing like this had *ever* happened to me before. This was the stuff of fairy tales. I gave a soft laugh, my eyes spilling over at the sight of the little bird, hopping closer and closer as it studied me once more.

I had gotten my wish. Now it was time to go.

For the first time since I'd been driving, I wasn't worried I would crash the car, prematurely ending my faery search, and we listened to music as we drove through the countryside.

"I'm so glad we recorded that ceremony," Raven mused. "When I get home, I'm going to play it back and see if we were lucky enough to catch anything."

"I'm so glad you recorded it."

"Wha—wait a minute," she said, thumbing through her iPod. "It's not here."

"What? What do you mean it's not there?"

"It's gone!" she exclaimed, bewildered. "The ceremony was there when I stopped recording, and now it's gone."

"Well, wait a minute. Are you sure you did it right? I mean, maybe you thought you were recording . . ."

"Signe," she said, throwing me a withering look, "I record my Equinox meditations practically on a weekly basis. I know how to work this machine."

"Right, right," I said. "Well, maybe *they* didn't want it recorded."

She sighed. "I guess maybe they didn't. 'Cause it's definitely not here."

After dropping off the car—and receiving a hefty assessment of nearly sixteen hundred dollars in damages—we returned to Jill's house for the night. As we grilled in the backyard, the practicalities of a spiritual traveling companion struck me. I may seem silly, but I was genuinely worried. What would *he* have for dinner? Where would he sleep? What was he doing when we were drinking wine and talking about men and marriage and other mundane life topics?

After cleaning up, I grabbed a dinner roll and walked barefoot in the yard. No sooner had I stepped outside than a little robin, the same type of bird I'd been so fond of in Glastonbury, landed on a branch above me. I'm sure they're all over the Untied Kingdom. They're called, after all, European robins. But it made me smile, and I broke the bread into small pieces, leaving it at the base of the tree before heading back inside.

The next morning Raven packed as I took a shower to accompany her and Jill to the airport. I was toweling off my hair when I walked back into the room to find Raven perched on the bed, waiting for me.

"You'll never believe this."

"What? You can stay?!"

"No," she said quickly. "Our ceremony . . . it came back."

I saw the iPod in her hands. "Lemme see."

Sure enough, where there had only been three recordings the day before, there were now four.

"But it has the wrong date on it," I observed. "You listened to it? You're sure it's the right recording?"

"Yes, it's us all right. But here's the weirdest thing," she explained. "The date on it is March third."

"I know! And we recorded it May twenty-fifth," I said.

"Right. All the other dates on here are correct, except for this one. But it gets weirder," she continued. "There's an old saying that when you knock on the door to faery land, you're supposed to knock three times . . . then three times again . . . then three times again. For a total of nine knocks altogether."

I looked at her blankly.

"Three times three is nine: 3/3/09! " she exclaimed.

"Oh," I said. So it wasn't the most convincing of evidence. I still thought any sort of electrical snafu could have occurred, no matter how well she knew her equipment. But it was something to note at least.

Saying goodbye was hard. It gave me that first day of kindergarten feeling, and predictably, I cried. But soon I was back at Jill's in a flurry of planning, booking a train from Oxshott to London, London to Liverpool, a hostel in Liverpool for the evening, and then an early morning ferry to the Isle of Man.

I knew that in choosing to go to Man, I was eliminating Wales from my trip altogether. I hated that thought, but the signs pointed to Man. I just hoped I wasn't missing anything by taking this leap of faith.

As I was saying my goodbyes to the ancient Chalice Well, I had felt like the waters whispered, *Stay awake, stay awake, stay awake.* In Glastonbury some part of me had been awoken, even more so than the unfolding that had begun back in Charleston. And I didn't want to slip into the unconscious again.

The next night, as I drifted off to sleep in a hostel in Liverpool, I wasn't thinking about how it was the home of the Beatles. I wasn't thinking about how the people spoke with accents I could hardly understand. I was thinking about something Raven had said right before she left. She told me that she had done a journey for me, while I was in the shower, to ask about my next destination, and if there was anything that the spirit world wanted me to know.

"I don't know what this means," she said, her brow creased, "but I just kept getting this over and over again. *The Isle of Man is for you, an Island of Masks. Nothing there will be as it seems.*"

The Isle of Man

13

The Isle of Masks and the Mystery of the Blue Jacket

They were all believing in faeries though. I heard my
father say my grandmother wouldn't go to bed without the
crock of water ready just for them, and bread in the house.

—MRS. KINVIG, RONAGUE

(QUOTE ON DISPLAY AT THE MANX MUSEUM)

TEN days on the Isle of Man. Now that I looked back on it, it seemed that the Isle of Man had beckoned from the middle of the Irish Sea. Of course, what first captured my attention was the fact that it was unbelievably rich in faery lore. There were reports that its great green glens echoed at night with faery music, that people would often get a funny feeling in the woods there, as though they were being watched, or sometimes even hunted by something they couldn't see. Adventurers in the wilderness would feel uncomfortable, then frightened, and some of them experienced problems with their vision, and a light-headedness that made them worry they might lose consciousness.

In her book *The Traveller's Guide to Fairy Sites*, Janet Bord writes that there have been such occurrences as recently as 1994. A man named John L. Hall and his friend were exploring an area called Glen Auldyn, just outside the town of Ramsey on the northern part of Man. They'd been walking for some time when they began to hear tinkling voices and strains of music blowing toward them on the breeze. Seeing as they were in the middle of a deserted forest, with nothing around for miles, they began to feel a growing sense of unease. They felt something was traveling along with them, watching them, but they saw nothing. They felt unwelcome, like they were trespassing. Agitation slowly grew into panic.

After deciding to press on, Hall noticed his vision growing fuzzy. He worried that, at any moment, he would black out. Unable to continue, the two turned back, abandoning their trek—not before, however, John snapped a few pictures. When the photos were developed, they were stunned to see what appeared to be a green man standing amid the tree branches.

Also associated with Glen Auldyn was the star-crossed love story of Phynnodderee, a handsome faery man who fell for a mortal girl who lived in the village of Glen Auldyn. Though he was part of the nobility of the faery world on the Isle of Man, his devotion for the young woman was so great that he left the faery court to be with his human love. But on the eve before Phynnodderee was to join his lady, he failed to attend an important faery event in Glen Rushen, deeply offending the king of the faeries. The king transformed the once-handsome Phynnodderee into a horribly ugly creature, banishing him to the mountains.

Isle of Man or "Manx" folklore, as it was called, was apparently rife with sightings of Phynnodderee, who, despite his terrifying appearance, was willing to assist humans who found themselves in trouble. On the Isle of Man, the faery world was so close that grandmothers told stories of their grandmothers seeing or speaking to beautiful men or women who behaved strangely on the roads at night, only to turn to find them vanished the next moment, seemingly disappeared into the moonlight or the eerie evening mist.

Folklore aside, there were other things about the place that made me wonder if it might be a particularly lucky location for faery research.

The entire island, for example, was simply one big 'tween place. Any island, of course, is an oasis between land and sea. But the Isle of Man wasn't just any island. It was an island almost exactly equidistant from four different countries: Wales, Scotland, England, and Ireland. And yet amazingly enough, despite its proximity to four different countries, the isle is a sovereign country of its own, with its own currency, language, postal system, and laws.

Though the island had enjoyed relative tranquillity for the past thousand years, there was still one ruthless invasion that took place every year, carried out by rough, bearded, powerful men. Their conquering was fast, furious, and it roared across the island for two weeks every summer. Since 1907, the Tourist Trophy Motorcycle Races, or TT as it is better known, has been held on Man, bringing tourists, tattoos, and the deafening thunder of roaring engines and squealing rubber to this otherwise quiet island.

I thought I was avoiding race week, as every tour book strongly suggests. But phoning a local hostel, I learned otherwise.

"Oh, hi there, need a room, hey? You coming for the TT?"

"What? Oh, no. No." I paused, utterly confused. "I'm actually coming to do some hiking." My statement was met with uproarious laughter by the man on the other end of the line.

"Hiking?"

"Yes." I cleared my throat, my fingers tracing the phrase in my guidebook. "I've heard the area around Ramsey is perfect for hiking, with its many glens and streams . . . you know, I'm just looking for some peace and quiet . . ."

"Yes, of course. We have lovely walks here. It's just that you've picked quite a time to get some peace and quiet."

"I don't catch your meaning."

"It's going to be TT week. Or didn't you know?"

What?

"The motorbike races?" the man on the phone continued.

"No, no. That was *last* week. *Bank holiday* week," I informed him. Silly man.

"You would be right," he said, failing in his effort to control a snicker of amusement. "But they've moved it this year. You'll be coming smack in the midst of it now."

"Oh, no."

"Oh, yes. But you're lucky. I don't have anything available for the first two days you'll be here, but I can get you in for June four through June thirteen."

"Okay," I sighed. "Please do."

I called dozens of places before I was able to book my first two nights in the only hostel left that had space. It was a music school that housed visitors in the summer, King William's College in Castletown, all the way on the other side of the island.

I came to terms with TT, or so I thought. Maybe I was *supposed* to be there during the loudest week of the year. After staying the night in Liverpool, I woke up early and caught a cab to the shipping port. The novelty of leaving England via steamboat was exhilarating. As we pulled up to the port I spotted the *Snaefell*, the huge white-and-red ship that would be ferrying me to Douglas, the capital of the Isle of Man. Ticket in hand and a smile on my face, I walked the gangplank that led to the outer deck of the massive steamer. Turning the corner toward the bow of the boat, I must have gasped out loud, because the whole gang turned in a single movement. To stare at me.

Oh. My. God.

The ship was packed, and I mean packed, with testosterone-fueled, beefy, leather-clad bikers, who were eyeing me quite openly. I scanned the boat in disbelief. I was practically the only woman on board.

Taking a deep breath, I tried to look confident as I made my way over to the ship's rail, but I could feel the curiosity all around me.

What's she doing here?

I was beginning to wonder the same thing myself. But as I took a seat on a nearby bench to better observe them, I began to relax. These guys were okay. On closer inspection they looked like teachers, lorry drivers, barristers. Nearly all the men had close-cut hair, many sprinkled with salt and pepper, and they were sporting sophisticated driving boots, T-shirts with long sleeves underneath, and thick leather jackets. They looked more like a bunch of giant horse jockeys than the rough-and-tumble, more menacing bikers you might see in the States.

The Irish Sea was black as tea, and even as the giant steamer cut through its choppy waves it wasn't hard to imagine how many times, on how many different boats, people had made this journey. All around me I could hear the bikers laughing uproariously, clapping each other on the back. Looking out over the gray horizon, I breathed it all in, and wondered what story I would find, what awaited me on this faery-haunted island.

Nearly three hours later, the island appeared before me. As the clouds broke I was met by emerald green trees, blue sky, and colorfully painted houses. The feel of the place was Victorian, I decided, my eyes settling on a light pink home with several steeply gabled roofs. I made my way down the ramp to collect my heavy pack from the luggage claim area, heaving it onto my back with a grunt. Without a doubt, this trip was going to give me sciatica.

I was lucky enough to have my own little dorm room on the second floor of the school. After an impromptu nap and improvised dinner, I set out for a bit of exploration. Across the street I noticed a ruin overlooking the ocean—sandy beaches strewn here and there with large boulders and flat rocks. I looked at the plaque posted by the ruin:

Hango Hill: Ancient Place of Execution. The ruins are those of a late 17th century summer house known as "Mount Strange."

How fantastically creepy. I was sleeping across the street from an ancient place of execution. The ravens certainly seemed to have gotten word, as they circled overhead calling to one another. Combined with the evening chill off the ocean, it was enough to send me back inside for the night.

The next morning I walked into town to visit Castle Rushen, which had stairways too dark and foreboding for me to even want to climb them. The town itself was charm personified, with exquisite white-washed buildings and curving streets. Between the buildings burst brilliant flashes of blue ocean.

Mostly, I slept. I slept all the time. I literally couldn't keep my eyes open. It was utterly against my will, and I couldn't explain it—like I was under some sort of bizarre enchantment. I walked around feeling spacey, light-headed. There were so many things I wanted to do, but there seemed to be perpetual confusion within me about where to start, when to go, and how to get there, and every time I tried to get up and get motivated, I fell asleep. It made no sense; I had gotten plenty of sleep prior to my arrival on Man. I am not, and have never been, a napper—it makes me feel too inherently guilty about all the other things I should be doing. And still I couldn't keep alert or awake. I began, of course, to blame the faeries.

"I don't know how you expect me to do anything in this state," I fumed, as I sat on the college lawn overlooking the ocean. "What is this about exactly, huh?"

Eat some clover.

Why was I feeling like I should eat some clover?

Above me the ravens circled. I ambled over to a patch of clover growing alongside the dunes by the beach and plucked it, giving it a rinse with my water bottle, supposing it was worth a try. It tasted clean and lemony. It could have been my imagination, but after a few minutes I actually began to feel better—more alert, a little more grounded.

Nonetheless, those two days were some of the longest of my life. I wasn't sorry to be moving on. Predictably, I fell asleep on the bus ride to the north of the island. I awoke as we were approaching Douglas. The bus had passed right over Fairy Bridge, from what I could see on the map. I'd slept right through it, meaning I hadn't even had the opportunity to greet the faeries as Ninefh had directed. I was beginning to feel like this island was conspiring to make me *earn* something before it would concede to my demands.

The town of Ramsey was nearly an hour by bus, the route taking me up the coast. This was the most I'd seen of the island so far, and it was breathtaking—undulating hills, grassy fields, forested glens with rushing waterfalls, sandy and pebbled beaches with towering cliffs.

Evening was setting in as we reached Maughold, the tiny village where I'd be staying, and the tall trees that lined the road were filled with songbirds chirping the evening rites. I found the office of the Venture Centre, and met one of its founders, Mike Read, at the check-in desk.

As Mike showed me to the private cabin I'd reserved across the street, I saw it overlooked the fields and, farther out, the ocean. It was rustic, to be sure, but comfortable.

"Now, you're going to be on your own for tonight, so it'll be pretty quiet over here," he warned. "But tomorrow we have a big bunch of guys coming for the TT, so hopefully they'll keep you entertained."

Oh, lord. "Fantastic." I managed a smile.

That night I dined on leftover cheese, some Irish whiskey I'd purchased in Castletown, and the three packets of biscuits that had been lovingly laid out in my cabin. With the bustling town of Ramsey two miles away, loneliness set in. It was dead quiet, and I'd been on my own without having much more than a passing conversation with anyone for four days. Compared to life in Manhattan, I felt like the lone survivor of a nuclear holocaust.

The next morning I headed out, sans map, to try and acquaint myself with the faeries living in Ballure Glen.

It was only down the main road a stretch, and I'd decided since I was crap at reading maps anyway I should try a new experiment—hiking by intuition. Normally (and especially in high-altitude areas where there are serious mountains and dangerous animals), this would be unadvisable. But here on the island, it was manageable. I kept walking until I came to a sparkling reservoir and decided to hike its loop, which I was unpleasantly surprised to find was dense with terrifying pines. There's simply no other way to describe such a desolate, utterly disturbing forest, one that left no question in my mind: *there be dark elves in yonder woods!* Thankfully, the loop took me alongside, not through it.

As I headed into an open meadow, I decided it was time to begin.

"Okay, fair folk, I'm all yours. Take me to your leader!" I laughed. "Seriously though. Today I'm going to let you take me wherever you think I need to go," I said aloud.

Ninefh had said I'd have nothing to worry about so long as I followed my intuition, so I did my best to quiet my mind and follow my instinct on which way to go, without questioning myself. I'm sure it was my imagination, but I really felt like I was being watched. Not in a bad way, just . . . noticeably. When I came to a fork in the trail, I paused, considering both options until a stone ruin nestled at the bottom of a sweeping hill in the distance caught my eye. It was a good distance off but I headed toward it, curious. After several minutes I reached it to find the walls intact, but the roof, windows, and door long gone. There was a gnarled tree by the edge of what might have been the side yard, and I touched its trunk. I had the feeling that whoever lived here had loved that tree, and I wondered how long they'd been gone. I felt a little spooked, yet stepped inside to find it was clear and clean with a simple stone floor. But something about the place gave me the creeps. Someone had left a cairn of rocks piled in the center of the room. And on the middle of the floor, a bizarre circular drawing had been etched in the stone.

Beating a hasty retreat back downhill, I continued on, forcing my feet to follow a wide path that ran through a dark, forbidding pine forest, ostensibly more foreboding than the one I'd passed before, because it looked to be the quickest way back to civilization. As the woods began to swallow me, I felt more and more certain that I *really didn't* want to meet the faeries that lived in these woods. I *sure could use an advocate now* . . .

I sang softly and tried to relax, but something was building. I felt the gnawing feeling that there was something right behind me, something that wanted to hurt me.

I was being followed by someone, and he was gaining on me. In a flash, I understood. It wasn't the faeries I needed to worry about—it was *people* that could cause me real harm. My heart pumping, I reached back and deftly pulled my pepper spray from my pack, putting it in my pocket, finger on the trigger. The next moment, I turned instinctively to look over my shoulder and nearly screamed.

In the middle of the dark pine forest, a blue men's jacket was hanging, suspended from a dead branch.

When hikers drop things, often a Good Samaritan will pick it up and hang it from a branch or signpost on the trail. But this jacket wasn't on the trail. It was hanging there, in the middle of the woods. Maybe it didn't make sense, but all I knew was in that moment, I wanted to get as far away from that jacket as I possibly could.

Leaving the trail, I stumbled through the woods, my clothing getting caught on branches until I finally found my way back to the reservoir. There were people milling around, and a fisherman was packing up for the day. I'd been hiking a good four hours. I went back down to the glass-framed map to figure out where I had been and something caught my interest. There was a point on the map marked "Site of Betsy Crowe's Croft," which looked to be in a field located past the top of the pine plantation, across the road. I'd been there. But who was Betsy Crowe? A local hero of sorts? Perhaps a female politician? She must be someone of importance if her house was marked on the map. There was something in this, I could feel it. I knew I needed to unearth the story of Betsy Crowe. It wouldn't be until I got home, at the end of my faery-hunting journey, that the true significance of the blue jacket would begin to take shape.

I was unpacking my hiking pack at the Venture Centre when I heard a great rumbling in the distance gradually approaching—the slow roar of motorcycles, an entire pack of them, pulling into the lot in front of my little cabin. It appeared my company had arrived, just as Mike promised. I peeked out my window and counted eight bikers, all clad in racing leathers and helmets. Well, this sure wouldn't be boring. I was just finishing dinner when Mike brought them into the kitchen on their tour of the facilities. There were seven men ranging in age from midthirties to late forties, and the eighth looked to be about twenty.

"This is the kitchen," Mike explained. "And this is Signe."

"Hi." I gave an all-encompassing wave. "I appreciate you coming all this way to entertain me. It's been pretty quiet here so far."

They laughed. We were off to a good start.

"I'm John," said a man with sandy, cropped hair and keen blue eyes, extending his hand. "And this is Joe, Paul, Huw, Sam, Wol, John, and Mark."

No way I was going to be able to remember all those names.

"We're, ah, planning on going to the pub later, if you'd like to come along," John offered.

"Oh! Well. I . . . I was thinking I'd . . . I have a lot of work to do, actually. I was planning on just staying here . . ."

"*Work?!*" John threw up his hands, completely exasperated. "What could you possibly be working on that's better than a pint?"

The man had a point.

"Okay. Yes." I surprised myself. "I'd love to come."

"Good then!" John exclaimed. "We'll come round you up when it's time."

And that's how I came to be friends with the bikers.

That night we walked into town together and got to know one another over . . . more than one pint. Dark-haired Sam was nineteen and his father, sporting a shaved head and goatee, was Joe. Sam had ridden on the back of Joe's bike on the trip, since his dad wasn't quite ready to have him out on the road on his own. Joe, John (who'd first introduced himself), and Wol, a rather quiet man with gray hair, blue eyes, and a closely trimmed beard, were brothers. Then there was Paul, a burly man with curly, dark hair and glasses, Huw, a blond-haired, blue-eyed EMT, and Mark, a compact man with an easy smile. Last but certainly not least, there was "other John," a tall, lanky bloke with dark hair and a weathered face. "You can call me Big John." He grinned.

Except for Wol, who was from Wales, the bikers hailed from Birmingham, England, and came every year to the Tourist's Trophy, the TT. I got plenty of good-hearted jeers as I told them about my purpose on the Isle of Man. As they taught me about the TT, I began to understand that this was more than just several days of racing—it was a huge social and cultural event. With the conversation flowing so freely, before I knew it, it was closing time. We packed ourselves into two taxis and headed back to the Centre. For the first time in what felt like forever, I wasn't lonely. And when John said, "Come on now, Sig. It's time to eat some chicken curry," I knew I'd found a new home. A little drunk and in soaring spirits, we fell upon the huge vat of delicious curry, regaling one another with stories from our pasts.

The next morning I woke up to stirrings in the kitchen and got up to fix some yogurt and fruit. I patted Wol on the shoulder, who was standing over the stove sautéing mushrooms, and said a cheery good morning to the rest of the boys, who were sitting around chatting and drinking tea.

"You'll have a full English, won't you, Sig?" John asked.

"Full English? Like as in a full English breakfast?"

"Yeah. Do you like it?"

"Yes! I love it, but—"

"Wol!" he called. "Sig'll have a full English."

I shook my head, smiling to myself. I may not have encountered any faeries on Man as of yet, but I was pretty certain that I'd just encountered eight guardian angels.

The faery search proceeded haltingly. I'd spoken to people everywhere I could strike up a conversation, and nobody had anything significant to relate. Sure, if you asked about the faeries, any Manxman on the street would obligingly regurgitate the story about the tradition of greeting the faeries when crossing Fairy Bridge. Even my bikers never passed by without giving a nod or a salute, though it was born purely of superstition. Beyond that, I was pretty much striking out.

With very few leads, I decided a logical place to begin might be the Manx Museum in Douglas. And to make things interesting, rather than languishing at the bus stop, I decided to give the ol' Manx Electric Railway a try. After all, the Lewaigue stop was only a few hundred yards from the Venture Centre.

The "tram," as they call it, was incredible—I was in love. You flag it down, it stops, you get on a rickety, wooden, caboose-looking thing, and sit back to watch the fabulous scenery go by. With only one stop in each town, it wasn't nearly as confusing as the bus. And the sheer abundance of enchanting glens between Maughold and Douglas was astounding. I watched as we whizzed past Ballaglass Glen, and Dhoon Glen, and fields strewn with four-horned Manx sheep and quaint thatched cottages.

It turned out that touring Man during TT was quite enjoyable, since I pretty much had the best places to myself. For example, I was one of four people in the entire, award-winning Manx Museum. My Manx Experience, as the museum called it, began in an auditorium, where I sat alone among a hundred empty seats as they showed a short film on the history of the island. Afterward I was set free to wander the exhibits with a far clearer understanding of what I'd be seeing.

The ancient roots of the Isle of Man, I learned, were Celtic. Suddenly, things were beginning to come together. England, Scotland, Ireland, and the Isle of Man were all countries renowned for their faery lore. And of course, all of them were Celtic in origin. No wonder the folk stories were so similar from place to place. I found a new energy as I realized that to truly understand where faeries might have come from, I first needed to understand the Celtic culture. Moving over to the library, which was conveniently located within the museum, I lodged myself at a table with a stack of books.

Now I was getting somewhere.

14

The People Behind the Faeries

Of all the ancient gods, one of the last to live upon the
earth with their ancient powers was Manannán Mac Lir,
the tempestuous god of the oceans . . .
—PETER BERRESFORD ELLIS, *CELTIC MYTHS AND LEGENDS*

T HE Celts were a mystical people, and as I sat there in the late afternoon hush of the library, letting the imagery of their ancient legends wash over me, their stories came to life. In a time before time, it
was said that the Tuatha Dé Danann came from the north. Children of
the great goddess Danu, they came from the four mythical cities of
Falias, Gorias, Finias, and Murias, where they had perfected the hidden
art of magic. Superior craftspeople, they were skilled beyond compare
at poetry, music, metalwork, and even war. But beyond that, they had
the magic at their fingertips to make themselves invisible to mortal
men, travel back and forth in time and between worlds. They could
change their appearance at will, and influence the weather. They
could heal themselves of any wound—they had learned the secrets of
immortality.

Listed as the fourth conquerors of Ireland in *The Book of Invasions*, the
Tuatha were followed only by the Sons of Mil—the ancestors of both

ancient and modern-day Celts. Some say the Tuatha came to Ireland by ship, others say on a cloud, still others say as a host of spirits on the wind, to take the land from the Fomorians, afterward battling the enigmatic people known as the Fir Bolgs.

The pantheon of the Tuatha Dé Danann is complex, and not without overlap, and there are volumes of texts and literature that detail their epic stories. But among the central figures was Danu, an ancient goddess of water (many believe the river Danube was named for her), mother of the Tuatha, and the goddess of all crafts. There was the Dagda, called the "All-father"; he was protector of the tribe and listed as the high king of the Tuatha Dé Danann. There was Lugh, the jack-of-all-trades: a warrior, a swordsman, a musician, a historian, a craftsman, and a sorcerer. Lir ruled over the sea. And there was Brigid. Daughter of the Dagda, she was the keeper of flame, wisdom, healing, holy wells. Later she would be so highly revered by the Celts that when Christianity gained footing, the mythos of St. Brigid was likely created to sway pagans into conversion—a saint associated with sacred flames. The Tuatha ruled in prosperity until the Sons of Mil came and ended their reign forever.

Also known as the eight sons of King Milesius, the Sons of Mil came from Spain, driving the magical Tuatha Dé Danann from their homes and thrones, and giving rise to the Celtic people. One poem in *The Book of Invasions* claims that some of the Tuatha Dé Danann chose to intermarry with the human invaders. But most chose to slip underground, into another dimension of space and time which would come to be known as Tír na nÓg, or the Land of Eternal Youth, rather than to continue living in the world of men. The gates to Tír na nÓg were within our mortal world—they were the very forts and portal tombs lived in by the Tuatha during their reign.

These places today are known as faery mounds or faery forts.

Now this is the stuff of myth, of faery tales. But it is here that the world of the gods who would become the Sidhe, or faeries, met the world of men. In an old manuscript known as *The Annals of the Four Masters*, there is an actual timeline to the rule of the Tuatha—stating they ruled Ireland from 1897 BC to 1700 BC. In fact, the Tuatha were considered a factual race of people/beings through the *seventeenth* century. I'm not kidding. And up to that point in Europe, *The Book of Invasions* was also taken as factual—it was even the basis of academic histories throughout the ages. It's interesting that *The Book of Invasions* claims the Sons of Mil were from Spain, because in *The Life of Agricola*, Tacitus writes he believed the people of southern Wales were descended from Spain due to their darker complexion and curly hair. The Caledonians (Scottish) had large limbs and ruddy hair, and he thought them to be of German or Nordic descent, which to me harkens the Tuatha, or people from the north.

But the sad truth is that we will never know the *exact* nature of many of the Celtic deities and myth. Since the ancient Celts believed the written word was sacred, they kept their historical records through oral tradition rather than written account. If words equaled power, to have the secrets of their culture fall into the hands of their enemies was akin to cultural annihilation.

We do know for a fact that at the heart of the Celtic community were the Druids and the bards. The Druids kept the collective knowledge of planetary movements, the natural world, plants that could be used for healing, judicial law, and domestic matters. They were so highly revered that if a Druid judged a battle clearly won, he could walk into the midst of the raging war with his arms raised overhead, and both sides would immediately cease fighting. The bards were the oral record keepers. Through elegant epic poetry, they cradled the stories of the Celtic people dating as far back as human memory itself. It is from their accounts that *The Book of Invasions* was first recorded by Christian scribes in the eleventh century.

It was, of course, tempered by Christian ideals, and in addition, one can imagine the stories themselves had already fallen victim to hundreds of years of embellishment while being carried through oral tradition.

So scholars and historians must rely instead on archeological findings and written texts from the Celts' conquerors: the Romans. Tacitus and none other than Julius Caesar himself told us much of what we know today about the Celtic people. When Caesar recognized that by annihilating the Druids he could bring the Celtic people to their knees, the unbridled fury of Rome was released and a massive effort was made to extinguish the Druids. Some survived for a time, fleeing to two small islands—Anglesey in Wales, and Iona in Scotland—before they were snuffed out entirely by the arrival of St. Columba, the Christian apostle of the Highlands. According to record, Druids disappeared from society entirely by the seventh century AD, but the bards . . . the bards continued on.

The Celtic religion honored nature as the giver of all things, and thus, ceremonies were conducted outdoors—in groves of trees, in stone circles. In old Brythonic Celtic, the word for a grove of trees was *llannerch*, from which the late Celtic word *llann*, or "church," is derived.

For the Celts, known as "the fathers of Europe," water was the gateway to the spirit world. Their votive offerings have been discovered in streambeds, lakes, bogs, and especially rivers as they sacrificed gold, ornate cauldrons, miniature statues, glittering jewels, and coins in hopes of appeasing their great gods. At its greatest height, the Celtic empire stretched from the Alps to Ireland, and east to Turkey, and from Belgium all the way to Portugal and Spain. Funnily, you may know more about the Celts than you think: their ancient custom of votive offerings has been unknowingly kept alive by the romantic—or superstitious— among us, who to this day toss coins into wishing wells and fountains.

The Isle of Man itself was named after one of the great Tuatha Dé Danann: Manannán Mac Lir, or Manannan, "son of Lir," who inherited the post of god of the sea from his father.

I found it fascinating, this link between god, man, myth, religion, and reality. *The Yellow Book of Lecan*, an Irish text from the late fourteenth century, states Manannan was not a god, but a real man—of sorts. The first Manannan, according to this text, was a man named Oirbsen, said to have been a Druid of the Tuatha Dé Danann—he went on to bear four generations of human rulers—all called by the name Manannan. There are rumors that he was a great wizard and was buried far beneath where Peel Castle now sits on the Isle of Man. Was Manannan a flesh-and-blood historical figure or a series of rulers? Or was he a god of mythic proportions? Perhaps in every myth we can unearth a kernel of truth.

The librarian cleared her throat and I looked up from my books, exhilarated by the discoveries I'd made. The Celts worshipped gods who became known as the Tuatha Dé Danann, who in turn became known as the faeries. Manannan was one of these gods. And I was here on his island.

"I'm sorry, miss," she called, "I'm afraid it's time to close."

"Could I just ask you," I ventured as I headed to the door, "I was looking for some information that I wasn't able to find today. Do you know anything about a woman who might have lived on the island by the name of Betsy Crowe?"

"Betsy Crowe, yes." She looked at me curiously. "I know the name well. She was murdered, you know, in the 1800s. It was never solved, thvat murder. But you can still visit the ruins of her cottage near Ballure Glen."

"Murdered? Wow. Thank you."

"You know, if you wanted to come back tomorrow, we might be able to dig up a few books. But not much has been written about Betsy Crowe."

"Okay, thank you. I appreciate that."

Unfortunately, I wasn't able to make the long trip back to Douglas again; the races shut down the roads and the tram. In fact, I wouldn't learn the real story of Betsy Crowe until I was home in South Carolina, where I received a few stunning shocks indeed.

~~~~~~~

That night at the pub John and I sat outside on a picnic table, talking about my dad, his wife and kids, Eric, and life in general. How do you explain meeting a group of people who after only a few days truly feel like family? Or the feeling of being so openly adopted that you feel entirely at home with a group of people who only days before were complete strangers? What about trying to imagine your trip without them? For the first time I realized a great risk of this journey—attachment. Over the past few days we'd shared so many laughs, so much meaningful conversation, so many stories. I knew I would miss the pool playing, walks into town, cramming into cabs to get back, watching the TT, and getting schooled in bike racing—not to mention the comfort of a shared meal between friends. I felt like I was being fussed about by seven father hens. And now that half of them were leaving soon, I felt inconsolably sad.

To take my mind off the imminent departure of my friends, I tried to refocus on the faery world. Something in Ninefh's story about throwing the pink quartz heart into the glen pool on the isle was echoing within me, and I felt on some level, perhaps if I paid a visit to honor Manannan on his mountain, my search might begin to turn up some more concrete findings. At the culmination of my time on Man were two major trips—Glen Auldyn and the Fairy Bridge. However, I couldn't undertake these until I'd paid a visit to Snaefell, the highest peak on the island, rumored to be the seat of the ancient god, where it was said on a clear day you could see all of the seven kingdoms: England, Ireland, Wales, Scotland, the Isle of Man, the heavens, and the sea. In a tradition I was told was still carried on to this day, the islanders would climb its slopes on Midsummer Day to leave tributes to the sea god for blessings, protection, and bountiful fishing on the Irish Sea. The weather had turned unexpectedly cold and bitter, but I couldn't delay my trip up the mountain any longer, so the next morning I put on as many layers as possible and ventured out into the whipping wind and biting rain.

I'd love to say I climbed Snaefell, but I rode the tram. I was disappointed in myself, but the grueling hike from Ramsey to the top of Snaefell was too lengthy to risk in such volatile weather—especially given my atrocious navigational skills.

Accompanied by only three other tourists, the ride to the top was stunning even in the lashing storm. The Manx landscape fell below us in a patchwork of lime and forest green, sprinkled with the yellow flowers of prickly gorse and the white elderflower that scattered across the crumbling stone walls.

As I exited the tram, the wind tore at me with punishing force, the rain needle-sharp, and my traveling companions retreated inside to the warmth of the café. Pulling up my hood, I leaned into the wind, pushing my way up the gravel path to the top of the mountain where Manannan unleashed his fury. The wind tugged my body from side to side with unimaginable strength. The air on Snaefell was significantly colder, probably in the midthirties (in June!), and it quickly chilled me to the bone. But at the summit I knelt down to fish out a small pink quartz heart that Raven had given me, some shells I'd collected from the beach in Castletown, a piece of sea glass from the beach in Ramsey, and a piece of the Glastonbury Thorn, said to have been planted by Joseph of Arimathea himself, that we'd found discarded at the foot of the famous tree. I was looking around, trying to find the perfect place, when something caught my eye. It was a black feather, half sticking out of the ground beside a large rock. Something told me I should try and lift that stone. To my surprise it lifted effortlessly, and underneath I found smooth bare earth. With numb fingers, I dug down a few inches and closed my eyes. Into the wind, into the rain, I sent my thoughts out to the Tuatha Dé Danann, to Manannan. I wished that they would come back to live among us in whatever way they could. I told them how desperately I thought we were all aching to find magic once again in our everyday lives.

If you've gone away, please come back. We need you.

With that I placed my items in the ground, along with the black feather. Gold aside, I hoped I was making an offering like those Manannan used to receive, but more than that, I was leaving a piece of myself there, hidden, a connection that no one could break between me and this mystical island. Replacing the rock, I made my way inside. I was enjoying the warmth, examining a poster board on Manannan, and sipping hot tea when I felt something cold trickling down the back of my pants. Puzzled, I tugged off my pack and, opening it up, resisted the urge to cry. The top to my water bottle had somehow come off, soaking everything in my pack—including my brand-new iPod. Cursing under my breath, I flipped the case open and pressed the On button to find the screen tragically black. *Death by drowning.* How had this happened? It hit me then, and I couldn't help but wonder. Could this have been the kind of sacrifice that Ninefh had been referring to when she told me about spraining her knee? If so, the faeries definitely knew how to hit me where it counts—the wallet. Aside from that, I'd have no portable music for the rest of the summer. But if I'd sacrificed something, it left me to wonder: What was going to happen in return?

That night after dinner and the pub, we sat around drinking cans of Boddingtons and passing around my flask of whiskey in the dining area of the kitchen. John told me he'd heard that Man was considering taking down the trinkets people left at Fairy Bridge.

"Why on earth would they do that?" I exclaimed.

"Well, Sig, it's a busy road, and they can't have people stopping their cars and bikes in the middle of traffic to tie a bit of ribbon on a tree, you know."

"But how *could* they? Can't they see that people are leaving trinkets there because they are desperate to feel a tie to something, a tie to their own histories, their heritage, to the *land?*"

And what would that do to our already diminishing ties to a magical world? I wanted to add. Instead I told them about how the bridge on the main road wasn't the *real* Fairy Bridge anyway, a tidbit of information I'd uncovered from speaking with a docent at Castle Rushen in Castletown.

"You know where the real bridge is?" Wol asked me.

"Well, the guy at the castle tried to describe it, but it was confusing. I might be able to find something online . . ."

"Listen," he said. "If you can find the location, we could take you. You could ride with me, on the trike," referring to his three-wheeled motorcycle. Big John gave a nod of agreement.

"Really? You'd do that? It could be miles and miles away."

"Sure," Wol said. "You can't write a book about faeries without having been to the *real* Fairy Bridge, now can you?" He gave me a grin.

"He's right," Big John said. "That just won't do."

"John! Did you hear *that*?" I said triumphantly. "We're going to find the Fairy Bridge!"

"Well, in that case, I'm only disappointed I can't join you. We're leaving tomorrow morning, remember?"

Oh. Right. Actually, I had done my best to push it from my mind. I looked around the room a little sadly. John, Joe, Sam, Huw, and Mark were all hitting the road. What could I possibly say to them? Thank you for being so awesome, thank you for the full English breakfasts and the laughs and for making me feel like family? I wanted to tell them that I would never forget any of them, and that I wished I could be a part of their clan forever. That they were some of the kindest, most endearing men I'd ever met, and the world was a better place because they were in it.

When John knocked on my door early the next morning, I shot upright, smacking my head on the bunk above me. *Shit!* I'd overslept! Damn all that Irish whiskey.

"Sig," he said through the door, "we're leaving . . ."

Leaving? Already? I was planning on getting up to have breakfast with them before they were gone. I was hoping to get some more time.

"Oh, no! Wait!" I called, flying out of bed in my pajamas and swinging open the door, squinting to see them without my glasses. I could see John okay. Behind him, the rest of the boys were just a fuzzy blur of helmets and coats, already astride their bikes. I hugged John. How I could possibly express everything so they would really understand? At a loss, all I could say was, "Bye! Bye!" Waving, trying not to cry. "Have a safe journey." John mounted his bike, and they drove off.

I closed the door and sat down on the edge of the bed, and the tears came.

Thankfully Wol, Big John, and Paul were still there until Saturday, which was, incidentally, my birthday. I was so glad to have them here for a few more days, but at the same time, the thought of having to feel this terrible feeling twice was unbearable.

I'd heard people say that as a traveler, you have to be careful not to get attached. Now that I'd felt it, I say that's garbage. If you are lucky enough to find people worth getting attached to, attach yourself with nothing less than all of your heart. Because if you find a companion to walk a stretch of the road with you, a person whose warmth and kindness makes your journey feel that much brighter, you have no other choice—you are among the very, very fortunate.

I found the boys in the kitchen.

"Find those directions, Sig," Wol said, "and let's get on the road, eh?"

Our first stop was the Home for Retired Tram Horses, where I unloaded a backpack full of sliced apples to feed the huge geriatric draft horses, all of whom had pulled the horse trams around Douglas during the prime of their lives. They were majestic, monstrous, beautiful, and mean, so incredibly mean! Their ears laid flat against their head, they snatched the apples without so much as a thankful whinny. The guys took a few apples from my sack at my prompting but headed to the gift shop after a while—apparently, it was time for tea. (Tea, I was beginning to understand, was similar to the Italian or Spanish siesta, except that there was no sleeping, just sitting, and you could always find an excuse to do it, and with cake, too, several times a day.)

From there we headed out to see the Calf of Man, a small, completely undeveloped island. I whipped out my camera and took a video of our ride through the countryside on the back of the trike behind Wol, my friend and fearless driver. Getting out to stretch our legs, I held out the camera and snapped a few silly pictures of all of us, smooshed together and smiling in the sun.

We went over the directions to the real Fairy Bridge that I had dug up online, but after two attempts, we still couldn't find the right road. I was disappointed to say the least, but on the way home, just before we came to Douglas, we passed the modern Fairy Bridge, complete with a sign marking it for all who passed over the busy road. The trees made an archway overhead, a tall, noble canopy, and there it was, a little stream running through. I caught a quick glimpse of ribbons and pieces of tattered paper. Were they notes? Dreams? Prayers? I saw Wol give a small salute in front of me, and looked ahead to see John and Paul do the same. Maybe it didn't matter what was real, or what was fake, what was old, what was new. What mattered was this nod, this salute, this respect of tradition. The wind rushing past as we zoomed by, I took a deep breath and shouted, "Helloooo, faeries!"

That evening I went to see Mike to borrow a topo map and get directions into Glen Auldyn by foot. Writing them down, I told him about our misadventures trying to find the original Fairy Bridge. The next morning, my penultimate day on Man, I was in my hiking gear departing for the glen, when Mike flagged me down in the parking lot.

"Listen," he said, "we've been feeling really badly that you weren't able to get over to the old Fairy Bridge. My wife, Ali, and I thought, if you were interested, we could go tomorrow—you know, and take the kids. Make a morning of it."

"Seriously? I mean, are you sure?"

"Yeah. It could be fun!" He grinned and turned to his boys behind him.

"Hey, guys, you want to go look for faeries tomorrow?"

The boys grimaced. "Blech! No!"

I turned to them in mock surprise. "No? You guys don't want to go and look for *faeries*?"

They looked at me, hesitantly. "Faeries aren't real," Mike's son Alex said a little triumphantly.

"Well"—I thought for a moment—"I suppose you could be right."

He considered this. My answer seemed to throw him. "Do *you* believe in faeries?" he asked me.

"Um, yes. I do, actually. But being a grown-up and all, it's really hard for me to see them. Kids are actually supposed to be able to see faeries, like, *ten times* more easily. That's why I could really use some helpers."

He assessed me warily. "All right." He shrugged at last.

"Excellent! Trust me." I grinned at him. "We're gonna have fun."

With that, I shouldered my hiking pack and headed out to see if I could track down a scary little green man of my own. From the beginning, the trek sucked. Even though I had perfectly clear directions, I got turned around going through Ramsey. Every time I stopped to ask a local, poised at the edge of the road to catch the race that day, they pointed me in a conflicting direction.

Again I got the feeling that I was being conspired against, that something wanted to keep me away from the glen, but it only made me more determined to get there. I finally made my way onto the marked trail, heading out across open fields. Folks had told me I would be lucky if I saw another human being up in the glen, and I understood now—as far as the eye could see, there was nothing but trees in the distance. It dwarfed me, and made Ballure Glen feel like child's play. I had Janet Bord's book with me, and my intention was to set out on the same trail that had so startled John Hall so many years ago. This was it, my one chance, and Glen Auldyn was the mother lode: aside from the green man in the tree, there were sightings of the Phynnodderee reported there, and another man had seen five small creatures dancing in a ring, hand in hand.

Even though I was in another country "faery hunting," for lack of a better term, I found these types of stories a little difficult to believe. The concept of faery creatures dancing in a ring rang too cutesy to feel authentic. When the road divided at the Methodist chapel, I took the road that forked to the right but ended up at a dead end. I would have had to cross a boggy stream; the trail on the other side was impassibly thick with brush and it was clearly marked Private Property. Thinking I might have taken a wrong turn, I went back the way I came and started over again from the church. Seeing a road that wound uphill to the right into the woods, I started in that direction.

I traversed a series of switchbacks, keeping a pine forest to my right. This one, however, was less threatening than the others I'd walked—too quiet and a bit unnerving, yes, but completely different than the forest in which I'd nearly lost my wits earlier. I could imagine the types of creatures that would love these woods—short, stocky, perhaps wrinkled . . . like gnomes. This wasn't the territory of airy faeries.

I continued my ascent, sweating now, hearing the occasional loud buzz of the motorcycles tearing through the island, picking up a few black feathers in my path until I could walk no more. There was a barbed-wire fence in front of me that wrapped around to my right, closing off the trail from a field. *Damn* it. And where was the running water? It dawned on me that I had not even made it into the glen. I had taken another wrong turn. I had been hiking now for three hours, and I was hungry, so I slipped under the fence and plopped down on the open hill, overlooking Ramsey, to eat my lunch. It felt nice to be out in the open, and more than anything I wanted to chicken out and head back to the Centre, but I couldn't quit now. I stuck the feathers in the ground and left a little of my leftover cheese by them, just like the peasants on the Isle of Man used to do, for the faeries. Even though it was now past two p.m., I headed back down to find the elusive glen once and for all.

Following yet another trail, I walked a well-trodden path along the side of a stream. I'd found it. The glen started off wide and beautiful, with a flat river that ran through, spiked with massive boulders. Unfortunately, the water was fenced off, so I could only walk on the trail beside it. Moving farther uphill, I climbed over a fence onto the Green Road, which took me along the edge of a cliff. When I reached a small waterfall with a pool, I laid out some chocolate as an offering and sat beneath it, reflecting quietly for more than an hour—during which I experienced absolutely nothing paranormal. It was now close to five, and I needed to get back—my legs were shaking from all the hiking and I was craving a pint with the guys.

I made my way back down the path from Glen Auldyn, feeling well exercised but deeply frustrated. Nothing. I had seen and experienced nothing. Where was the "westerly fork"? I had followed my instincts and ended up at a dead end. Typical. Where had John Hall been when he experienced the green man in the trees, the singing, the light-headedness, the feelings of paranoia? It seemed much more likely that he was experiencing fear—fear of nature and the dangers it can hold for any man. That's why we built shelters and made fires, put roofs over our heads and doors through which to enter. We willingly made the choice to step away from the natural world and all its discomforts and vastness.

The late afternoon sun was warm on my back, and it lit the fields that edged the hillsides with a golden glow. As I reached the last field on the trail, I spotted a man in the distance, coming toward me with a tremendous beast of a black dog. After my startling encounter with the blue jacket I was oddly nervous to come upon strangers, and he had an impressive stature to him, even from this far away. But seeing me, he veered off the pathway into the waist-high grasses of the field, following his dog, almost as though he were trying to set me at ease. It looked as though he was searching for something—discarded golf balls, perhaps. Relaxing, I proceeded through the field with a brave, friendly smile on my face.

As I got closer, I could see the dog was taking great vertical leaps across the field, his head popping into view for a moment as he strained to see above the high grass, before disappearing again in a sea of golden yellow. It was so hilarious I couldn't help but laugh. Pollen drifted gently on the breeze, and I called out to the creature. He lifted up, ears cocked, and then took off toward me, bounding enthusiastically, his owner following behind. I knelt down, waiting for him as he emerged from the field shaking himself, but he stopped just short of me, clearly waiting for his master.

As the man approached, I studied him. Tall and rosy-cheeked, he had grayish, nearly white hair that was slightly shaggy, not unlike his dog's. He wore a thick ivory fisherman's knit sweater, but it was his eyes that stopped me: they were the bluest eyes I'd ever seen. And when he smiled, they sparkled with a curiously captivating intelligence. There was something in them that didn't seem quite . . . human.

Faery. No, that was ridiculous. Of course this man wasn't a faery!

"Go on," he told the dog, in a deep, clear voice. The shaggy monster of mythic proportions made its way over to me and I buried my fingers in his thick tufts of fur.

"He's a fluffy beast, isn't he?" The man chuckled.

"Yes, indeed," I murmured. After a quick pat the dog lost interest and resumed its investigation of the field. I stood and brushed off my pants.

"How was your walk?" he asked me, matter-of-factly. I couldn't quite place his accent, but it could have easily been from Scotland or the Isle of Man, I supposed.

"It was great," I said. "Really beautiful." I paused. "But I wish I knew where I was, when I was up there," I continued, gesturing to the hills. "I mean, I was trying to find this one trail, and I just . . . I wish I knew exactly where I *went* today. It's so frustrating not to know if I was in the right *place*."

He gauged me for a moment, his eyes dancing with a humorous sparkle, but then grew serious, and for a moment I found his gaze uncomfortably penetrating.

"No," he said, a little fiercely. He softened a bit, his eyes holding mine.

"You just enjoy it." It managed to be both an admonishment and a plea of sorts. Of course! He was right. Up there in the hills I had been so on edge, searching so hard to find something in every crevice of rock, every shuffle of leaves, that I had missed the experience of it entirely. Just being in nature, being alone. My cheeks flushed involuntarily, and I gave him a nod, wanting him to know I understood. Adjusting my pack, I moved toward the fence at the end of the field. At the gate, I turned back—half expecting both man and dog to have disappeared into thin air. But I saw him, walking slowly, his silvery hair lit bright with sunshine, hands tucked into his pockets.

He was gazing up into the hills.

15

Finding the Ancient Fairy Bridge

The fairies went from the world, dear,
Because men's hearts grew cold:
And only the eyes of children see
What is hidden from the old.

—KATHLEEN FOYLE

TWENTY-NINE years ago, in a hospital in Ithaca, New York, a woman went into labor with her second child moments after a volcanic eruption. It was Friday the thirteenth, and to her great surprise, her child was born with copper-red hair.

I always thank my mother for not measuring the weight of these bad omens against me, not trying to push me back in to be born on a more auspicious date. She in turn jokes, "Why on earth would I want you *back in*? With all that bad luck, I wanted you out as quickly as possible."

My mother can't help but smile when she talks of going into labor a few minutes after the *second* eruption of Mount St. Helens. (The first eruption was known as the deadliest, most destructive volcanic eruption in the history of America.) Since my mother believes this specific volcanic event and its subsequent timing in relation to my birth has informed my character, I suppose that I (and the rest of world) are fortunate I was born after the second eruption, not the first.

It was an unusual sensation, waking up in a foreign country on my birthday. There would be no phone calls from friends or family. No gifts, cards, or flowers, no dinner out at a fabulous New York restaurant. But I didn't miss all that stuff. Mostly I was excited to be going on an organized faery adventure, thanks to my very generous hosts.

I threw on my cargo pants, a sweatshirt, and one of Eric's T-shirts I'd brought to comfort me. Outside, Mike, his wife, Ali, and Emma, Mike's sister-in-law, were working on wrangling five children into the Venture Centre expedition van. I had given Mike my directions from yesterday, and he seemed to know what had gone awry. We hadn't been able to find the Old Castletown Road because that was merely what it was referred to as. As will happen on a small island over hundreds of years, the road now had another name completely. It was about a forty-five-minute drive to find the entrance to the public footpath to Oakhill across from the Kewaigue school from Maughold, and I was amazed at the transformation of the boys' attitudes—they were practically bouncing out of their seats to look for faeries this morning, and it was really quite touching. We clambered out of the van and crossed the road heading toward a big barn. Past the building the driveway became a footpath. Mist hovered above the fields, giving the path a haunted feel.

Ali, Emma, and I walked together with Emma's youngest, George, while Mike and the rest of the boys were farther ahead.

"Manannan's cloak," Ali murmured, gazing out across the meadow. "People believe that in times of danger, or really any old time at all, he draws his cloak about the island to enshroud it, protect it."

"People still think about Manannan?" I asked.

"Yes." She smiled, as if considering it for the first time. "I guess we do."

The boys were having a blast, running about and swinging sticks, looking into all the bushes. Alex and his brother came running back toward me, excited.

"I just saw a faery!" they exclaimed.

"You saw a faery?" I asked.

"Yes." They both nodded. "Well," Alex explained, "it was a dragon-fly, but it told me it was a faery!"

"Well, that is excellent. Very good work, both of you—I told you I needed your help." At this they beamed and ran back to the head of the pack. None of us had any idea how far we'd be walking until we found the bridge, or even what would be left of it. At my best moments on this trip, I imagined it fully intact, with two dozen stately members of the faery race awaiting our arrival in their full regalia on the bowed arch of the bridge. In more realistic times I imagined three large stones, original purpose long forgotten, stranded in a dry field. Ali, Emma, Mike, and I were all happily chatting when four-year-old George stopped dead in his tracks and turned to us quite sternly, putting his fingers to his lips.

"Shhhh!" he hissed. "We have to be very quiet now . . . We're al-most there!"

We glanced at each other, surprised. "All right, George . . ."

I think it's fair to say we were all a little taken aback when, after less than a minute of walking, the path dipped down and we came to a stream. At first I was confused—straight ahead there was a big con-crete chunk of the bridge that looked more communist bloc than faery rock. But then Mike pointed. "There it is."

An ancient-looking bridge, fully intact, arched across the stream to my right. Orange silk lilies had been wound into the greenery that cas-caded down from the top of the overgrown bridge. I could hardly take it all in—*everywhere* there were gifts and offerings. On the well-trodden bank beneath the bridge there were artfully arranged ceramic teddy bears, miniature statues of faeries, beach shells, coins, buttons, hand-beaded necklaces, gnomes, origami cranes, and even a Spider-Man action figure.

There were iron faeries perched on sturdy rock ledges. There was even a canister of ashes, and nearby was a laminated note: *Here lie the ashes of our mum and dad . . . may they rest in peace in this beautiful place.*

Above the bank overlooking the bridge, someone had hung a sturdy green hammock, weaving more silk flowers into its mesh. The sheer swelling of belief here, the trinkets left, the incredible care taken to create something of beauty, the wishes made—the impact of it all brought tears to my eyes. I wondered what my father would have made of it. Obviously, he was no believer in faeries, but the power of this place was undeniable. And I knew he would have felt it, too.

The kids had exploded in sheer delight, and their shouts brought me back to myself. "Hey, guys! Come here a second," I called out, kneeling down as I waited for them to gather.

"From the most ancient of times," I explained, their five little faces gazing at me intently, "people would come to this very spot, and when they did, they would leave something for the faeries. They believed if they left something to show the faeries that they still believed in them, they could then make a wish, and the faeries . . . they would make that wish come true." I rummaged around in my bag until my fingers closed around a bulky package. "So I have a biscuit for each of you, and you can find your own special spot to leave it. Each of you can pick your own spot, and each of you gets to make your own wish. Okay?"

"Yeah!" they exclaimed and, taking their biscuits, ran to find their spots. I turned to Ali, Mike, and Emma. "Of course grown-ups get one, too!" We laughed, but they seemed pleased. I extracted some chocolates from my bag and left them in a few places that seemed right. God, I wished I had discovered this place sooner. I would have loved to come at twilight, sit in the hammock, see what might happen.

"Signe," Ali said, finding me among the ferns, "I have this friend I really wish you could meet. She's . . . a very magical sort of person, and she's really into all this stuff."

"Oh, that's sweet, Ali, thank you. If only it weren't my last day here!"

"I know," she murmured. "It's really too bad . . ."

We wandered around, exploring, taking photos. Of course we had to get a picture of me with all my fabulous faery-finding helpers lined up on the bridge. I knew it was almost time to go, and I was saying my goodbyes when Ali came up to me, her cell phone extended.

"Signe, I've called my friend. I'm sorry, I just thought . . . I should do it. So it's Charlotte on the line. You two should talk," she said, handing me the phone.

We said hello, and explaining my search, I asked her if we could meet. Despite my time constraints, Charlotte agreed to meet me at the Venture Centre for tea in a little over an hour.

I flipped the phone shut and smiled at Ali. "Thank you. This is shaping up to be a pretty spectacular birthday."

"It's your birthday?" they exclaimed.

"Yup. So far it's been pretty unforgettable."

We collected the kids, who were now wandering with Mike a little farther upstream, and headed back up the path. We'd been walking for a few minutes when something occurred to me. I had really wanted to ask permission to take something with me from the area of the Fairy Bridge. Not someone else's tribute, of course. Just a fallen leaf to press, a twig, a stone, something. The place had felt so magical, it *was* my birthday, and most important, it would forever serve to remind me that I'm not alone. There are other people who believe, and who want to believe, and seeing the bridge had given me a new surge of hope that this journey I was undertaking wasn't going to be in vain. I let out a sigh and looked down at the dirt path. Nothing but old paving pebbles here. Nothing special.

Oh! I lamented. *I really wish I could have taken a stone . . .*

Back at the hostel, I freshened up and went outside to wait for Charlotte MacKenzie to arrive. Soon I heard the crunching of shoes on gravel, and Ali came toward me accompanied by a pretty lady with a button nose and a broad white smile. Something about her radiated an elegance, even though she was wearing jeans, hiking boots, and a T-shirt. She looked at me in surprise.

"Looking for faeries?" she said, laughing. "You *are* a faery! Look at her," she said, turning to Ali. "Doesn't she look just like a faery?"

Me? Look like a faery? Ali left the two of us together, and Charlotte sat down across from me. We had an instantaneous rapport that took me completely by surprise.

"So. Here I am, and my time is yours. Where do you need to go? What do you need to do?"

"Well," I said, "I actually have no idea. It's my last day on the island and I feel like there's so much I haven't seen. What are some places that you might suggest?"

She squinted at me, and thought for a moment. "There's Ballaglass Glen, which isn't too far from here, and it is, in my opinion, a pretty magical place . . . but then there's the Point of Ayre. A very powerful place. It's at the northernmost tip of the island, and to be honest, the two places couldn't be more different."

"Oh, goodness," I said, contemplating. "I don't know . . ."

"What do you *feel*?" she asked me. "When I mention them, does one place pull you more than the other?"

God, all this feeling stuff was really hard! I tried to turn inside for a moment, and Point of Ayre popped up.

"Then that's where we'll go," Charlotte replied.

The car ride was stunning—miles and miles of pristine Manx countryside, and the mist had burned off, splashing the open fields in sunshine. The white-washed thatched huts with brightly colored flowers adorning them slipped by, and glimpses of the ocean flashed through the distant trees. As we drove we talked about my trip, my search, and Charlotte's take on the faery world. She'd spent summers on Man growing up, but had only become aware of faeries as an adult, when she moved to live on Man full-time.

"I spent a lot of time just walking in the woods here," she told me. "I was healing from a lot. And I guess I just became aware of this energy, all around me."

"What do you mean, energy?"

"The more you look inside, and begin to trust what everyone refers to as 'intuition,' the more you'll become aware of the way places feel. The more you tune in, the more you begin to know things." She tapped her head. "Not with your head, this is a different kind of knowing. You'll know things in your heart."

"So this energy you felt, what did it feel like?"

"It felt earthy, ancient, wise, and . . . sentient. After that I had a big phase I went through, where I wanted to know everything there was to know about faeries. But ultimately, the faery energy connected me to the work I'm doing now. Even bigger energies, divinity."

Listening to Charlotte, I considered the feeling I'd experienced when I saw the sparkling lights in Glastonbury. It wasn't until I had let go of my fear of the unknown that I had seen something—and I had no doubt of what I was seeing. I'd recognized the otherworldly nature of it in my heart. Since then, my head had reclaimed its hold. I was afraid again, so afraid of everything. Just when I thought I had banished my fear, it roared back.

I was afraid the faeries would scare me to death, blind me, possess me—who knew? Steal me away to the land of the undead. But how could I be so intensely afraid of something when I wasn't even convinced it *existed* yet?

"We're almost there," Charlotte announced, pulling into a large parking lot at the edge of the ocean. It was unlike any of the other beaches I'd seen on Man; it was completely composed of smooth stones. Millions of perfectly shaped pebbles and rounded rocks in all different shapes and colors. We strolled along the water, my feet sloshing through the stones. Charlotte bent down and scooped up a huge piece of washed-up bone—it looked like some sort of animal pelvis that had been bleached in the sun.

"This is for you," she said, matter-of-factly.

"Thanks." I shrugged, thinking, *What the hell am I going to do with an animal pelvis?*

"You know, sometimes, I just need to come out here for, I guess it'd be an adjustment. Energy-wise. This is a really powerful point because all the energy that circulates within the island meets right here, at this point, surrounded by the water. Maybe you should just take a seat for a little while and just . . . be."

"All right," I said. I walked for a bit, out toward the point, and then, feeling like I'd reached a good spot, I sat down on the sun-warmed stones.

I began to feel somehow different after a few moments. Clean. And then something hit me as I gazed around. *Millions of perfectly shaped pebbles and rocks.* I laughed out loud, like a lunatic. What was it I'd said?

I really wish I could have taken a stone . . .

It was my birthday, and apparently now I'd been given free rein to take my pick. I closed my eyes and reached out my hands, feeling the stones, until I decided on one. A beautiful, deep copper stone. It reminded me of the color of the rock at the Chalice Well, like the color of my hair when I was a little girl. I noticed with some curiosity that in front of me were also two black feathers. I picked them up and put them in my pack with the pelvis, tucking the stone into my pocket.

"Well," I said, making my way back to Charlotte, "I think I got what I came here for." I told her the story of the bridge, and my wish for a stone, and she laughed. "Of course. This means you're in, you know. 'You want a stone? Here, pick a stone!' This is great news for you, Signe. Great news."

Perhaps it was, I thought. We had so much time left, the afternoon still yawning open for us, to do with it what we would, so I asked Charlotte if she fancied a walk in the woods.

"What do you have in mind?"

"I'd like to see the spot you were, when you first started to believe."

She smiled at this. "Okay then. Let's go."

I'd seen the signpost for Ballaglass Glen while riding the Manx Electric Railway to Douglas and the Manx Museum. Getting the chance to visit Ballaglass on my last day made me feel as though my trip had come full circle. There are seventeen major glens on the Isle of Man, and having seen only a few, they were so varied I could assume that each glen would be different—in feel, light, remoteness. Depending on the glen, the trails could be muddy and wet, dry as a bone, precariously steep, or gently sloping. Ballaglass was compact, only fifteen acres big; cut deep into rock, it instantly reminded me of a gorge I'd loved to visit in Ithaca. The Cornaa River ran through it, rushing down to join the sea, and the trees created an arched canopy that gave you plenty of room to breathe. The sun came through the leaves, creating dancing patterns of shadow on the rock. Lilting ferns lined the banks of the river, which was filled with spongy, moss-covered rocks. The glen felt open, friendly, cozy. And yet still mystical.

"We can stop and sit anywhere you'd like," Charlotte said. When we came to a fork in the trail, she asked me which way I wanted to go.

"That way." I gestured to the left. After a few minutes, the trail began to climb up, the river spilling into a crystal pool, sheltered by rock cliffs on either side that obstructed the view from the trail. It looked private. In comparison to the rest of the glen, this place felt forbidden. I had to go down there. Charlotte waited on a bench farther along the trail as I climbed down the slippery rocks to the belly of the river. The water came tumbling down a narrow split in the rock in front of me, creating a perfectly concentric pool. The only sound was that of rushing water echoing between the two cliff walls that reached high overhead. The rock was slick under my boots, but I was drawn farther in—ahead of me there was a massive log that had fallen, creating a dry area behind it that bordered the cliff wall. The tree was too massive to climb safely over—as my dad had said, "If you have to think twice, don't do it. That's a good way to break a leg."

Checking to ensure it was well lodged against the rock and couldn't slip to crush me, I slithered under the tree trunk to the other side. Brushing the dirt from my pants, I took in the sheltered surroundings. Now I was standing well beneath the trail, looking back into a funny-shaped cave in the rock. It was only about three feet high, and too narrow for a person to do much but stick their arm in, but it exuded a distinct feeling of age and foreboding. It looked like a good place to find a hoard of goblins. I forced myself to stay there, looking into its inky depths for a few minutes.

I was so sick of being afraid.

I bit my lip in frustration, and after a moment the frustration built into a powerful torrent of anger. This had to stop. I had to face this, own it, embrace it, banish it. I stood there, looking into the cave, and imagined every terrible thing that could dwell within it. I welcomed them, challenged them. They could do nothing to touch me, because I was stronger. I understood, then, something about the nature of evil. There was no such thing as evil in nature. There was balance. Death, destruction, these things were necessary to sustain life. Nature was devoid of mal-intent. It was humans; humans were the ones truly capable of evil. Without really thinking about what I was doing, I took the bone, the animal pelvis from my pack, propping it up to the right of the split in the rock so it was resting on the mossy shelf. Taking the two black feathers, I placed them at the top of the pelvis, one at either side. I imagined this thing I created held all of my fear inside it, and I was leaving it there, where whatever it was that was here could help me with it, transmute all those feelings into something positive. I stepped back to admire my impulsive handiwork. The pelvis had a ridge running through the center, which looked like a nose. Combined with the placement of the feathers, there was no denying it. I had just made a mask.

I scurried back under the log and up the rocks to join Charlotte on the bench, feeling like I just dropped a boulder I'd been carrying around on my shoulders. Walking through the glen, I could actually feel the joy of everything around me once again, just as I had that evening in Glastonbury. The sparkling light of the sun reflecting off the water, the sweet fresh air, the sound of the swiftly rushing water. I was able to let it all in, become part of it. We arrived at the top of the glen, and the trail crossed the river on a high bridge, a set of stairs moving up to the railway tracks above.

We stood there a moment, shoulder to shoulder.

"So what type of work is it you do exactly?" I asked Charlotte as we gazed down at the peacefully moving water.

"Well," she said, "I use various techniques, but essentially what I do is help people rediscover their true selves, restore their inner balance and peace. You know, just improve their general quality of life."

I was going to tell her about the mask, the moment by the cave, when she turned to me, giving me a pat, and said, "Maybe that's why you found me. You just needed a little tune-up, that's all."

As we prepared to head back, I felt a rush of gratitude. Ballaglass Glen had taught me what lay at the core of the Isle of Man: only the sparkle of the natural world and the energies within it. There was nothing to fear. I looked up into the towering maple tree above me and thought, *Goodbye . . . thank you.* Then something caught my eye. It was a single maple leaf moving back and forth, waving at me. All the other leaves were perfectly still.

"Charlotte, look!" I whispered.

"Oh my God!" she exclaimed. "It's waving!"

Feeling like a couple of fools, we waved back, laughing, only to see the leaf really going for the gusto now. After a minute or so it finally stopped, and a breeze picked up, making the leaves softly rustle once again. The action over, we shook our heads in disbelief and turned to go.

I thanked Charlotte as she dropped me off with a warm hug, but we both had the feeling we would see each other again. I turned the key to my room and there, sitting on the bed, was a beautifully wrapped gift. *Who could have done this?* I wondered, pulling apart the gift bag. Inside was a glass bottle of elderflower liquor, obviously handmade and bottled, and a rustic ornament carved from wood in the shape of a fish that read "Isle of Man." I read the card:

Happy Birthday! From Mike, Ali, the kids . . . and the faeries. I melted. I had gone into the day expecting nothing and had ended up with one of my most memorable birthdays ever. The kindness of others was simply astonishing—I was the luckiest girl in the world.

That night was my last with Wol, Paul, and Big John, and we were going to the pub for one final evening out. But I needed to say goodbye to Mike and Ali before leaving for the night. I found them outside with the kids.

"You guys are incredible," I said. "Thank you so much for the gifts. You didn't have to do that!"

"Of course!" Mike smiled.

"You can mix the elderflower liquor with Pimm's, seltzer water, or vodka . . . it's made from the flowers of the Elderflower trees, which have long been considered sacred to the faeries." Ali grinned.

"It's amazing, thank you. I love it."

"Thank *you*," she said, "for giving us the chance to discover something that we didn't even know existed in our own backyard."

That made me feel pretty special indeed.

Little George was standing in front of a brown dish tub, blowing bubbles into the courtyard. "Hey, George, I want to say goodbye now, because I probably won't see you before I leave."

He froze, dropping the plastic bubble maker, and turned to me, a shocked, heartbroken look on his face.

"*Why?*" he asked, his voice tiny.

"Well, I'm leaving very, very late tonight. And you'll be fast asleep in bed! I just didn't want to miss you."

He processed this for a moment. "But when are you coming *back?*"

My heart swelled. "I'm going to come back as soon as I can again, to visit. Maybe next summer, or the summer after that. America is pretty far away, you know, but I really do want to visit soon, okay?"

He looked down at his toes, stricken, and his upper lip began to quiver. *Don't cry,* I willed silently, *please don't let him cry!* How this little boy loved so openly, and saw so many people come and go, I just don't know.

"Listen, George," I said, placing my hand on top of his blond head, looking at him quite seriously. "I wanted to ask you for a favor." I paused, to allow the gravity in my tone to sink in. "Do you think you could do something for me?"

Ever the brave boy, he straightened and, looking up at me, nodded his head slightly.

"You were the very best faery helper today . . . so I wanted to ask you. Do you think you could keep an eye out, for me, you know, until I come back? And let me know if you see any more faeries?"

He beamed. "Yup, I can do that."

"That would be wonderful. I hope I'll get to hear about your adventures someday." Giving his hair a tussle, I turned to head back to my room, lest I suffer from my own case of the quivering upper lip.

I was only blowing gently on the flame of imagination he already had kindling within. Someday he was going to grow up, like the rest of us. But maybe, when he was walking in the woods, he'd see something that reminded him. And just for a moment, he'd remember the day the red-haired lady came, and he and his cousins and his mom went off into the woods, looking for faeries. Maybe that was all that the faeries were trying to connect us with—a flash of magic, if only in a memory.

I met up with Wol, Big John, and Paul in the kitchen.

"So," Big John said, as I detected the slightest smirk on his face. "Did you have any luck? Did you see any faeries?"

"No," I replied, "I couldn't say I *saw* them . . ."

"Well, we did," he said. "We saw a faery."

"Ha-ha. Very funny," I said, crossing my arms.

"No, really, we did!" exclaimed Wol.

"And we brought it back for you." Paul was smiling broadly now. They stepped aside to reveal a small white box.

"Happy birthday," they said.

"You guys!" I exclaimed, flipping it open. Inside was a beautiful little pewter faery with pink wings and an Isle of Man symbol on her chest. "Oh my God!" I swallowed the lump that was forming in my throat. No crying allowed in front of bikers. Wol passed me a greeting card. *For your birthday, we thought you'd like something that makes you feel loved, admired, and appreciated!* I flipped the card open. *So here we are!* They had all signed it, and at the bottom was written simply, *We are waiting. —The Faeries.* Then Big John handed over a jar of Manx Knobs (very funny) and I burst out laughing and crying all at once. It was the perfect end to a magical day.

"Okay," I said, recovering myself. "I'm ready to celebrate!" The TT was over, and most everyone had left, so we had the pub pretty much to ourselves. We didn't stay out too late—I had been planning on just staying awake until two thirty a.m., when my taxi was scheduled, but my adventures of the day had caught up with me, and I felt my eyelids closing of their own volition. We took a cab back to the Centre and I said my farewells.

Before the tears came, I managed to give them one last hug and disappeared into my cabin. I was on my own again. But little did I know, I *had* seen a faery. Rather, my camera did.

At the end of my journey, looking back at my photos from the old Fairy Bridge, something caught my eye. A tiny glowing dot on the bottom left of the photo. Zooming in, it gets blurry, but I swear, within the glowing bubble is a little form with wings.

IRELAND

16

The Last Battle of the Fir Bolgs

*Everything exists, everything is true, and the earth
is only a little dust under our feet.*

—WILLIAM BUTLER YEATS

I T was three thirty in the morning, but I couldn't sleep on the ferry ride from the Isle of Man to Dublin. I'd been thinking a lot about the old saying that there is nothing new under the sun. More often than not I've found this to be true. Even as we discover new species of plants and wildlife, we tend to forget that these things are not new at all—they're simply new to us. The problem is that as humans we have an annoying habit of making a big deal of ourselves. It's been estimated by an organization called the UN Global Diversity Assessment that Earth supports close to 13.6 million species. Of which human beings comprise . . . one.

What does this have to do with faeries, you might ask? Lots. We aren't certain about the existence of faeries, so we conclude they don't exist. But just like some undiscovered exotic species of plant or animal, they could exist whether we see them or not. It made me wonder once more how so many people believe in the existence of God and angels but laugh at the notion of faeries, ghosts, and other spirit-world characters. You'd think they were part and parcel, would you not?

Now as I roamed from place to place, I couldn't utter a word about my search without people entering into a full-fledged debate over the existence or nonexistence of a world outside our range of human perception. It was fascinating and, after a while, exhausting. I grew tired of hearing people argue that God was real but faeries weren't. That angels were real, faeries weren't. I would ask them why they felt that way, and the funniest thing was, no one knew. "Because God is real and faeries are fictitious," came the common response.

So perhaps by the same logic, God could be fictitious and faeries could be real. But if you ask me, the existence of one only serves to support the existence of the other.

Apparently, insomnia on a ferry in the middle of the Irish Sea wasn't a bad thing. I had nothing but time to think. Now that I was headed to Ireland, I had been reading a lot of William Butler Yeats, and I was surprised to discover that he and I had more in common than I thought. First of all, we had the same birthday—June 13. Of course, he was born in 1865, making him 115 years older than me. But hey, I'll take it.

Also, when my parents split, my mother moved to West Yates Street, which is probably why I grew up spelling his name wrong. If those commonalities weren't enough to bind us together as kindred spirits forever in my mind, there was the subtle fact that we both were interested in the world of faeries. Yes, that's right.

You may have read his poem "The Stolen Child," which was one of several Yeats wrote about the faery kingdom. Not only did he write poetry about it, Yeats truly believed faeries existed. He made a lifelong study of mysticism, occultism, spirituality, and astrology. "The mystical life is the centre of all that I do and all that I think and all that I write," he wrote in 1892. And like W. Y. Evans-Wentz, Yeats's interest in faeries spurred him to travel the Irish countryside collecting local folklore and supposed firsthand accounts of faery encounters, which he presented in his book *The Celtic Twilight* (1893).

At the turn of the twentieth century, much of Ireland had been devastated by the potato famine of 1845–1851, which claimed the lives of more than one million people and caused another million or so to leave Ireland for better hopes of survival abroad. Ireland was struggling to retain its autonomy against British rule, and nearly everyone who lived outside the major cities still believed in faeries. So actually, the fact that Mr. Yeats wandered the countryside chitchatting with locals about "the kindly neighbors" and "the good people" was quite unremarkable. Mysticism was on the rise at the turn of the twentieth century, as many people participated in séances and created the famously mysterious occult organization the Golden Dawn, in which Yeats was an active member. During this time, faeries had yet to undergo the Victorianization that was to come. Instead, faeries were considered, much in the way the Frouds consider them today, mutable spirits connected to the land that should always be respected (and were best left alone entirely).

Yeats's involvement and belief in this world of faeries was widely known, but it's interesting to see how public opinion of him was influenced by his beliefs as time went by. He was a Nobel Prize–winning poet, but after his death in the late 1930s, his popularity swelled to even greater heights. Later, his worldview was rashly criticized for being too "fascist," and his occultist tendencies were frowned upon. And yet no one has ever called Yeats a madman. No one has questioned his sanity due to his belief in faeries. (Lucky for him. The adamant Christian Joan of Arc was burned as a heretic for her connection to the "Charmed Tree of the Fairy of Bourlement," where she used to visit and leave garlands in the spring.)

Yeats would spend hours walking through the woods "pre-occupied with Ængus and Edain, and with Manannan, son of the sea." Sure, he was perhaps susceptible to the power of suggestion, and as a result, some of his writing, especially in *The Celtic Twilight*, is pretty far out there.

He describes being entranced, bearing witness to things that can't be seen by the naked eye. Yeats "saw" things upon waking. He writes of one late night encounter: "I awoke to see the loveliest people I have ever seen. A young man and a young girl dressed in olive-green raiment, cut like old Greek raiment, were standing at my bedside. I looked at the girl and noticed that her dress was gathered about her neck into a kind of chain, or perhaps into some kind of stiff embroidery which represented ivy-leaves. But what filled me with wonder was the miraculous mildness of her face. There are no such faces now. It was beautiful, as few faces are beautiful . . . it was peaceful like the faces of animals, or like mountain pools at evening, so peaceful that it was a little sad."

It was this that reminded me of faery.

The ferry arrived in Dublin at dawn. I caught a cab to the train station and hopped on the first train to Galway.

I watched from the train window as my first glimpses of Ireland whizzed by—a blur of green grass, cows, sheep, and horses. Located three hours from Dublin by train, on the western coast of Ireland, Galway is well known for its "Irishness," mainly due to the fact that it has on its doorstep the Galway Gaeltacht, a center devoted to keeping the Gaelic language alive.

I would be there five days researching and writing before my friends Liz and Stephanie arrived. Two of my best friends from New York, I hadn't seen them since I shipped off for Charleston. Liz came to Ireland often and wanted to introduce me to her Irish friend Peter Guy, who was, according to Liz, one of the most brilliant people she'd ever met. Peter knew more about Irish history and folklore than most, and he was going to be our host for a few days in our search for faeries.

Even though I hadn't slept in nearly two days, I felt oddly energized arriving in Galway with its quaint winding streets and gorgeous shopwindows, a vibrant, buzzing hub filled with locals and travelers alike. By the time Liz and Stephanie arrived to meet me, just seeing their faces was a welcome dose of home. Liz looked me over from head to toe and concluded, "You look like somebody who's been looking for faeries!"

After cleaning myself up and doing some much-needed catching up, we set off to meet Peter. And the first thing Peter Declan Thomas Guy did was present me with a large manila folder. He'd gone to the library and photocopied hundreds of pages of research that he thought I might find helpful on Irish folklore and faery tales. While Galway had not gotten off to the most productive start research-wise, I had a feeling that if Peter had anything to do with it, all that was about to change. A tall, striking man with piercing blue eyes and dark hair, Peter had a quick wit but a quiet manner of speaking that radiated intelligence. Rather eccentrically, he avoided eye contact altogether. Born and raised in Ireland, Peter earned his doctorate in literature and psychoanalysis. He was curious about my interest in Irish folklore and faeries, and even though he himself hadn't given much thought to the manner of their existence, he didn't think me mentally deficient for pursuing them. Instead he opened himself up to our will, saying, "All right, girls, tell me where you want to go and we'll go there."

That's how we found ourselves on a bus to the tiny town of Ros a' Mhíl and from there on a ferry to the Aran Islands. I rode out on the upper deck with Peter in the biting wind as the boat slammed up and down against huge swells in the mighty Atlantic.

"You've heard of the Tuatha Dé Danann?" Peter asked over the crashing of boat against water.

"Yes, absolutely." I shouted to be heard over the wind and waves.

"Well, there's a middle Irish text called *The Book of Invasions*, that was recorded first in the eleventh century, but its origins are thought to be oral, and far earlier."

I nodded enthusiastically. It was so exciting to meet somebody on the same page.

"In *Leabhar Gabhála Éireann*, as we call it in Gaelic, it recounts the five conquerings of Ireland."

"Yes," I said. "As I understand it, the first four of these conquerings technically would have occurred in prehistory, is that right? The only timeline, as far as I can figure, is that of the Milesians. That was the fifth and final conquering, and it must have taken place, since they are said to be the ancestors of the modern-day Celts, well, that must have taken place around the Bronze Age, if not far, far earlier."

"Perhaps. It's important to remember," Peter said, gripping the railing of the boat as it pitched through the turbulent water, "that The Book of Invasions, no matter how seriously some take it, is in fact considered to be a fictional text." I felt like Peter and I had suddenly landed in The Da Vinci Code of the ancient Celts, figuring out a history that had been so long forgotten.

"Right," I said. "Okay."

"So the fourth conquering of Ireland occurred in what you would call prehistory, and it can't really be dated. During that invasion, the Tuatha Dé Danann over took Ireland from the monstrous Fir Bolgs. The Tuatha had magical powers, and they pushed the evil Fir Bolgs out of Ireland, all the way out to the Aran Islands. Their final battle, it is said, was at Dún Aonghasa. At Dún Aengus, as we call it in English, the Tuatha battled the Fir Bolgs to the edge of the cliffs where they were forced to choose: they could turn and fight the Tuatha, or leap to their certain deaths in the sea, hundreds of feet below."

"And that's where you're taking us?"

"Yes." He smiled shyly. "That's where I'm taking you."

I'd done some research on Dún Aengus the night before we left. The name meant "Fort of Aonghas" and referred to the Celtic god Aengus, yet another member of the Tuatha Dé Danann—he was the son of the major deity Dagda. Built on a towering cliff that overlooked the sea, the date of the fort has been largely contested. It was the first fort I'd see, and I didn't really know what to expect. Inishmore, the home of Dún Aengus, was the biggest of the three Aran Islands, laid out between Galway Bay and the Atlantic Ocean like a short strand of pearls. The islands, I'd read, were isolated enough that they remained untouched by tourism for longer than one would have expected. At the turn of the twentieth century, few of the inhabitants even troubled with English at all. Tourism had since crept in, and the islands had been overtaken by the rest of the world. Peter warned me that I wasn't likely to get much from these folks about the faeries. He'd spent long winter weeks here, nearly months, on the smaller islands, and even then the locals had parted with very little folklore. But I didn't mind the challenge.

The island was a mass of green, cut only by gray stone and sandy beach. White cottages with thatched roofs stood stark against the clean landscape. After a short van ride, we walked a gently sloping path uphill and found ourselves suddenly at the foot of the fort. The ancient stone towered above our heads, monstrous, imposing, impenetrable from the outside, bolstered by thick stone buttresses. It was protected by four rings of what must have been, in ancient times, towering walls of stone. To conquer one would be to greet another. There would have been lethal, jagged stones set between the third and fourth walls, an excellent way to slow the enemy before they'd even reached the third line of defense.

On the interior of the fort a huge rectangular slab had been found, larger than any of its kind found in prehistoric ruins. This led some scholars to believe that Dún Aengus had a particular sacred, ceremonial use. With its breathtaking views, it wasn't hard to believe. I walked to the edge of the cliff as if pulled. Could this have been where the Fir Bolgs and the Tuatha truly had their last stand? I leaned over the edge to see the writhing waters of the sea nearly three hundred fifty feet below. It was captivating, the power thrumming there—the sun, the height, the Atlantic expanding for eternity before me, the heavens crashing over the windswept fort. I felt . . . at home. And yet nothing here was familiar. I sat at the cliff's edge for what seemed like an eternity, dangling my feet over the edge of the chiseled rock. When it was built, the fort was several hundred meters from the cliff's edge, but since then, the frothing sea had swallowed nearly half of the original construction. All that history, reclaimed by nature.

We headed back down the hill to grab some lunch, and I noticed a miniature house, larger than a dollhouse, smaller than a playhouse, situated in the corner of a small field. "What the . . ."

"Maybe it's a faery house, Sig!" Liz called. "Want me to take your picture by it?"

"Sure!" I tossed her my camera.

Below the fort, cattle were grazing, and below the grazing fields, just above the museum, I spotted some moss-covered trees just over the stone wall. Stephanie and I peeked over the wall, looking down onto the wild grasses beneath the trees. Perfect territory for faeries. Under their tight canopy the sunlight filtered through in delicate patterns, and the leaves whispered in the wind.

Just as we were about to turn off the gravel path to head into the museum, a rounded stone ruin pulled me to it.

"Wonder what this was . . ." I murmured aloud, stepping into the high grass to investigate.

"It looks like a cattle well," Peter said, coming up behind me.

No, not just a cattle well. This was important. This was a very important, ancient well at the foot of the great fort. People would come here . . .

"Sig, we're going to head inside," Liz called.

"Okay. Coming." I shook my head in confusion.

Inside we read up on Dún Aengus. My favorite museum board was a re-created drawing of the stone altar, with an image of gracefully robed figures standing on it, facing the sea, their arms raised to the sky above. *Druids.* On our way out the door I stopped in front of the admission desk.

"Can I help you?" the woman asked kindly.

"Yes, thanks. I just had a question, actually. I noticed that well outside. Do you know the story behind it?"

She smiled. "Yes, people do ask about that well from time to time. It's a very, very old well. I've always wondered if it didn't have a connection with the fort. Maybe some sort of old holy well. But now it's just used for the cows."

"Thank you." I smiled. That was weird. How had I known? I thought of Charlotte. *There's knowing something with your head, and knowing something with your heart.*

We stopped into a tourist shop where they sold Leprechauns in a Can for six euro fifty, complete with a lock and key, and then spent the rest of the afternoon driving around the island in the van, visiting ruined churches that overlooked the sea. When I asked our tour guide about the wee house we saw, he informed me that it was a leprechaun house.

"Really?" I balked. He pointed out a few more as we were driving.

"And why do you think people put these out?"

"Oh, you know, for the tourists, mostly."

Well, gee. That was disappointing. We stopped on the beach for a photo, and I stooped down to collect a few pretty shells. With that, our tour was over. The ocean swells had picked up while we were gallivanting so the ride back across to the mainland was rough. I'd gone to Inishmore looking for faeries, and I'd come back with a memorable visit to an ancient fort and a pocketful of shells.

One thing was certain. If the tour guide *had* known anything, he certainly wasn't going to share it with a day-tripper. I would have needed at *least* a week completely alone on Inishmore if I was going to have the slightest chance at cracking its code. Peter kindly assured me he didn't think I'd get anything at all, no matter how long I stayed. People didn't believe anymore. And if I was lucky enough to find someone who did, they'd never discuss such things with a tourist.

The girls and I had a fabulous time in Galway over those three days. We had lavish dinners out, went shopping, and spent the evenings laughing, dancing, and listening to music in the pubs. The problem was, even though Liz and Steph had paid for our hotel room, which was amazing, this lifestyle wasn't in my budget. I was running out of money, fast—damn exchange rate. Plus, everything in Ireland was twice as expensive as it had been on the Isle of Man. On the fourth day we were supposed to leave by train to Dublin, and then travel up north to Belfast and beyond.

Who could blame my New York girls for not wanting to stay in hostels on the remainder of the trip? Hostels weren't exactly luxury accommodation. But the morning we were supposed to leave, my stomach was in knots. We tried to figure out some way to compromise, we nickel-and-dimed the costs, again and again, adding them up. Just to travel another three days with them would mean parting with at least three hundred euro when all was said and done. That was four hundred fifty dollars. I couldn't go. I felt wretched having to abandon the rest of my time with them, but I had to get real. I had no job, no income. That was my choice. And now I had to deal with it.

The girls left, and I returned to the hostel, where cold pasta awaited me.

As I lay tucked in bed, listening to the peaceful breathing of my fellow bunkmates that night, I wondered if what Peter had said was true. Had the faery faith completely fled Ireland? Since my arrival here, I'd been "woman about town," striking up conversations with pub goers, taxi drivers, hotel receptionists, waiters. And so far, at the mere mention of faeries, people in Ireland looked at me as if I were bat-shit crazy.

"Do I believe in faeries?" they'd echo. But the answer was definitive. "Ahh . . . No."

Still, I refused to give up hope. The faeries would lead me in the right direction, help me find the right people to talk to.

All I had to do was believe.

17

Caring for Your Kirsten Pike (and Other Survival Tactics for Faery Hunting Abroad)

I HAD allowed a little over three weeks in Ireland, and my sister, Kirsten, was coming to keep me company for two. An experienced hiker, with her I could safely venture into the wilds of Ireland with no concerns for my safety.

We were raised by the same father, suffered just as much in the outdoors at his hands. There were the cross-country ski trips in the Adirondack Mountains on a six-inch-wide ski track, boulders and trees on one side of us, a five-hundred-foot drop on the other. There were the camping trips with nothing to eat but ramen noodles and rancid, freeze-dried beef stroganoff. Although, thinking back, she had missed the time Dad and I climbed the fourteen-thousand-foot Grand Teton in Wyoming, reaching the top only to discover Dad hadn't brought a long enough rope to get us back down. We had different reactions to our outdoor childhood traumas. In college, Kirsten dove into the outdoors with even more vigor—she became a Wilderness Reflections Guide at

Cornell, taking groups of freshmen in the wilderness. She spent a summer in the White Mountains of New Hampshire. She joined the Peace Corps and roughed it in Ivory Coast. It was during all these adventures in the outdoors that she became known simply as KP, and the name had stuck.

I graduated college and moved to Manhattan.

For our Irish faery-hunting adventure, we decided to wing it. Kirsten would drive, and I would navigate—wherever the faeries wanted to lead. KP, I should divulge, is not a believer in faeries. Or angels, or God, or life after death, or ghosts. But she wanted to be a supportive sister, and she was willing, for my benefit, to keep an open mind during our time together.

The morning of her arrival I was sick with excitement. I hadn't seen KP since Christmas, now that she and her husband were living across the country in Seattle. I waited inside, then outside. Inside, then outside. I checked my watch fifteen thousand times. Finally I spotted her turning the corner carrying a huge pack with a rolling duffel in tow. She'd brought a tent and an extra sleeping pad for me. Her ash blond hair pulled into two low pigtails, she was wearing her favorite jeans with a wide brown leather belt and a bright yellow cardigan. Our faces split into smiles at the same time and we ran to each other, nearly knocking each other over. People on the street stopped and stared. They could kiss my ass. KP was in Ireland!

There are three things about caring for the KP that must be done, or, I'd learned the hard way, I would be very, very sorry. I'd come to think of it as a survival manual of sorts.

1. You must always feed the KP *before* she got too hungry. Otherwise, it was bad.

2. You must always let the KP go to sleep when she was tired. Otherwise, she would fall asleep wherever she happened to be. Bartend-

ers, particularly, tended not to like this. They just never understood that she could have zero drinks or five, and the result would be the same: a sleeping KP.

3. You must exercise the KP every single day. Do not miss taking your KP for at least one very long walk each day, or you will have a very grumpy KP on your hands. And the grumpy KP is no fun. No fun at all.

Rules in mind, I immediately made some lunch, we walked some of the sights in Galway, and she took a nap, in that order. We'd heard that the small town of Doolin in the County Clare was one of the best places to see traditional Irish music sessions and decided that would be the first stop on our trip. Doolin was also home to the Cliffs of Moher, better known to most as the Cliffs of Insanity in the movie *The Princess Bride*. *Aillte an Mhothair*, they were called in Gaelic—cliffs of the ruin. So far most ancient places I'd visited were connected in some way to the faery world, so this was promising.

Just over a quaint stone bridge across the Aille River in the heart of Doolin, we came to the scenic little yard where we'd be camping, on the grounds of a charming old hostel. That was the plan, at least, until we discovered, to KP's horror, that she'd forgotten to pack the tent poles. Tough to pitch a tent without the poles. I stood there watching as she turned her things inside out into the trunk of the car.

Finally, plopping disillusioned down on the grass, I decided it couldn't hurt to beseech my faery friends. *Oh please . . . isn't there anything you can do? I know you can't, you know, make tent poles reappear . . . but this is really bad. I can't pay for the hostel . . . I'm running out of dough here, guys, and I don't know what I'm going to do . . .*

I sat there stressed-out for about twenty minutes and was headed to see the hostel owner about a room for us when KP reappeared, an embarrassed smile on her face.

"Uh, I found the poles."

"What? But how?" I'd watched her dig inside her bag. They weren't there.

"I don't know!" she said, astonished. "I just . . . I thought I should look one more time in my duffel bag, and so I did, and they were right there, in the bottom of my bag."

"Ha!" I said, reaching up to give her a high five—though I wasn't convinced that my sister had much to do with recovering them after all.

The hike that took us from the hostel along the Cliffs of Moher was several miles long, rising from ocean level all the way up to more than seven hundred feet. As we walked, we saw the cliffs rising ahead of us, and we rose with them. The sun beamed overhead in a vivid afternoon sky, and I noticed my skin was brown from all the hiking I'd done on the Isle of Man. With our detailed map, we navigated the trail with little difficulty. We stepped lightly, two sisters with big feet on a narrow path, the ocean stretching out below us. Gulls glowed white and tipped their wings in the distance, their shrill cries echoing against the rock. A place like this could make a girl religious, I thought.

The Cliffs of the Ruin were twice the height of the cliffs at Dún Aengus. I was learning that place names held secrets. And this place name must have been quite old. But there were no ruins on the Cliffs of Moher, just a tower that was built in the 1830s, and another that was built during the Napoleonic Wars. What had been here? Was it a fort like Dún Aengus? And why was there was no information, no speculation, on the prominence this place must have had on an island so alive with history?

There were three music pubs in the tiny seaside town of Doolin: McDermott's, O'Connor's, and McGann's, and that night we went to all three to get our fill of Irish trad sessions. Fiddle, guitar, tin whistle, the music throbbed, filling the room, seeping into the floorboards of each pub, reverberating in our glasses. Walking back along the road to the Aille River Hostel and our tent, the moonlight shimmered in the fields, and it was easy to understand how many a person, back in the time of

Yeats, could have imagined they saw something, on a night like tonight. Before settling into our tent, I looked out to the river.

"Goodnight, faeries," I whispered. "Thank you."

I'd read that there was no place in Ireland quite as eerie as the Burren. If ring forts were truly connected to the faery world, as the Irish believed, I supposed one would be hard-pressed to find a place more populated with faeries: the Burren had no less than four hundred ring forts in ninety-six square miles. I'd asked around at the pubs about the Burren and its reputation for faeries, and one local man told me that the name Burren comes from the Gaelic meaning "great rock"—he said it was "quite lonesome." When I asked him what that had to do with faeries, he explained that the Burren was composed entirely of limestone, and that it was bedrock. Some delicate wildflowers, some grass, but mostly just miles of desolate gray rock. Limestone is soft, so when it rains the water erodes it, creating fissures in its surface. These cracks in the rock, which sometimes become water-filled caves, are thought to be portals to the faery world. Needless to say, a hike in the Burren was a must.

We consulted with the manager of the hostel, who mapped out a Burren hike that would take us up a hill called Black Head, and if we climbed higher still, we'd come to an ancient ring fort. A girl at the hostel was kind enough to lend us her pedometer so we could keep track of how far we were hiking. The Burren wasn't a death zone, by any means, but it was known to be tough to navigate since much of it looked the same.

"Just keep your back to the Black Head Lighthouse," our host advised, "and you won't have any trouble finding the fort."

Apparently this was easier said than done. Black Head rose in steep plateaus, and after we'd gotten a good amount of height underneath us, the lighthouse disappeared from view. The Burren was as desolate as its reputation forewarned. Areas of high, dense grass hid treacherous pot-holes that could easily cause an ankle sprain. When we weren't walking on the uneven ground, we were treading on fissured gray rock. And yet halfway up, we came to a flat green plateau.

"Look at this, Kirst," I said with alarm. "This was a *road*." There was a clear avenue along it, made by hundreds of years of tromping feet that cut its way wide and bold across the hill. "We're getting close, I know it."

We climbed several more minutes and then suddenly it was before us, thrust up from the bedrock it was built upon. The tightly lain rocks raised like ancient brickwork to form a perfect circle, though time had collapsed one side of it. The walls were still about twelve feet high. It looked to be about one hundred fifty feet in circumference.

"Want to go in?" KP asked me.

"Actually, not just yet." I wanted to walk around it, get a feel for the place. I told her quickly about Jo in Chagford, about asking permission to enter places.

"It can't be a bad idea," I continued, "especially when you're all the way up here in a place like this." I left her to make her own decision.

The day was clear and the view, incredible. I stood between the fort and the ocean, marveling at who could have possibly built this place. Gazing out to sea, miles in the distance, I saw two distinct lumps of land, long and flat, one next to the other. Those had to be the Aran Islands—Inishmore and Inishman. The sweeping beauty took me, and I don't know how to explain it, but in that moment, I felt someone. I was alone, and then I wasn't—but at the same time, he was there but he wasn't, next to me, admiring the view with a certain amount of pride. I was looking ahead, but I could see him perfectly in my mind—a man about a head shorter than me, with long, dark red hair and a sizable dark red beard. He looked to be in his fifties, and he was wearing clothing of a long-ago time. His face was tan and weathered, and his eyes, I knew, were brown.

All this was my kingdom.

I knew no one was there. But all the same, I let the words sink in and looked out, as far as I could see, all the way to Inishmore. In that moment, I was quite sure: on a dark night, you could see a fire lit at Dún Aengus from here.

I wanted to know the name of this fort. I wanted to know who built it. I knew these things, at least right now, were impossible. So instead I went to enter the fort through the fallen piece of wall. It made the perfect doorway. I paused before I went in, asking permission, and caught my breath. *No way.* There at my feet was a black feather. I bent and picked it up, supposing this was my cue to go inside. Within the walls, the air felt different, stiller somehow. I guess that's no surprise since rock blocks wind. But it seemed to create an atmosphere, and I felt safe, surrounded by all that stone. I didn't see KP and wondered if she'd tucked herself somewhere outside the fort and was already digging into lunch. I walked toward the center of the fort, where there was a small stone circle, built up about two feet high so that it resembled a well, and sat gingerly at the edge. Not wanting to disturb anything, I placed the black feather on a protruding rock halfway down the small stone ring.

All this was my kingdom.

The Aran Islands seemed so distant. Could this all have been part of one man's kingdom? I was wishing I had something else to leave, aside from the feather, when something told me to look in my pack. That was silly—I'd just cleaned it out that morning. Something told me to look in the smallest pocket. Feeling stupid, I did it, even though it would be fruitless. Then my fingers pulled out the shells from the beach of Inishmore, two white swirls with an exotic red-and-white striping. I'd forgotten all about them. Obligingly, I placed them by the feather on the stone. It looked better now—less lonely. I went to zip up my pack and clumsily knocked my little head lamp out. It tumbled to the ground and I bent quickly to pick it up, then stopped, my fingers frozen in midair. Underneath my head lamp, lying in the grass, was a small scattering of seashells. They were identical to the ones I'd just left.

I found Kirsten sitting outside the fort, her back to it, eating her sandwich, and sat down to unwrap mine. I told her about the feathers.

"I know this sounds weird, believe me. But I don't know . . . I feel like it's no big deal, just to, you know, follow my urge. This whole search has become so . . . intuitive. I feel like now all I can do is try to listen."

"I think that makes sense," she said. "I mean, here you are, trying to contact what could be an invisible world. How do you communicate with it? How will it communicate with *you*? I don't think there's any other way to find out."

"You're sounding very woo-woo." I nudged her playfully.

"Your mom's woo-woo. Seriously though. I'm just trying to be . . . open."

"I appreciate that. Hey," I said, switching the subject. "How far did we climb just now?"

She reached into her pocket.

"Shit!"

"What?"

"The pedometer."

"Don't tell me you lost it."

"Damn. I put it on top of the car. On the roof of the car."

"Where?"

"I don't know. Either here, just as we were getting out at the lighthouse, or back at the hostel."

"Fabulous. Now we have to buy that girl a new pedometer."

"Where the hell are we going to find a pedometer around here?"

"That's an excellent question, KP."

"Damn!"

We sat there a moment, bemoaning her incidental absentmindedness yet again. It really wasn't like her to be this forgetful, and I honestly didn't know what had gotten into her. She was always the responsible one. Oh, how the tables had turned. Little sister was all grown up! I *almost* delighted in it.

"You know," I said, "there is one thing you could try."

She raised her eyebrows expectantly.

"Well," I continued, "it's lost. So you have nothing to lose. I bet if you were to make the faeries a deal, they might help you out here."

"What kind of deal?"

"I don't know." I thought a moment. "Maybe you could say, if they somehow can return the pedometer, you would agree to acknowledge there might just be something to all this faery stuff. You know, give them the chance, if they want to take it, to prove to you they exist."

"Mmm-hmm," she said.

"But, KP, if you do this, and it's totally up to you if you want to . . . if something *does* happen, you need to accept the responsibility of it. If you're going to ask for a favor, you can't go back on your word. 'Cause that would be really messed up, you know what I mean? To promise one thing and do another?"

"Okay," she said simply. "I'll try it. Do I need to . . . say it out loud?"

"Oh, God. I don't know. I'm new at all this stuff myself." I considered it. "You could probably just say it in your head." *That's what I do.*

She closed her eyes briefly. "Okay. Done. Now let's head back to the car. It's hot enough to swim—I wanna hit the beach."

18

Guinness, Faery Tales, and the Slopes of Ben Bulben

Faeries, come take me out of this dull world,
for I would ride with you upon the wind,
run on the top of the disheveled tide,
and dance upon the mountains like a flame.

—WILLIAM BUTLER YEATS, *THE LAND OF HEART'S DESIRE*

I WAS reluctant to leave the fort, especially with so many unanswered questions. Who built this fort and why? What was it used for? Was there a battle here? History, I decided, is the ultimate tease. It gets you interested, then leaves you wanting more.

Back at the car we looked high and low for that stupid pedometer. On top of the car, under the car, on the road, in the trunk. Finally, we admitted defeat.

"Maybe it's in the parking lot of the hostel," KP said, seeing my subtle look of disappointment. So, maybe I *was* hoping for a little faery magic.

We were hot from our hike and the sun was beating down. We stopped at a sandy beach, busy with tourists. Ever prepared, KP changed into her suit. I hadn't even thought to bring one on the trip. *Dummy.* I'd just go swimming in my clothes, I decided, rolling up my yoga pants and stripping down to my tank top. As we waded into the clear water I was grateful for the extra material—the weather may have been hot, but the water was cruelly frigid.

"My feet are stinging," I noticed after a minute.

"Mine, too," KP said.

"It's because our nerves are slowly dying."

"I think you're right."

"We really should just dunk under."

"Come on, girls," KP said, lowering her voice, "you've just got to splash a little water on your neck. Adjust the thermostat!"

"Very funny."

"Let's do it on three."

She reached out to take my hand.

"One . . . Oh, Jesus, this is cold . . ."

"Two . . ."

"*Three!*" We squealed, pulling each other under. We didn't have to say it, but we both knew. We needed to swim, not for us.

This swim was for him.

Clean, showered, and dinnered, we headed out for our last night in Doolin. We'd had a little wine with dinner, and that tended to bring out the "the Talker" in my sister. I was familiar with the Talker, not only because I'd been at the butt end of it throughout my life on vacations with my sister, but also because I had a little Talker in me, too. We got it from our father. The Talker is most interested in talking to strangers and pursues an interesting conversation with passionate abandon. Luring the stranger into a conversational trap, the Talker will speak with them the length of the night, obliviously ignoring the people who matter most—in this case, me. This night, KP had snared a group of three men—Sam, Rory, and Allen, and they were tour guides, the kind that lead busloads of people around the Cliffs of Moher. As a result, they were actually interested to hear what had brought me to Ireland.

"Whatever," I said lightly, after explaining. "Nobody believes in faeries anymore. I might as well sit back and enjoy the Guinness."

But Sam looked especially serious, even while the other two snickered. They noticed and quieted down, turning to him.

"Sam believes in faeries, don't you, Sam?"

"No," he said, flushing slightly. "I mean, not really."

"Oh, come on, Sam, tell her the story, the one you told us."

I looked at Sam expectantly.

"Oh, well, you know. It was just something weird, you know? Like something that happened that was a bit off. Unexplainable."

"Tell me, please. Really, I'd love to hear it."

Sam told of his upbringing by a devout Catholic grandfather. But despite being religious, his grandfather was constantly telling them stories about faeries.

"Granddad," they'd ask, "do you believe in faeries?"

"No," would come his gruff reply. "And they've the nerve to exist all the same." Sam's family lived near Ben Bulben, a "hollow hill" that's thought to be a place of the faeries, and before Sam and his brother went out to play on the slopes, their grandfather would warn them to be careful. It wasn't them falling off the mountain that he was afraid of. He was worried that they might fall in.

As a teenager Sam would meet his friends on the mountain, to spend the night drinking and camping in the woods. On one such night, he'd agreed to meet his friend at an old miner's shack so they could find a place to camp from there. But the time came and went, and there was no sign of Sam's friend. Darkness fell and it started to rain, so Sam figured he'd just spend the night in the shack and head home in the morning. The rain pelted down through the night, and all alone in the creepy old cabin, Sam was nervous, but he eventually drifted to sleep.

He woke in the middle of the night to the creaking of the cabin door, and sat up to find two men standing in the doorway. One was tall and slender with long hair blown wild by wind and rain, and the other was a stocky little man between four and five feet tall. They seemed very surprised to see Sam there. Sam couldn't think how on earth two men had ended up at the old miner's shack in the middle of the night. Unless they had a tractor or something. Now that he was listening, he thought he could definitely hear the sound of a tractor idling outside the door. After a moment, the tall man seemed to recover himself.

"Hello."

"Hello," Sam replied.

The shorter man then whispered something to the taller man, who cleared his throat.

"Do you mind if we ask who you are?"

"Uh, my name is Sam Healy, of the Sligo Healys."

The tall man considered his answer, then turned to the shorter man, as if to explain.

"He says his name is Sam Healy, and he's of the Sligo Healys."

The stout man nodded gruffly and murmured once again to the tall man.

"And do you mind if I ask who your father is?" the taller man questioned.

It seemed an odd request, but Sam answered. "My father is Seamus Healy, of Healy's Pub down in the valley."

"He says his father is Seamus Healy," the tall man repeated to his companion, "proprietor of Healy's Pub down in the valley." At this the stout man nodded sternly and whispered once more to the tall man. The tall man cleared his throat.

"And do you mind if we ask you what you're doing here?"

"I was supposed to meet a friend to camp in the woods, but he never came and it started to rain, so I thought I'd stay the night here."

The tall man narrowed his eyes at Sam and then related this, too.

The short man nodded and then the pair looked at one another.

"Well," said the tall man carefully, "I think we're going to go now."

"Okay," Sam said, bewildered.

"Good night," the tall man said.

According to Sam, the two men then closed the door and left. When he awoke in the morning and the rain had stopped, he wondered if it had all been a dream. On his way out of the cabin, he looked in the fresh mud for tire tracks. He was sure he had heard the sound of a tractor after all. But there were no tire tracks. To make matters more confounding, he realized in the light of day that the path in front of the shack was too steep (and far too narrow) for a tractor to pass through there.

"And that's it," Sam concluded.

"So, do you still think it was a dream?" KP asked.

"I can't be sure," he replied. "But I'll tell you one thing. When I hear your sister talking about how there are no faeries left in Ireland, I remember that night. And in my opinion, the faeries up on Ben Bulben are alive and well as ever."

The next morning KP decided that since the pedometer had still not turned up, it was time to fess up that we'd lost it. We'd simply have to buy her a new one, ship it somehow. I was hoisting my pack into the trunk of the car, when something nudged at me just to look one last time. Halfheartedly, I moved a few of KP's things aside, and there, in the corner of the trunk, was the pedometer.

"Aha!" I shouted out loud. "Aha, aha, aha!" I ran with it, lofted in my hand, over to Kirsten—who'd just walked up to our hostel pal—doing a little dance around her.

"You are never going to believe what I just found . . . in the trunk!"

"No."

"Aha, yes!" I exclaimed, holding out my palm.

"You did this."

"I did no such thing."

"But I looked in the trunk!"

"Well, maybe you didn't look *hard* enough," I said, insulted. The girl was looking on, bewildered. "I think you owe somebody an apology," I continued.

KP looked at the girl. "I'm sorry—"

"Not her!" I exclaimed. "*Them.*"

"But why did they have *you* find it? Why not me? That's mean! It's like they had *you* find it just to spite me."

"Well, maybe you couldn't find it because you never *really* believed they would help you in the first place. And I did."

"It was mean."

"Whatever. They proved it to you, and now you have to give them props."

"Fine! I give them props," she conceded.

But she wasn't truly convinced.

I had been trying in vain to get in touch with famous storyteller Eddie Lenihan all summer, and had only succeeded in doing so right before we left Galway. It was regrettable because Eddie lived in Crusheen, which was much closer to Galway than Doolin. So although we were now on our way to KP's friends' house in Kells Bay, we would detour back north to meet yet another man I'd seen interviewed in the documentary *The Fairy Faith.*

As we drove, I told KP another story from Ben Bulben in County Sligo. It was a story related by Yeats in *The Celtic Twilight*, told to him by villagers there. One night, a little girl disappeared. There was excitement in the village because it was rumored that the faeries had taken her. One man had seen it happening and tried to hold on to the girl in vain—he found he held nothing in his hands but a broomstick. The town constable instituted a house-to-house search and ordered all the ragweed in the field where the girl had disappeared to be burned, because ragweed was sacred to the faeries. I read aloud.

"In the morning the little girl was found wandering in the field. She said the faeries had taken her away a great distance, riding on a faery horse. At last she saw a big river, and the man who had tried to keep her from being carried off was drifting down it—such are the topsy-turvydoms of faery glamour—in a cockleshell. On the way her companions had mentioned the names of several people who were about to die shortly in the village."

"And did the people die who the faeries predicted would die?"

"Yes, according to the townspeople, they certainly did."

I told KP about my meeting with Peter Knight in Glastonbury, and how he believed a lot of the danger in these stories that surrounded interactions with the faery realm could just be Christian propaganda. We sat in silence for a while, watching the scenery pass by. Sam's story from the pub fascinated me. It provided a glimpse into the world I wanted so badly to experience. But there was no way we could make the long drive up to County Sligo to walk the haunted, hollow mountain. I could only hope that a visit to Eddie Lenihan could provide me with what I so desperately needed—some answers.

19

The Secret of the Black Dog

. . . Lady Wilde records black dogs that belonged to the Cave
Fairies, the diminished and conquered Tuatha Dé Danann.
—KATHERINE BRIGGS, *THE FAIRIES IN ENGLISH TRADITION*
AND LITERATURE

EDDIE Lenihan was practically Ireland's National Treasure. He'd appeared on television, in all the major papers, and he'd published numerous books—one in particular about faeries entitled *Meeting the Other Crowd*. He was a bit of a celebrity in America as well, at least in the storytelling world—he'd been featured on NPR, and the *New York Times* had singled him out as one of the few traditional storytellers left in Ireland. He was the folk heartbeat of the country, and I imagined there wasn't an eyewitness account of a faery sighting that Mr. Lenihan hadn't heard in his years of recording stories around Counties Clare and Kerry. He was a wild-looking man with curly, shoulder-length hair and a great bushy beard that gave him the appearance of being part man, part lion.

I felt an instant kinship with Eddie, and not just because I liked his frankness and easy spark of humor. I was only a young grasshopper, and he was a seasoned storyteller of epic proportions, but we had one thing in common—we were both digging for any stories that local people might share about supposed encounters with faeries.

Lenihan is so much more than a storyteller. Sure, when he tells a tale, you find yourself glued to the edge of your seat. You're nearly afraid to blink, that you might miss the slightest facial inflection, or worse, that you might carelessly break the spell he has so masterfully woven with his words. But more than that, Lenihan is a story collector. Sitting in his living room, KP and I were surrounded by cases and cases of mini-tapes, cluttering every available surface, each holding years, lifetimes of stories that Eddie had recorded. So it was only natural that he wanted to know, as soon as we sat down, how my story collecting was going.

"Have you found many faery stories since you've been in Ireland?"

"No," I answered simply. "Truth be told, aside from one story about Ben Bulben, I haven't had much luck."

"Yes . . ." Eddie leaned back in his chair, letting out a long sigh. "They're getting harder and harder to find. And you can't believe all the stories you hear. You just can't. When it comes to faery stories, or even ghost stories for that matter, I always say two things. One, if the person is a big drinker, I don't necessarily believe them. Two, if a person is on drugs, forget about it. You'll see anything you want to see when you're on either drink or drugs."

"So how do you know which stories to believe?" I thought, thinking back to Sam's tale from Ben Bulben.

"I'm more inclined to believe a story when it comes from a person who is not afraid of the dark. Because look, imagination is a wonderful thing, and when a man is frightened, it can make him see things that aren't truly there. It's when you meet practical people, who have been out at all hours . . . I listen to those people. And very often you'll find out that what they have to tell you is not easy to dismiss."

"Like what?" I asked, leaning in.

"Well, for example, even today, if you were to ask most young people, especially those living in the countryside, 'Would you bulldoze a fort?' most of them wouldn't. Of course they'll laugh it off. 'Ah, not that I believe in the faeries or anything, but, but . . .' They've all heard stories about people who have interfered with these places and who have come to some misfortune or even death within a short distance of time after destroying an old fort on their land. Now, it has to be said, those misfortunes might have happened anyway. But when you've been collecting stories as long as I have, you see after a while there's too many coincidences for it to be coincidental. There's something there. Whether it's the belief in these things that brings on the consequences, or whether faeries are factually and actually there, there's something to it." Eddie looked at us intently.

Eddie explained that he often gets calls from people who are having problems of a bizarre nature, something they just can't explain, and that most of them are folks who don't believe in faeries and ghosts and the like. He'll typically ask if he can come out and see the place for himself. "Just to make sure they're not pissing around." He winked.

One man was accidentally decapitated while trying to remove a white thorn, a tree sacred in Ireland to the faeries. Building a home over a faery path was another frequent trouble in Ireland. Recently, a man in Kerry had called Eddie after building a brand-new house at the back of his old family land. It had all the modern conveniences, but he was having a very perplexing problem. Despite everything he tried, there was a bedroom at the center of the house that was always freezing cold—even when the heat was on full blast. After going out to the house to see for himself, it was clear to Eddie that the man wasn't making it up. So he suggested he call a priest to come in and bless the house. When that didn't help, Eddie figured the house had been built on a faery path. When Eddie declared his verdict, it jogged the man's memory, and he told Eddie something he'd completely forgotten: many years ago, before his mother passed away, she had pulled her son aside. "Listen to me," she'd warned. "If you inherit this house when I'm gone, whatever you do, you mustn't build down *there*," she said, pointing downhill to a pretty spot of land at the back of the property. Of course that was precisely where her son had built.

"See, the old people knew," Eddie explained. "There were precautions he should have taken."

According to Eddie, in the olden days, before people built a house, they would get four hazel sticks—good, solid ones—and place them at the four proposed corners of the house. They'd hammer them in so that cattle couldn't knock them, and if the sticks were disturbed in the morning, they knew they'd better reconsider where they were building—the faeries were communicating that was their place. They'd move that stick to another corner, leave it overnight, and see how the newly oriented house fared.

"Now, who I am to say," Eddie added, "perhaps the old people believed in faery paths because those are the cultural circumstances under which they were raised. Nowadays people might say it's a ley line, I suppose. But try telling that to one of these older people. They'd say you were talking absolute nonsense: you put your bloody house in the way of the faeries, and you won't block them!" He paused a moment to take a sip of his tea.

"The faeries will have their way, one way or another," he continued. "Because after all, what chance have you against a people who can only be seen if they want to be seen or can take any shape they like?"

Valid point. We wouldn't have very good chances at all.

"Have you ever had an experience with the faery world?" I wanted to know.

He smiled at this, and I noticed KP lean forward in her chair.

"You know, it's an odd thing. In all my years of collecting stories and writing books, I've had only one. When I was teaching in Limerick, I used to have to drive up and down the highway to get there every day. One particular morning I was passing near Bunratty, past an old farmhouse with a big field in front of it, when something caught my eye. I looked and in the middle of the field I saw this *huge* monster of a black dog. And as sure as I saw it, the next moment it was gone. I could hardly believe my eyes; it was quite a shock. I got into the staff room and one of the lads said, 'Jesus, you look like you've seen a ghost!' I told him what happened, and of course they all laughed. 'You were tired, you were asleep,' they said. But I knew what I saw."

It was the disappearance of the creature that hadn't made any sense to Eddie. There were no bushes nearby, no ditch it could've slunk into. It was in the middle of a flat field, so where had it gone in one second? He never saw it again and soon forgot all about it. About six months later, he was visiting an old man in that area, and they were talking about "the black dog" in general. In Ireland, apparently, the black dog was a favorite shape the faeries took. The old man told Eddie that in the 1950s, in front of that very farmhouse, in the same field where he'd seen the dog, there used to be a faery fort, but the farmer had bulldozed it.

"It would have been *highly* unusual back in the fifties, when people still believed, for a farmer to do such a thing," Eddie said. "But that was the fort where the black dog used to be seen. Many of the locals had seen him. He'd be lying there at the mouth of the fort, paws spread out in front of him, a huge dog, watching people on the road. He never interfered with anybody, and nobody interfered with him, either. You see, all the locals knew—he was no simple dog. He was 'one of the boys' guarding their property."

I recalled running my fingers through the fur of the monstrous black dog on the Isle of Man. But as quickly as the memory flashed, I brushed it away.

Curious to understand what he'd seen, Eddie made more inquiries and was stunned at what he discovered: that black dog had been seen in that very spot for well over seventy years.

Eddie raised his brows at the two of us. "Dogs don't live to be seventy years of age. So, I still believe to this day, that what I saw, it was something more than meets the eye."

I'd met a man at the Aille River Hostel who'd also encountered a massive, rather eerie black dog, this one when he was walking near an old fort just outside of Doolin. This dog had also "disappeared." It could be easy to dismiss such stories when you consider that Ireland is still quite rural in areas, and farm dogs are known to wander. But whatever it was these men thought they saw, they truly believed in their hearts that they had witnessed something that just wasn't "normal."

I tuned back into Eddie, who was continuing his train of thought. "At least with the black dog you knew what you were facing, and you could just avoid it." He lifted a single finger. "But if you ask me, the more frightening stories you hear are of faeries being able to take human shape. The person that is sitting next to you could be one of them. And you'd never even know it."

It hit me before I was aware of it—a flash of a familiar face—with a pair of crystal blue eyes that strangely hadn't seemed . . . human. The man I'd spoken to with his giant black dog, in the middle of a field on the Isle of Man. Just like that, pieces of a puzzle clicked together. I could only describe it as a sense of knowing. I'd asked Ninefh in Glastonbury how the faeries might try to communicate with me, how they might try to prove, if they wished, their existence.

You'll experience something only to find out much later what it all meant. When they want you to know.

Just when you think you've forgotten it, or just when you've given up trying to figure it out, you're slapped with a verification. I realized there was always a key, a sign. Experience, verification. It was almost as though something was trying to help me believe.

Like in Glastonbury when I was wondering where to go.

You're going to the Isle of Man next, aren't you?

Here the key was the black dog. The dog was at the heart of my connection with the man in the field. If it hadn't been for the dog, I wouldn't have spoken with him. Now I'd heard two stories in the past twenty-four hours about sightings of black dogs and their connection to the world of faeries. Why hadn't I encountered stories about them previously? Likewise, I hadn't read that faeries could shape-shift into human form. Yes, in folklore people "saw" them—the man who came to fetch the midwife, for example, but it was never explicit that faery had become a man. Rather, I figured it was some sort of specter. So why now? Why through Eddie Lenihan?

I had to hand it to the faeries—their timing was impeccable. It was because Eddie Lenihan was someone I believed. He was a critical thinker. He was a skeptic whose interest in this subject compelled him to collect stories. He was an educator, a folklore expert.

"Those stories you heard about faeries taking human shape," I ventured. "Did any of those stories seem . . . authentic to you?"

"Very much so. I got to know some of the men I interviewed extremely well. The old people weren't stupid. These faeries they'd encountered were dangerous lads. You messed with them, and you were dead. Simple as that. Or what, carried away? That would be worse. They take your spirit and you're the living dead then. Whether that was true or not was neither here nor there. The fact is, people believed it to be true, which shows you that the belief in faeries was very strong."

The rosy-cheeked man hadn't seemed dangerous to me. A bit otherworldly, but not dangerous. But maybe I'd proven myself, or maybe it was even my advocate. Who knew? I let out a breath I hadn't known I'd been holding.

"So after all the stories you've listened to, all the people you've met—what do you believe?" I asked.

I saw a flicker of something in his face, and then he chose his words carefully. "People can believe what they want, but I'd have great respect for these faery places myself. I wouldn't interfere with them. I'd bring nothing out of a faery fort, I don't care who laughs at me for that. You go in, have a good look around, measure them, photograph them, sure. But I'd bring nothing out—not even a leaf out of one of the bushes. Because that's not my property. That's *theirs*. I've heard too many stories of people who have interfered in one way or another and ended up the worse for it.

"Right now," Eddie continued, one finger aloft, "there's a murder a day in this country—probably two or three. It's not that long ago that a murder in Ireland would have been very unusual. Something's gone wrong. And I would much prefer to be listening to these old people—call them superstitious, call them what you like. They were interesting, and they had respect. They had respect for certain places and there was a reason behind it. The reason was that they had inherited a system of values, and I think that is something worth keeping."

These days, the demand for Eddie's storytelling was cutting into the time he'd like to have for his writing and his collecting of folklore. But he can't refuse to go places to tell his stories, because that's what keeps them alive. He was worried that if a new generation can't hear them, where they came from, and the context out of which they came, something could be lost.

"I have always said, and I am not a bit ashamed of it, that Ireland was always a third-world country with a little dab of white-wash on it," he said. "People thought that they had nothing. But that's not true, they had something. They had their beliefs. They had their stories. And they threw it all away for money."

He was referring, I knew, to the economic boom Ireland experienced beginning in the 1990s.

"People wanted a bigger house, a bigger car, three holidays . . . they tried to substitute things for things that you can't substitute anything for. Helpfulness, kindness, charity, human decency. It costs you nothing to help people," he said vehemently. "Nothing at all. These"—Eddie held up a tape—"these are invaluable. They cannot be replaced. Money can buy a lot of things. But not these." We gazed around the room, taking in the hundreds of stories surrounding us from a generation whose memories were turning into dust. Then Eddie looked down at Charlie, his dog, who was flopped at my feet with his legs open, angling for a belly rub.

"Sometimes I think that's why I admire dogs so much. They're better human beings than we are." He reached over to stroke the dog's head.

"Charlie," he murmured, "you might be talking to the faeries every night and regard it as a very natural thing. While we have to go looking for them."

We said our goodbyes and I turned back to give Eddie and Charlie the mutt a final wave as we pulled out of the drive. I looked at KP, feeling like a kid who'd brought my parents to show-and-tell at school.

"So what'd you think?" I asked anxiously.

"It was pretty awesome," she said. "So that's how your interviews typically go?"

"Yes. And no. There's always something different that intrigues me. It's as though all the people I'm meeting . . ." I paused. "Well, I know this sounds completely ridiculous."

"No, Sig, go on . . ."

"Well, it's as though all the people I'm meeting I was somehow *meant* to meet. Believe me, I know how crazy it sounds. I'm following my instincts about where I need to go, who I need to talk to, who I need to meet, and every single time I have an interview, it's as though I'm given a clue. Or a piece to a puzzle would be a better way to describe it. They'll say something—something almost out of the blue—and in the course of the conversation it means something to me, helps me to figure out something mysterious that I've experienced. I noticed it first in Glastonbury, and from there it's just happened over and over again. It's just like Eddie said: after a while there are too many coincidences for things to be coincidental."

"Hmm," she said. "I think I can see what you mean."

I looked out the window, watching the countryside go by, just thinking about the black dog. I could almost see him, lying dutifully in the field with his paws crossed, reminding all who passed: this was once a faery fort.

～～～～～

September 27, 1989

Dear Dieary,

These pages in the middle of you are for things I needed to write so this is what I have to say. Sorry I haven't written in so long I promis I will write in you every day!

    How are you?

    I am fine.

    I wish you were a real person because than, I would have a real best friend that would talk back to me and never talk about how chubby I am. And if you were a person you would be my very best friend because you would be so nice and never tell secrets that I told you. Dieary, I love you.

I was sucking on a watermelon Blow Pop when my dad opened the door. Clicking the lock on my diary I took out the sucker and sat on it. I could feel it sticking to my comforter . . . and my leg.

"You're eating candy at this time of the night? Jesus, Signe," he said, shaking his head. "Throw it in the trash."

Busted, I reluctantly extracted it from my leg, wrapping it in a tissue so I could pick it out later, and dropped it into my wastebasket.

"Now you've got to go and brush your teeth again."

"I don't mind," I answered defiantly, moving past him into the bathroom. He followed me and leaned against the doorframe.

"Sig, have you noticed that your clothes aren't fitting so well lately?"

"Nope."

Yes. But I didn't care.

"Why don't you come running with me tomorrow?"

"I don't want to go running."

"Signe, don't be perverse. It's the best exercise you can get. It works the whole body—every muscle group."

I paused, midbrush, to look at him.

"I don't like running."

"You've never tried it."

"I only like running in soccer."

"Damn it, Signe!" he exploded, banging his fist on the doorframe. "Why are you so goddamn argumentative?"

I looked back at him, and he had that really scary look in his eyes like he always got when he yelled.

Because you always make me do things I don't want to do.

"I don't know," I said quietly.

Mom tucked me in. I tried to fall asleep, and I even had my polar bear, but I was worried. What if I fell asleep and accidentally rolled over on him and then he wouldn't be able to breathe and he'd die? I sadly relinquished him to the floor. Everybody thought that stuffed animals weren't alive, but I knew that when we weren't really looking, they were. So you had to be careful. There were probably lots of girls who killed their bears by accident in their sleep.

The next morning Dad took me to the bike path behind the house. Normally I loved the bike path. My favorite days I would steal carrots or apples from the fridge and follow the path to where it cut through the fields—that was where the Cornell polo ponies were kept. There were always a few horses waiting by the fences in the pasture, and I fed them treats while I stroked their velvety noses.

Today Dad was teaching me how to jog, but he was running too fast, singing a Navy song to try to make it fun. It actually felt like I was trapped in a box with no air.

"Your left, your left, your left, right, left," he sang, his voice intoned with some weird accent, like a drill sergeant. "Your lef, your lef, your lef, raght, lef!" he droned.

It reminded me of an evil marching song that the Orcs would chant when they were hunting hobbits in *The Lord of the Rings*. They were going to catch me. My lungs were burning and his legs were so much longer than mine and he kept running, running. He tried to teach me how to breathe.

"Come on, Sig! We're going to run for forty-five minutes. Look, I'm timing us on my watch." He jogged in place next to me, showing me his Casio watch. I glanced at the timer. It'd been six minutes and I couldn't breathe.

I stopped and he continued to jog in place.

"Come on, Signe. Don't be a wimp. Don't be a quitter . . ."

I could feel how hot my face was, and I hated him for making me do this.

"Signe," he sang, "don't be a quitter."

I hated him for making me feel like a quitter.

"Signe . . ."

"Dad!" I shouted. "I'm not doing this. I hate it . . . you go too fast!"

His face got tight, and I could tell I'd made him angry.

"Fine," he said, after a moment. "Go home then. I'm going to finish my run." I watched him run down the path in his stupid short little shorts until he got smaller and smaller and smaller.

Tears stung my eyes as I turned to walk back home. This wasn't what I wanted. I wanted to get out of running, but why did it have to feel so bad? I found my mom weeding in the front garden.

"You're back early," she said, straightening, brushing the dirt from her gloves.

I told her about Dad running too fast and feeling like a quitter. She thought for a while and said, "Do you think you might like running if you could do it on your own?"

"I don't know, maybe."

"Well, maybe you could save up some allowance and get your own stopwatch. Then you could time yourself, and do your own runs?"

I considered this. "Okay. But how much do they cost?"

"Hmmm . . . I bet we could find one for five dollars or so."

Oh, brother. That was going to seriously cut into my candy money. Big time.

"Jeez!" I exclaimed.

She laughed. "Well, if you want to do this, maybe we can think of a couple of extra chores to earn you the extra money. I'll give you two dollars for mopping the kitchen floor."

I thought for a moment. If I did this, maybe my dad wouldn't think I was such a loser. Maybe I could learn to run in my own way, a way that didn't hurt.

Maybe I would even like running!

"Deal."

~~~~~~

October 15, 1989

Dear Dairy,

I can't wait for Holoween because I am going to be a fairy that looks like every kind of beautiful fairy there is. It's going to be so NEAT! <u>NO ONE</u> will guess what I am!

I hide candy everywhere in my room, so my parents don't know! I save all my allowance from my chores and buy candy after school from Short-Stop Deli. Lemonheads are what I usually buy. Any kind of chocolate is good too— Snickers or M&M's, or Reeses Peanut Butter Cups. Or Reeces Pieces. Also the ones in the shape of half limes and lemons that look real, with the rind and everything, and they're coated in sugar. Those and the Rock Candy might be my favorites. My favorite place to hide them is in my shoe rack—don't tell! But I like it because then nobody can tell me what to do! And I can have candy after dinner too!

Your friend,

Signe Singer (I just like to write that sometimes because I think it looks neat.)

I was drawing flowers over the i's when suddenly my bedroom door burst open, and I nearly jumped out of my skin.

"Goddamn it, Signe!" My father stood in the doorway, his arm raised, and I could see he was clenching something in his fist. He was waiting for me to look at him.

I thought as fast as I could. *What did I do this time? I didn't do anything!*

His body looked like a spring that was being stretched too far.

"I told you to get this out of the goddamn living room!" So loud that my neck automatically tucked into my shoulders in a cringe.

"Alan, give her a break, will you?" I could hear Mom rushing down the hallway.

"Linda," he said as he rounded on her, "stay the hell out of it!"

She melted away. He looked at me, his jaw clenched. The next moment I saw his arm fly back, and I watched in slow motion as my brand-new stopwatch came sailing from his fingers. It arced across the room, sailed over my head, and hit the wall, nearly colliding with my pink African violet. There was a sharp crack and its guts spewed onto the floor. I clenched my fingers. Open and closed, open and closed. His eyes were piercing mine.

"You live like a goddamn pig. Learn to clean up after yourself."

He turned and left. The house was still again. I turned my face into the carpet and pulled my polar bear over my head. His soft fur protecting me, I could imagine we were just hibernating until spring. I heard a shuffling on the carpet and hoped it was my mom. She gathered me in her arms, her sweater smelling sweet and clean like Navy perfume.

"Siggie, we can get you another one," she murmured into my hair. "We'll get you another one, okay, sweetie? Don't cry . . ."

I pulled my head up from her shirt. "I don't want another one. I *don't want another one ever again!*" I drooled through my tears.

I hated him. I hated him and his stupid running. I hated him so much that sometimes I wanted to kill him.

20

Climbing the Lost Druid Mountain

Is it madness to believe, as I now believe, in the
existence of the subterranean realm?
—JOHN MATTHEWS, *THE SECRET LIVES OF ELVES*
AND FAERIES

I LOOKED over at Kirsten and her pretty golden hair, gleaming in the sun. I always wanted to have blond hair like hers. She seemed almost unaware of me as I sat there, admiring her profile as she concentrated on the road.

"Sig."

"Yeah."

"Put something else on. We've heard this CD like seven times."

"Mmm, okay. You want Mix One, Two, or Three?"

"Don't you have any CDs we haven't listened to already?"

"No. These were all from Eric. And I'm traveling light."

"How about the radio?"

"Mmm, okay." I fiddled with the tuner.

"Can I ask you something?" I turned to her.

"Sure."

"You remember the time Dad broke my stopwatch?"

"No. He broke your stopwatch?"

"Yeah. When I was nine. He threw it against the wall and it shattered into pieces. He never apologized or anything."

"Wow."

"Sometimes I wonder—why didn't Mom do anything? Why didn't she stop him from acting like that, yelling at us the way he did?"

She thought a moment. "I guess she was like me. She stayed out of the way." It was true, Kirsten was always somehow better at avoiding Dad's fits than I was.

"I wish she hadn't."

"You know, Signe, interfering only made it worse. I think she could have pushed him to physical violence if she had gotten in the way. I mean, don't you remember? Can't you hear her? She'd say, *Alan, just leave her alone! Linda, stay the fuck out of this. This is not your business.* I can hear those voices in my head. I mean, can't you?"

"Yes." I turned to gaze out the window. "Yes, I can."

"I think she *did* try," she said, after a moment. "But the reason you can't really remember is because it was so ineffective."

"She couldn't stop him?"

"No. No one could."

"I remember he never wanted anybody in the family to comfort anyone else," I said.

"Nope. Because that would make it seem like he'd done something wrong. If we had to . . . console each other against his wrath."

"But where did it all come from? All that anger? I think about it sometimes, and I just can't understand why leaving a pair of shoes in the hallway could justify that kind of reaction."

"It might've had something to do with the fact that he was smoking all that pot."

"Self-medicating for some kind of depression . . ."

"Yes. He was also a control freak. That didn't help, I'm sure."

"But after the divorce, it was like everything changed. I guess it must have happened more slowly than that—probably in retrospect things got better once they told us they were getting a separation. He realized that now we could choose. If he lost his temper, we just wouldn't want to be around him."

"The old Dad and the new Dad—they were like different people," KP said. "I guess after the divorce I just wanted to leave the yelling one behind. So I did."

My sister has always had a way of deciding something, and then making it so, when it comes to her emotions. It's a behavior I'm not able to summon. I couldn't decide to forget how it made me feel, even though so many years had gone by. I still hated running. With a passion. And after all those years of practice, I still couldn't stand to be yelled at. Where some people could handle it, I still had to fight not to burst into tears in a conference room filled with people. I blamed him for that. In fact, I realized I still blamed him for a lot of my fears. Maybe that was a part of why I was having so much trouble getting over his passing, letting him go.

There was too much anger, too much regret.

I could never reconcile my two fathers. After the divorce, he became more of a dad, and more of a friend. He told us he loved us, that he was proud of us. He hardly missed a home soccer game, he fixed us breakfast before school. He pulled all-nighters to help me finish papers, he took us skiing at midnight. He let me have parties while he hung out at the neighbors'. He let us have wine with dinner. But what about the old Alan—the one we so feared? He'd melted away and in his place was this gentle man who literally caught bumblebees on his fingertips. Perhaps we'd been so amazed by the transformation we didn't want to jinx it. Nothing was ever said.

I was twenty years old when I sat down to remind him of "old Dad." I'd composed the conversation with the help of a therapist so that he might acknowledge that his mistakes had made my childhood at times really, really shitty. So he'd finally understand what it was like to grow up with Dr. Jekyll and Mr. Hyde. Was it the weed? My mother said he smoked several times a day. Was it the depression? Depression was never something he'd acknowledge having. I was still so broken, so angry about the past, and I desperately wanted some closure.

I could feel my heart in my throat, I remember, when I got up the courage to ask. "Dad, can we sit down? I'd really like to talk to you about something."

He looked worried. I could see him thinking, *Oh, no, what has she gotten into now?* Taking a breath, I reminded him of everything—the spankings, the yelling, the stopwatch, the tears every morning before school. He just sat there at his kitchen table looking dumbstruck. After a moment, he reached across for my hand. I looked to see tears—there were tears flowing down my father's cheeks.

"I'm so sorry, Signe. I am so, so sorry." He shook his head in bewilderment. "I don't remember any of that. I'm sorry, but I just don't remember."

So it was all gone. Repressed. Memory loss maybe, due to the drugs? People who say marijuana is harmless, marijuana isn't addictive are full of crap. I lived it in more ways than one, and I know. Kirsten and I, we were left with the memories. Such a proud father. So brilliant and beloved by his students. So charming. So adventurous. Such a great mentor. Such a storyteller. Such an angry bastard. And then such a sad, sad man.

All of these things were true.

And six years later, he was dead.

"Sig!"

"What?" I managed, irritably.

"I need you to navigate here. We're coming up to a roundabout."

I unfolded our directions.

"We're taking the middle exit."

"Thanks," KP said, and let out a long sigh. "I guess I like to remember the Dad who went to Stewart Park with me when I was in eleventh grade to play in puddles when we got too tired of being inside, or the one who threw dinner rolls at me when I was on the phone too long with my boyfriend freshman year."

"Ha! I remember that. *We* were cleaning up and you were gabbing away . . . man! You used to talk on the phone for *hours!*"

"Shut up." She threw a halfhearted whack in my direction. "I liked the Dad who took us cross-country skiing Christmas Eve . . . that made us do things that we always liked having done afterward but at the time we weren't always happy to have done."

"Yes. And we did a lot of singing."

"A *lot* of singing." I could tell we were both considering bursting into spontaneous song, but then both decided against it. It took too much heart to sing like we used to.

"It's amazing how much, if you just love people to death, you can redeem yourself."

"Yup," I said. "He did love us." That was never a question. "He just had so much more to figure out about himself."

We arrived in Kells Bay with time to freshen up before dinner. KP's friend Vicky had been the head of the English Department at Nobles and Greenough, the private school where KP taught prior to her move to Seattle. Tad was Vicky's husband, and a teacher as well. His parents had built the house in Ireland when he was growing up, and he'd summered there. Both of them were also artists. Tad painted watercolors, and Vicky designed glass jewelry.

Just south of the Dingle Peninsula, Kells Bay was a charming little fishing village surrounded by beach and mountains—part of the touristy "Ring of Kerry." But Vicky and Tad's place was off the beaten track. Because they would sometimes lend their house out to artists in exchange for pieces of their work, the home was a well-decorated, creative refuge. The woods surrounding the house looked like the perfect habitat for faeries—all big, mossy oaks and ivy-covered greenery. Across from their house was an old estate that had been turned into what was called Kells Gardens—forty acres of rare plants including Europe's largest collection of ferns and Ireland's largest palm tree. As Tad toured us around the property, I was amazed to see that they had several ruins of old houses in their backyard, where an old road used to be. The area was separated from the rest of the property by a low stone wall with a series of steps that led into it. It was covered in an arching canopy of trees.

"I do my best to keep the weeds out," Tad said. "Most of my time here is spent up in these ruins."

"They're incredible," we agreed, gazing around. The first chance I got, I was going to dive in and see if anything happened.

After dinner—whipped up by Tad, who prepared it while sipping a glass of wine and listening to the soundtrack from *The Secret of Roan Innish*—Vicky and Tad warned that I should wait until morning to head outside, or else be devoured alive by midges, teeny biting insects sent as a scourge from the depths of hell.

Having experienced my share of blackflies, in the morning I coated myself in bug spray, foolishly thinking, *Right. How persistent could they be?* The atmospheric beauty of the space was undeniable. The foundations of the houses stood three feet high, covered in ivy. There were ferns, one taller than a human, everywhere, and loose leaves fell here and there from the tall trees. I sat and watched them drift down in shafts of golden light. The feeling of this place, though so close to the house, was completely different from the rest of the property. It felt eerie—there was, Tad had shown me, a short square opening that seemed to lead nowhere but into the hill behind it. Can you say, *entrance to the faery world?* I'm sorry to disappoint you, but I wasn't brave enough to stick my head in there. In my defense, no one in Tad's family had ever done it, either.

But the bugs, the bugs! They crawled in my eyes, my ears, up my nose, down my throat. They buzzed at me aggressively, biting into my neck. I tried to stay calm and open.

I had a greater purpose! I could not let them win! I tried asking the faeries to make them go away. Soon they were joined by bizarre-looking buzzing creatures that reminded me of bees or wasps, but darker, and a little smaller, more like large houseflies. I noticed that the tree trunk I was perched on was covered in larvae or some sort of nest, just as three of the buzzing creatures formed a tripod and hovered over my head, investigating. Then they dive-bombed me. I wanted to stay, really I did, but in the end, the bugs were victorious, and I the lump-ridden loser.

I tried to console myself. If the faeries really wanted me to undertake this adventure, it would do no one any good if I were devoured by vicious, flesh-eating insects. Right? I went inside, defeated.

"Sig, you can't expect something to happen every time," Kirsten said. "I mean, if that were the case, wouldn't everybody believe in faeries?"

"Yes," I conceded. "I guess you're right."

We spent four days at Vicky and Tad's, and there wasn't much time for faery searching, so I dialed it back a bit and enjoyed being a tourist. Maybe KP was right, and a break was what I needed. They made it easy, what with Vicky's heart-shaped biscuits, glass-working demonstration, Tad's beautifully prepared dinners, lunches at seaside cafés, beautiful walks, and driving tours of the countryside complete with more stone forts. I allowed them to spoil me in the warmth of their generosity, truly enjoying myself. And I plotted our next move.

In Ireland, faeries and spirits are often connected to mountaintops. There was Ben Bulben, of course, way up north in County Sligo. In my research I'd come across several spirits that reportedly guarded wells or ancient sites on mountain peaks, thought to be members of the faery kingdom. KP and I were itching for a big climb, but we needed to find something not too far, something in the general area of Dingle. We settled on Mount Brandon, the second-highest mountain in Ireland outside of MacGillycuddy's Reeks, a series of peaks within the Ring of Kerry, farther afield than we were able to go.

As we hit the road to drive back up the coast to Dingle, I began to notice that Ireland was no longer so much a place of myth as it was a place of numbers. One road sign warned "141 People Have Died in Co. Galway in the Past 4 Years," advising drivers to drive carefully. Hostels tried to lure tourists with highly emphatic signs with ratings and exclamation points galore: "#1 Hostel in the West of Ireland!" or "Voted #2 Hostel in all of Dingle!" "Dining Pub of the Year, 2005!" "Mt. Brandon! The 8th Highest Peak in Ireland! The 2nd Highest Peak Outside MacGillycuddy's Reeks!"

Even Kerry Radio blasted "The Top Ten Reasons Not to Have a Mobile Home Tax!" And everywhere we went, the radio broadcasted sad stories of desperate people with no work. Collapsed economy, pay cuts, halts on development. Legions of workers had lost their jobs. The country was in the middle of the biggest depression it had seen after such an impressive period of economic boom. The economic tidal wave had struck Ireland, all the way from America. There was no better time to set up camp in a tiny remote village and climb a mountain.

We camped in the backyard of a pub at the base of Mount Brandon. The proprietor showed us to the back where we could pitch our tent by the edge of the bay, telling us not to worry about the barking dogs.

"It'll be me sheeping dogs," he explained.

"Oh!" I exclaimed. "Can I meet them?"

"No," he said, crabbily.

The weather was soggy the morning of our departure, and he and his wife warned us not to go.

"You'd best not be climbin' Brandon in this soggy weather," she admonished. "And two girls, all the same."

But up we went. Mount Brandon was supposed to have some of the most incredible 360-degree views in Ireland. It was so foggy I could hardly see three feet in front of my face.

"Maybe it'll clear," KP said. "You know, unpredictable Irish weather and all that."

"Yeah. Maybe." I wasn't holding my breath.

During the Ice Age, glaciers had scooped a series of cauldrons out of the rock on the eastern side of the mountain. Now, in a line nearly all the way to the summit, a stream connected a series of glacial lakes that braided together, the largest of which was called Loch Cruite. Brandon was named for St. Brendan, who lived circa 484 to 577. He was one of the early monastic Irish saints. He built monastic cells at the foot of Brandon, and it was said that he climbed the mountain to view the New World, before setting sail for it. Of course, I immediately thought that it must have been a pretty important place to the pagans. The pagans being the pre-Christian Celts. The pre-Christian Celts being the ones who believed in the Tuatha Dé Danann: the faeries.

We reached the foot of the mountain and were about to begin our ascent when we were greeted by a charming sign:

Going climbing? Are you prepared for tough ground, wind, rain, mists, accidents, etc.? You should have map, compass, torch, whistle, food, water, first-aid kit, stout boots, protective clothing, and spare clothing. It is 10 degrees colder at a 3,000-foot summit than here. A breeze down here is a strong wind up there. Do not climb alone. A party of **FOUR** is recommended.

KP and I looked at each other. "We've got most of that stuff, right?"

"Right. Apart from that party-of-four thing."

"Right. Let's go."

We followed a steep path into the mist. It wasn't long before we came to a stone shrine to St. Brendan, looking forgotten in the fog. As the slope got steeper, we soon found ourselves on the beginning of "the ups." I'd missed how mountain climbing made me feel so tough.

"Those are my girls," our father would declare. In the Tetons, the Adirondacks, on the slopes of Mont Tremblant in Quebec.

We passed three men making their way down, warning us, "Can't see a damn thing up there! You girls should wait until it clears. We got down just in time."

"Thanks," we said, pressing on. The higher we got, the thicker the mist became, soaking our hair, our faces, adding to the moisture caused by our increased sweating. Still it made me feel fresh, somehow clean, rugged. Eventually we were completely enclosed by the sheer rock walls, and the boulders and split fissures in the rocks were easy homes for elves and dwarves. I felt like we could be ambushed by Orcs at any moment. I hoped Orlando Bloom would step out to save me.

The altitude gain and my pumping blood made my fingers swell, until my engagement ring, which had been getting gradually looser on my finger as the weeks had gone by, was constricting the blood flow to my fingertips. We reached the eastern ridge, where the lakes began, a silver chain up the spine of the mountain, silent and still. There were slugs the size of my little camera case, and the only other sound was the haunting call of a single bird, trilling from nowhere and everywhere at once. It was exhilarating. Eerie. The breath off the water was ancient.

"I have a curse, I think, involving mountains that are supposed to have spectacular views," I grumbled, thinking of my windy, cold, wet trip up Snaefell on the Isle of Man. "Sure would be nice to have a view . . ." I hinted to the rocks and pools around me.

"Well," KP said, "maybe the faeries are trying to tell you something."

"What? Like I should have kept my day job?"

"No, maybe they're saying that you should stop looking outside, and try . . . looking within."

"Could it be," I gasped, in mock awe, "that the faery within is the faery that I've been looking for?!"

"I'm serious," she said. "You've been getting so frustrated with things not 'happening.' Maybe things *are* happening. You just don't know it yet."

"Okay. So you think I just need to relax?"

"Yes."

Maybe Kirsten had a point. Maybe, like the tall stranger in the field on Man had said, I just needed to enjoy it.

At the top of the mountain, which we reached at long last, the wind whipped, and we tossed our packs down to zip into some more layers. We'd been planning lunch on the summit but it was too damn cold, so we just walked around. I picked up a few red rocks. "These are cool," I mumbled, stuffing them in my pocket. Then I caught myself, and thought, a conciliatory gesture, *I hope it's okay if I take these?* There was a strange stone structure dug into the top of the summit—definitely a ruin of sorts, but it almost reminded me of some of the burial tombs I'd seen photos of in Devon. A portal tomb, was that what it was called? It looked like it led down into the ground, but it was now covered in earth. Could it have been a monastic cell? Even the pagans probably weren't crazy enough to live up here.

It was then that I realized the entire time I'd been hiking, I'd been seeing them in my mind. Lines and lines of people, trekking up the hill, their feet coming before mine on the ancient stones. I could see their faces. They looked like Celts. Up and up, but only in certain times of the year. Something whispered, *This was a special place, a place of pilgrimage, just as it is now, in Christian times.* But was it really? Or had I let my imagination get carried away?

We stopped to eat on the leeward side of the mountain, then climbed back down the slippery wet rock in the mist. At the bottom awaited dinner and a pint, and another night of sleeping underneath the stars.

Months later, in South Carolina, I wrote a letter to my new friend and partner in historical mystery, Peter Guy.

Dear PDT Guy,

I have come across something in my research related to Mount Brandon in Dingle. I have a crazy hunch that mountain was an ancient pagan place of wor-

ship, and I think there may be a few clues left in the place names, but have only been able to (with my nonexistent understanding of Gaelic) take my research so far. It all stems from the very un-scientific fact that when I climbed it with KP, I had a strong feeling. So back at my desk, I undertook a small amount of research to see if I could turn anything up.

The largest lake on Brandon is Loch Cruite, which means "harp?" in Gaelic. So literally it could be referred to as Harp Lake. Funny thing is, the lake doesn't resemble a harp in shape, not from memory, nor from the topographic map. I think it's more likely the place name contains some older clue or connection to the true history of the land . . .

What I stumbled upon was my own etymology-based theory. In antiquity, it became custom for those who didn't know any better to refer to any pre-Christian Celts simply as Druids. As more people converted to Christianity, the term Druid was demoted further, to the title of "bard." (From that point on in Christian texts, we find examples of bards who are in actuality Druids, making this a proven fact.)

Of course in Celtic society, the word Druid actually denoted a particular and specific high-level position (that of teacher, judge, peacekeeper, etc.), yet in Christian records, monks refused to give any credence to the societal distinction. Druid came to represent the entire pagan Celtic population and their beliefs. A thread of this Christian propaganda still lives today: there is still a common misunderstanding that Druids were a cultural people.

A harp player was called a Cruitier. A bard was a traveling poet or musician. In many cases, these "bards" were actually Druids, on the run to avoid further persecution. Fighting to keep their sacred culture alive, they traveled among pagan communities recounting oral history, in many cases posing as simple poets or musicians to avoid death. It was during this time, perhaps, that the terms became somewhat interchangeable. If we can accept that, Harp Lake was likely to have been, in essence, a pagan holy lake that was strongly connected to the "Druids."

Lake of the Bards, or Lake of the Druids. After all, what did you look for when looking for an ancient pagan site? You looked for its strongest established Christian church. Or in this case, an entire mountain named after a Christian saint. History would tell us that if this was the case, the mountain must have held a very real cultural or religious significance to the ancient Celts.

We need look no further than written history to find evidence of this blurring of the lines between bards, pagan Celts, and Druids. In 1283, Edward I ordered the massacre of hundreds of "bards and harpists in Wales, Scotland, and Ireland." Edward was a Christian crusader and was also responsible for expelling the Jews from England seven years later. So, as late as the thirteenth century, a high king of England was ordering the massacre of a group of musicians? It seems certain that in these areas, the Druids still held the loyalty of the local populace—a power that a king found threatening enough to want to exterminate. A contemporary historian, Adam Ardrey, contends that the countryside functioned as strongholds for the pagan religion, and the carriers of its oral history, the Druids, for several hundred years after AD 500. Essentially, Edward I was rooting out the pagans.

This was a topic that Peter and I would debate. But in my opinion, KP and I were sleeping at the foot of a 300-million-year-old mountain that had most likely been worshipped by the ancient Celts. I wish I'd known that at the time. It would have made being there so much more poignant, and so much less . . . frustrating. And perhaps I would've further explored my vision of the lines of ancient people. It was just one more part of my experience that was validated when someone or *something* deemed the time was right.

Even though we were physically and metaphorically in the dark, it *was* magical. Outside the tent the stars were bright, and I was aware of how amazing it felt to have all that beauty hovering up there, directly over our heads. I let out a soft sigh and tried to adjust my bumpy "pillow."

"Signe?" Kirsten whispered.

"Yes?" I whispered back.

"Do you think we appreciate Dad more now, now that he's dead?"

I thought for a moment. "Yes. I think it's a very hard thing, sometimes, to appreciate people while they're here. Especially, for some reason, family."

We were quiet for several breaths, both locked in memory.

"Kirsten?"

"Yes?"

"Do you ever . . . sense him?"

"No. Well, I mean, just in the same way I did when he was alive. When I was doing something outdoorsy and cool, I would always think, 'Dad would totally love this.' It's just that now I can't tell him about it. But I guess I take a lot of comfort in one thing."

"What's that?"

"Well, there's half of Dad in you, and there's half of Dad in me. So when we're together, we make one whole Dad."

Tears sprang to my eyes, and for a moment the lump in my throat kept me from saying anything at all. Taking my silence as non-agreement, she whispered it out for me, in typical KP logic. "You know . . . Dad is fifty percent of the genetic material that created me. So technically, he is half of me, therefore, if I am hiking, then he is there, enjoying the hike."

I bit the edge of my lip to keep from laughing. She had actually just used an "if/then" statement. Leave it to my sister to describe her philosophy of our father's presence using conditional predicate logic.

"You know, in a literal sense," she continued in a low voice, "because your children technically *are* you. So . . . maybe I feel him. But maybe it's just me, so . . ."

"No, I get it, I get it!" I laughed.

"Kirsten," I said after a long moment.

"Yes?"

"Can I ask you another question?"

"Mmm?"

"Why are we whispering?"

She paused a moment, then whispered, "Uh . . . I don't know."

It was one of those moments, like you have in sleepovers when you're little, where one person starts laughing and soon no one can stop. The tent exploded with our laughter, which grew into irrepressible cackling. We laughed until we cried, until our stomachs cramped, futilely trying to muffle ourselves in our slightly damp, irregular pillows.

More than a hundred years ago Yeats wrote, "In Ireland there is something of timid affection between men and spirits. They only ill-treat each other in reason. Each admits the other side to have feelings. There are points beyond which neither will go . . ." As I traveled Ireland it seemed this mode of thinking, this close relationship between man and spirit, was a thing long forgotten in the collective consciousness. I was following such a cold trail in trying to find people who still viewed the world in this way—as sentient, and reached out to it with a spirit of collaboration, a spirit of respect.

One hundred years' time and a girl comes to pick the threads. If only I could have plucked one thread that could take me back to the source. I guess that was the saddest thing about Ireland. It was such a beautiful, paradoxical country where faith in God coexisted with a belief in faeries. Each was a part of the other. And there was suffering then, terrible suffering. Poverty that would rip your guts out it was so pervasive, so unjust. But they had something then. They had their beliefs, and they had their stories. They could have one loaf of bread to their whole family, and they would still leave a few crumbs for the Sidhe; they would still leave a few crumbs for the good people. An old peasant woman in Yeats's time said, "The faeries are always looking out for the poor." And who's to say they weren't, in whatever way they could?

Perhaps there was an exchange there, a kindness, in thanks for being recognized and remembered. Perhaps then, if they had a chicken, it would give a few more eggs every once in a while, but it was those extra eggs that gave enough to keep the family fed. Perhaps if they had a cow, it gave sweeter milk. We don't yet know, and may never yet know, the ways in which their world reaches out to us. But I had begun to see it. I had begun to understand that when the worlds intertwined, the faeries' touch was subtle. And in that subtlety we always have the right to choose. We can choose to believe or not to believe. I only knew that the stories of fear and dread and violence that made up our folklore hadn't shown themselves to me. Instead, I found that the more I was willing to walk toward belief, the stronger my own intuition got, and the more gifts and kindnesses I received, even if it was only because I was now more aware, faeries or no.

But thinking back over my path, thinking back to where it had led me in that very moment, sitting in Shannon Airport, waiting to board a plane, I knew that my journey since undertaking this book had been nothing short of miraculous. In carefully picking up my own thread in the faery story, I saw that there had been signs all along.

They were silly little things. The ease with which I met my book agent, how quickly the project sold, Eric and I finding the one little house in our suburban neighborhood with a wild, almost mystical backyard—at a price we could afford! All of the incredible people I'd met who had accompanied me on a piece of my journey so far, each one contributing something to my search for the meaning under everything, each one of them magical in their own way. This was the enchantment I'd found in following my own faery path, whatever that meant. And I couldn't help but wonder what the people of Ireland were losing in leaving theirs behind. I'd quizzed shopkeepers, bartenders, patrons. Children, mothers, bus drivers. I'd spoken to more than a hundred people in passing through Ireland asking them all the same thing: *Do you believe in faeries?* The answer had been no.

In Ireland, the storytellers cling to the dusty fabric of the old days even as the new generations absentmindedly sweep everything under a new three-thousand-euro rug. They don't wonder what will happen to their culture when there is no one left to tell its stories. They don't wonder what will happen to Eddie's treasure—his trove of tapes—when he is no longer alive to protect them. Would they forget altogether? There were struggles in the newspapers between believers and local government, when they wanted to chop down sacred faery trees to build the new highway to Shannon Airport. But the new generation beats back the magical mist from their shores with every "I don't believe" that's uttered from their lips.

I envied them their enchantment even as I watched them ignore it. I had heard it stirring in the untamed echoes of a night's entertainment, in the haunting whistle and frenzied bowing of an evening's music session. In hearing and in dancing, it was enough to make me wild with it. To be Irish, with that ancient Celtic drumbeat thrumming through your veins, thousands of years of connection within you, between you and the land, the land and its spirits. I felt a pulse buried beneath it all, and it gave me hope. The Shining Ones have slumbered for hundreds of years, relegated to a forgotten corner in the country's collective nursery, but perhaps there was still a chance that once again people would stir them, reigniting the mysticism of ages past.

I wondered if they ever remembered, if even just in sleep, the ancient secrets that still lay within them, whispering through their bodies in the deepness of their dreaming.

SCOTLAND

21

The Faery Queen of Aberfoyle

The good people . . . are said to be of a middle nature
betwixt man and angel . . . of intelligent, studious spirits and
light, changeable bodies (like those called astral), somewhat of
the nature of a condensed cloud and best seen in twilight.
—THE REV. ROBERT KIRK, *THE SECRET COMMONWEALTH OF*
ELVES, FAUNS AND FAIRIES

SCOTLAND is immense, desolate, awe-inspiring. It rains while the sun shines fifty yards away. There, the faeries are known as the Sith (pronounced *shee*). In lore they reflect the landscape around them. Waterfalls crash down deep splits of black rocks, and the mountains stand like mythic giants, their faces cragged with age, the rock weathered by centuries of wind and rain. Walking the hills, you can feel the ghosts walking alongside you—those who climbed the slopes before, some to feed and shelter their sheep or cattle, some to honor the land that bore them. Here, people remember what they are—human, yes, but in actuality, they remember that really we are all animals. And when you remember what you are, your connection to the land, and to the other animals that we are charged to share it with, your viewpoint changes forever.

I'm not saying that the people of Edinburgh run through the streets worshipping cattle and singing about rainbows and butterflies. Edinburgh has its charms, and in truth it is one of my favorite cities in the world. But it has its share of ghosts. There are haunted tours that take you through dank dungeons and underground communities, bricked up with people alive in them during the plague. Like all bustling cities, there is a certain remove from the natural world. So upon arrival, I sought the remoteness right away. Saying goodbye to Kirsten in Shannon Airport was another tough parting, but there was a freedom in being back on my own, continuing my quest.

From the start, one man's story in particular had intrigued and terrified me, more so than any other. He wasn't a social scientist (like W. Y. Evans-Wentz) or a poet (like Yeats). Rather, Robert Kirk was a humble Scottish minister who had devoted his existence to the pursuit of the faeries. And it cost him his life.

A well-educated man, Kirk served at the parish of Aberfoyle until his early death in 1692. One year prior to his untimely departure, he had taken an interest in his parishioners' fascination with the Sith. He began traveling the countryside, speaking to people who claimed to have encounters, questioning seers about the unseen world, and compiling a manuscript, eventually entitled The Secret Commonwealth of Elves, Fauns and Fairies.

It's a nonfiction essay on the nature and actions of a people that Kirk describes as subterranean and "mostly" invisible—the faeries. In it, he details both intimate and mundane facts about faeries: how they reproduce, what they look like, what they eat. Shortly after completing the book, his dead body was found on the nearby "Fairy Hill," where he would often walk while researching his book. He was wearing only his nightshirt.

Villagers believed he had been struck dead by the queen of the faeries for divulging too much privileged information about them, imprisoning his spirit in a tree atop the hill, known today as the Minister's Pine. It was certainly radical for a minister to study the world of faeries. Kirk's successor, Rev. Grahame, wrote of his death, "As Mr. Kirk was walking on a *dun-shi*, or fairy hill, in his neighborhood, he sunk down in a swoon, which was taken for death." Was *taken* for death. His specter was later spotted at a family christening, a last-ditch effort made by Kirk's spirit to be rescued before he was whisked away for all eternity.

I'll admit it. I was afraid to go walking alone at the place where Rev. Robert Kirk had so mysteriously died. Wasn't I doing *exactly* what had allegedly gotten the man *killed*? That's why I planned this part of my trip when Eric was coming to visit. We were renting a car, and we'd be driving together to Aberfoyle to climb Fairy Hill.

Waiting for Eric at the airport was one of the most excruciating hours of my life. We'd arranged to meet at the hostel in Edinburgh, but as his arrival inched closer, I realized it wasn't humanly possible for me, having not seen him for over two months now, to refrain from seeing him right away. So I wrote down his flight number, kept my secret, and took the bus to the airport to surprise him. At nearly every appearance of close-cut brown hair my heart skipped a beat. I put one leg in front of the other. Now leaned. Pulled out my compact to check my makeup. Put in a piece of gum. Spit it out. Finally, he appeared, with a big pack just like mine. His face broke into a smile of utter delight.

"I knew you'd be here," he murmured into my hair.

"I couldn't wait," I explained.

"Neither could I." He grinned.

I took him on a mini–walking tour of Edinburgh, and we dined on fish and chips and sticky toffee pudding. The next morning we took a cab to the rental car place and were on our way to Aberfoyle. It was to be our first and only stop on our way up to the Scottish Highlands.

We checked into our B and B, borrowed a hiking book from the proprietors, and set off for Doon Hill, otherwise known as Fairy Hill, home of Robert Kirk and his eternal tormentors.

"E, listen," I began. "I know you're . . . on the fence about this stuff, but I just want to stress: a man studying faeries *died* here."

"Okay . . ."

"So, it wouldn't hurt to be a little extra careful, you know, show some respect."

"Okay," he said patiently. "Like what?"

"Well, like you know how you always spit a lot when we hike?"

"I don't know what you're talking about."

"Well, don't do that. Or if you do, warn them in your head or something."

He took my hand and raised his brows at me. "All right. Ready?"

"Yes, ready."

We began our walk through the woods. It was evening now, but the sun would be up for another three hours at least. The woods below the hill were peaceful, and airy, the ceiling of trees was high above, giving the forest beautiful light. There was something about the place that made you want to walk softly, to whisper.

"It feels . . . enchanted," Eric said.

"I am so writing that down. That you said that just now."

He laughed. "Well, it does! There's just something about it."

There was no one else in sight. We had the hill and the surrounding forest all to ourselves as we climbed. The hill was broad and steep. I wondered for a fleeting moment whether we were tramping on top of the home of the faery queen, in her subterranean kingdom inside the hollow hill.

After being apart for so long, just walking through the woods together was wonderful. Soon I could see we were reaching the top of the hill. I didn't know what to expect. But I think it's fair to say that we were both utterly blown away.

As we crested the hill we entered a clearing. The first thing I registered was a towering pine tree front and center, with a wide ribbon around its trunk and dozens of scraps of brightly colored cloth tied to it. In the next second I saw a little red-breasted robin on the ground, a butterfly fluttered in front of us, and there were dragonflies *everywhere*. The entire hill was one huge, human-decorated tribute to the faery kingdom.

"Wow," I whispered, just as a dragonfly alighted on Eric's arm. I heard a buzzing and looked up.

Flying just above the level of our heads was a tripod of buzzing insects, exactly like those I'd seen in Vicky and Tad's ruins.

"Holy shit," Eric said. "Look at this place!" Every tree, every bush, every sapling was covered with colorful offerings. To my right was a tree, the length of its trunk tied with shimmering ribbons of gold, white, pink, and silver. At the base of the pine, delicate figurines of faeries were placed lovingly amid the moss. In each spot was a different gift to behold—a bracelet, a miniature car, a few squares of beautifully patterned cloth. On a piece of lined paper I peeked at a child's secret wish to the faeries: *I wish I had a Lego Batman.*

"These represent hundreds of people's wishes and prayers," I explained to Eric. "Each one of them probably asked for something, and in exchange, they left a gift." Just as I finished speaking, I felt something brush my neck and spun around. Hanging from the tree behind me was a key chain depicting the Vesica Piscis symbol—the same one I'd been wearing around my neck since purchasing it in Glastonbury.

We wandered around the hill for almost an hour before our stomachs started to gnaw at us, and we decided it was time to head home. But not before Eric pointed something out to me. "Look," he joked, "faery goo."

All along the moss on the trees throughout the forest were delicate, sparkling crystals, catching the glow of the evening sun.

As we headed back down the hill, I looked over my shoulder at the tree. Was the spirit of Rev. Robert Kirk really somehow trapped inside? The hill felt like a place of beauty, peace, hope, not torment. I smiled and nodded my respect to this faery queen, whatever or wherever she may be.

Rev. Robert Kirk was a silly man, I heard on the breeze. Or was it only in my head? I was so spaced-out, I barely registered Eric calling to me, "Watch out!"

"What?"

"Look!" He pointed to the ground, right where I was about to step. The road was covered with hundreds of tiny little frogs, the size of our thumbnails, moving off into the underbrush.

The next morning, as we set off into the Highlands, I stopped at a local shop called Fairy Rade & Pet Trade. Pushing open the door of the tiny store, I wasn't quite sure what to expect. A woman with long brown hair streaked with gray stood behind the counter. At first glance, I wasn't sure she looked like a faery type. Then I observed her feet: Birkenstock sandals with socks and a skirt. This lady might have something to tell me. I perused the shop for a few minutes. It was quite an interesting combination of merchandise. There were racks of T-shirts depicting, alternately, painted faeries and wolves, backs arched, howling at the moon. The shelves were stocked with faery figurines and ceramic dragons. On the other side of the store were pet collars, leashes, bowls, eating mats, and sweaters for toy dogs. Diversification, I guessed.

I took a breath and introduced myself. Her name was Diana Carmody, and she was the owner. Originally from Kent in England, she'd now lived in Scotland for almost thirty years.

"People here in town don't like to talk about the faeries," she told me, leaning over the counter, her voice low.

"Why not?" I asked.

"Well, they don't believe, first of all. When I came here and opened this shop people were angry. They'd come up to me and say, 'What do you think you're doing opening that silly store?' But I've always been interested in these things, and there are plenty of people who come to Aberfoyle and want to take a little piece of the faery world back with them. That's why I'm here."

"They come to visit Doon Hill?"

"Yes," she said, "of course. Have you been?"

"Yes, it was incredible. We went last night."

"I've been up there," Diana said, "at night. Three of us decided we'd go up there at midnight. It was something, really something. One of my friends claimed to have seen faery lights, but I didn't see them. I had a different experience," she paused, a little uncomfortable.

"What was it?" I nudged her.

"I can't explain it, but I felt something that wasn't *good* back in the bushes on the far side of the great old pine," she said, a little vacantly. She shook her head, as if to shake herself awake. "I'm an investigative type of person, always exploring. But I'll tell you, I wouldn't go wandering about in that area behind the tree, and especially not at night. I just didn't like the feel of it; there was something off about it, something . . . not good lives there, I think."

"Did you see anything else that night?"

"Yes." She smiled. "In fact, we did. Just as we were leaving, we saw a bright ball of light go streaking through the trees in the clearing, so fast that none of us could begin to explain what it could have been."

Thanking her, I found Eric and we climbed into the car, ready to head into the hills. As we maneuvered the twisting road toward Glen Coe, I ruminated on our visit to the faery haunted hill. Sure, the sheer force of faery faith present on the hilltop had been astounding. That Diana from Fairy Rade had seen lights atop it was not surprising. More than that, it was the shape of the hill itself that still haunted me—the way it rose so quickly up from the ground. Just like Glastonbury Tor.

There was a similarity, a tie, that I couldn't quite isolate. And yet I felt in my core I was on to something very real. I hoped, if my faery friends wished it so, that I'd discover the connection when the time was right.

22

Fantastical Faeries of the Scottish Highlands

We call them faerie. We don't believe in them. Our loss.
—CHARLES DE LINT

THE Highland faeries seem to have their own reputation. I remembered reading something in old Scots-Gaelic that translated roughly, "Don't you call me a faery, 'cause if you do, I'll smack you in your freaking head." I'd learned of course that people in Ireland, the Isle of Man, Scotland, and Wales didn't like to call faeries "faeries." They were "themselves," "the fair folk," "the good folk," "the blessed folk." Apparently Scottish members of the faery world were particularly sensitive on this topic. The more I understood about the vast possibilities of species of beings in an unseen world, the less the term seemed adequate. It'd be kind of like an alien race coming to earth and insisting on calling every creature on our planet "cats."

Nestled out to sea on the west coast of Scotland, the Isle of Skye is the largest of the islands that make up the Inner Hebrides. This was my second trip to Scotland—Kirsten and I had taken a "sisters trip" the summer after our dad passed away. He'd headed to Scotland after he got out of the navy to visit his best friend Richard, who was living there at the time. They drove from the lowlands to Loch Ness in a search of the Loch Ness monster, hoping to dive in, find it, and bite it on the nose. He told tales about trying Talisker for the first time on the Isle of Skye, nearly falling out of his chair from the strength of it. As a mountaineer and avid naturalist, he spoke of Scotland with a reverence that was awe-inspiring. He was as infatuated with the landscape as he was with the people, especially the rugged and epically heroic Highlanders. And the man could do a spot-on impression of the Scottish Highland accent. It was really quite astonishing. After he died, we decided a trip might be in order. As though we could somehow find his footprints on the main street in Portreigh. As if we could stumble into a bar and find him there.

So much of our relationship with my father revolved around hiking or eating. We ignored the elephant in the room—his mysteriously failing health. Everything was quitting on him—he had nearly crippling pain in his back and neck, blurred vision, dizziness, loss of circulation to his hands and feet, loss of balance, loss of bladder control. And he was only sixty-five years old. We told him he needed to take a break from teaching. His days in retirement were crowded with doctors' appointments to address each troubling new ailment. Pills were prescribed, tests were run, and nothing was discovered. When KP and I were home for Thanksgiving the year before he passed away, we'd gone out to eat in College Town. It had rained and when evening fell the ground froze. From the driver's seat Dad mused about dinner.

"I wonder if tonight I'll have the steak teriyaki . . . or will it be the tatiki roll?" We were glad to be eating out. His house was devolving into a wood-hermit's bachelor pad, reeking of dog urine and cluttered with papers, magazines, and bills. After the warmth and buzz of Mom's house, Dad's felt like a mausoleum.

We were both noticing that everything for him was getting harder. I forced myself to smile, trying to show him that for tonight, instead of being absorbed with the cacophony of ailments, he could concentrate simply on being with us. There were six types of medications on the cracked tile table, and I had watched his thick fingers shaking to clasp their tiny centers as he methodically sorted them into the appropriate days. *Monday, Tuesday, Wednesday, Thursday* . . .

He was gloomy as we pulled into the parking garage. We were moving together down the driveway one moment, and he was looking at me. The next he was slipping, his feet out from underneath him. It's a split second I play over and over again—that split second I had to react: I let out a noise as I reached for him—his arms didn't come out to break his fall and I heard a sickening crack as his face hit the concrete.

In an instant we were bending over him, seeing blood gushing from his nose.

"Goddamn it!" he shouted, holding it with his hand. "I broke my goddamn nose!"

I turned my head as quickly as the tears sprang up, biting my lip. Oh my God. What should we do? Call an ambulance?

"Come on, Dad . . . We need to get you to the hospital . . ." KP urged, helping him to his feet.

"No," he said, his voice muffled but stubborn. "I'm fine. It's a broken nose. What the hell are they going to do?"

"Dad," I insisted, "you're being crazy. We need to get you to the doctor's. It's broken—"

"Signe, I'm fine," he nearly shouted. Softening then, he pulled his handkerchief from his back pocket.

"I just want to have dinner with my daughters," he said quietly. The driveway was still empty and there was no one around, only the soft yellow lights from the Plum Tree Restaurant glowed from across the street.

So we had dinner then, the three of us, with our father's nose bleeding onto the white tablecloth until the confused waiter offered us ice in a towel.

As Eric and I drove through the Highland countryside it dawned on me that something of significance was happening: I was remembering. I hadn't been able to face the dark corners—I'd grieved for the death of my father, but that couldn't aid me in coming to terms with the loss. Because what I really needed to grieve for was his life. It had been, toward the end, so unbearable to bear witness as he suffered. I was completely helpless, and all I could do was tell him I loved him even as I watched him deteriorate in his loneliness.

I had dinner with my father ten days before he passed away. As we drove from Bundy Road into town, I noticed his coordination was off. He looked down for one moment to adjust the radio, and the next we were swerving into oncoming traffic. It was two days after Christmas. As we pulled into a parking spot, he drove over the curb, nearly striking the parking meter. We ordered wine with dinner, he had the surf and turf, and I regaled him with stories from Random House, trying to learn the ropes, trying to find my way amid all the talent there. We must have talked about books. Mostly I just remember his warm brown eyes, and how they somehow seemed a little duller, but how they still looked at me with so much love. The following Wednesday I was back in New York when he called.

"It's snowing here," he said, "and I'm looking out the picture window in the kitchen. I've got cardinals at the feeder today. I wish you were here, Signifer."

"Me, too, Dad."

He paused for a long moment. "I've been . . . seeing things."

"What do you mean, seeing things?"

"I've been seeing patterns in everything lately," he said, his voice sad yet somehow filled with a curious wonder. "I see faces in the bushes, in the snow. I'm seeing patterns in everything."

I didn't know what to say. Hearing him like this broke my heart. I was thinking, *I should move home.*

"Anyway, I went to the eye doctor today and they said I had ocular hemorrhaging. They sent me straight to the hospital for more tests, so I'll probably be getting results back next week. They did blood work, scans, the whole nine yards."

"*Ocular hemorrhaging?* Dad, that's serious. They don't have any idea what's going on?"

"Oh, you know doctors. They don't tell me a goddamn thing," he sighed. "I just wish I knew what the hell was going on with me."

"I know, Dad. Me, too. They'll figure it out. I know it. Just hang in there."

He told me about how an old student of his, from back in the 1970s, was coming to stay with him on Friday for the weekend. My dad's filthy house flashed in my mind, and inwardly I cringed. It'd been a long time since he had entertained an out-of-town guest. But the hardest thing was how painful it was for him to walk, how he couldn't straighten his spine enough to look up at the sky anymore, couldn't see his cathedrals of trees.

That Saturday the sun went down, and Dad's friend Roger was still out and about from the day. My father's car was in the driveway, but it was pitch dark in the house. Concerned something might be wrong, a neighbor let herself in. Flipped on the lights. Called out to him.

They found him in the bedroom, still under his sheets. The dog was lying on the bed next to him, her eyes moving side to side. Side to side. Dogs always know. They stay anyway. When my mother called to tell me, I locked myself in my own bathroom like it was the safest place to ride out this storm, like clutching the tub could somehow keep my world from imploding.

I closed my eyes for a moment as Eric and I drove across Skye Bridge. There was water underneath me, and we were headed into the mountains. The thought soothed me. There was something beautiful in remembering his end, no matter how hard, when I was in the safety of his church. Maybe, I thought, this was the only place I could allow myself to remember.

I'd been so quiet for so long, Eric seemed to understand I was processing something. It was as if he could feel my temperature change. Something caught his attention and a moment later he pulled over onto the side of the road. Across it was a foamy white waterfall cascading over a tumble of rocks.

He turned to me. "Hey. Want to take a look at that waterfall?"

I took his hand in mine. "Yes," I whispered. "I really do."

We bounced around various B and Bs all over the island. It was a luxury to have a full Scottish breakfast every morning (hold the haggis), but the biggest luxury was being able to sleep next to Eric again. And I was delighted to be on an island where there were more faery sites than anywhere else on my journey: There was Dunvegan Castle, home of the Fairy Flag. There was Skye's own Fairy Bridge. There were the Fairy Pools in the Cullin Mountains. There was Fairy Glen above the town of Uig. We certainly had our work cut out for us.

Legends, however fantastic or far-fetched they may appear to be, are rarely without some trace of historical fact, read the message on the Dunvegan Castle website. And the legend of the Fairy Flag of Dunvegan goes something like this: Long ago, when faeries and men still wandered the earth as brothers, the MacLeod chief fell in love with a beautiful faery woman. They had no sooner married and borne a child when she was summoned to return to her people. Husband and wife said a tearful goodbye and parted ways at Fairy Bridge, which you can still visit today. Despite the grieving chief, a celebration was held to honor the birth of the newborn boy, the next great chief of the MacLeods. In all the excitement of the celebration, the baby boy was left in his cradle and his blanket slipped off. In the cold Highland night he began to cry. The baby's cry tore at his mother, even in another dimension, and so she went to him, wrapping him in her shawl. When the nursemaid arrived, she found the young chief in the arms of his mother, and the faery woman gave her a song she insisted must be sung to the little boy each night. The song became known as "The Dunvegan Cradle Song," and it has been sung to little chieflings ever since. The shawl, too, she left as a gift: if the clan were ever in dire need, all they would have to do was wave the flag she'd wrapped around her son, and the faery people would come to their aid. *Use the gift wisely*, she instructed. *The magic of the flag will work three times and no more.*

As I stood there in Dunvegan Castle, gazing at the Fairy Flag beneath its layers of protective glass, it was hard to imagine the history behind it. The fabric was dated somewhere between the fourth and seventh centuries. The fibers had been analyzed and were believed to be silk from either Syria or Rhodes. Some thought it was part of the robe of an early Christian saint. Others thought it was a part of the war banner for Harald Hardrada, king of Norway, who gave it to the clan as a gift. But there were still others who believed it had come from the shoulders of a beautiful faery maiden. And that faery blood had flowed through the MacLeod family veins ever since. Those people were the MacLeods themselves.

"Pardon me, miss . . ."

"Excuse me . . ."

"Frank! Frank! Do you see it? That's the Fairy Flag!"

I moved out of the way. Visitors were allowed entry into the bottom room of the Fairy Tower, as part of the museum, but Dunvegan Castle was still inhabited by the clan chief—now the strikingly handsome Hugh MacLeod, the thirtieth MacLeod. And the room in which the faery mother was rumored to have visited her crying son so long ago was directly over my head, still a part of the private residence. I looked up at the ceiling. Crazies like me were probably the very reason that the room was closed to the public in the first place. But if anything, it made me exceedingly happy that the flag was still so prized, that the tower was still kept private. I scanned the crowd for my own sexy Highland chief, Eric MacLiebetrau of the German Liebetraus. A girl can dream, can't she? He'd look awfully fetching in a kilt . . .

On the way out I stopped to speak to the disarmingly charming castle curator, Maureen Byers. She lived in the castle year-round, and often at nights and during the long winter months she was the only one there. She was well suited for the job; she's not afraid of the dark. And she did, in fact, believe in faeries. Ms. Byers suggested we visit both the Fairy Pools and Fairy Glen, and was kind enough to give us directions to both places.

"You must see them," she enthused. "They're magical." That was endorsement enough for me. But first things first. Since we were following the story of our faery maiden, the next stop on my tour was Fairy Bridge.

The bridge was unmarked and unpassable. It was similar to the original Fairy Bridge on the Isle of Man, but here no one left trinkets. Stretching our legs, we went to explore. I felt nothing. It didn't feel ominous, it didn't feel strange, it only felt . . . forgotten. I crossed the stream and climbed the opposite bank where I discovered a black feather lying in the grass, of course. Pulling out my plastic bag full of trinkets, my fingers naturally found the perfectly round, deep copper stone from the Point of Ayre on the Isle of Man. How could I have forgotten? I'd learned in the Manx Museum that the Isle of Man, in antiquity, was actually considered to be the southernmost island that composed the Scottish Hebrides: Mull, Isle of Skye . . . Isle of Man. This kingdom was once linked with that one. And yet on one bridge faery history was being honored—and in the other, it seemed long forgotten, save the name. I left the copper stone on the far side of the bank, lodged in a crevice, and slogging back through the stream, nestled back into the car. Something— some relationship, possibly beyond my ken—was taking place. On the Isle of Man I'd left a trinket from Glastonbury. In Ireland I'd left shells from the Aran Islands in the old fort, sitting its lone vigil on the top of

Black Head. All without even thinking. Here I felt compelled to leave something from the Isle of Man. Perhaps so these two bridges could remember, through this simple copper stone, their common past once more. Or maybe, as Ninefh suggested I should, I was just doing as I was told.

It is a very sad fact that there is no good live music in Scotland. Well, at least not in Edinburgh. Or Glen Coe. Or on the Isle of Skye. We tried, Scotland, every night. We were there in high season. We gave you our best. You have stunning scenery, men who aren't afraid to wear skirts, sexy accents, funny comedians, and a really sad music scene. At least for traditional music, that is. If you want to hear a cover band play hits from the 1970s, Scotland is the place to go. If not, buy a bottle of expensive Scotch and head to your rented room after dinner with your clock radio or a couple of CDs. I mention this not to play amateur music critic, but to prove a point. It was a testament, perhaps to the validity of all those who claimed to have heard faery music echoing at night through Scotland's glens. It couldn't have possibly been the natives.

The next morning we took the road that led to the Talisker distillery, then branched off toward Glenbrittle. After a couple of miles we passed a pine plantation, then dipped down to an open valley floor. Before us, the Cullin Mountains loomed dark and massive. A simple green sign to the right said "Fairy Pools." We parked the car and headed out into a field, following a rushing stream that soon became a series of tumbling waterfalls with cold, crystal clear pools, passing quite a few hikers along the way. Were they, too, hoping to spot a faery?

Despite the crowd, there was something enchanted about these pools. It had been sunny and warm minutes before, but suddenly it grew markedly cooler and began to mist. As we climbed higher above the pools into the foothills of the Cullins, we began to feel the magic of the land. An old giant of a mountain towered ahead of us. Perhaps this was where the faery people retreated when the tourists came out to play.

We couldn't go up any farther without a map, so we had to turn back. If Mount Brandon was "dangerous," the Cullins were downright deadly. On the way back down, all I could do was laugh when Eric made a real splash with the faeries, stripping down to his boxers and jumping off a ledge in the rock into the deepest of the pools.

It seemed to me that if there were faeries on Skye, they were taking quite a nap. I was attempting to follow KP's advice and not expect something to happen everywhere I went, but come on! These places had these names for a reason, right? Or was this like trying to find the real Santa by visiting JCPenney's Annual Christmas at the North Pole?

I'd heard nothing about Fairy Glen from anyone other than the curator at Dunvegan, so as Eric and I took the winding road up past the Uig Hotel, I didn't know what to expect. Or how we would know when we arrived. It wasn't in any of my tour books, and it didn't appear on any map that we'd seen. But as we rounded a twist in the road, suddenly it ound us.

"Stop the car," I said.

"I'd say we found it."

One moment we'd been driving up a snaking, narrow road, and the next we were staring at faery land itself. Before us were clusters of bizarrely cone-shaped hills covered in green grass, with what looked like terracing or ridges running along their sides. A deep, dark pool of water lay at the base of the hills, clearly a loch. Everywhere were thick, gnarled thorn trees, covered in moss and sheltered by a soft carpet of fern. Never in my life had I seen any place so inherently . . . *mystical.*

Eric and I set off like two kids in a candy store, each in our own direction. I wandered where my feet wanted to lead, up the steepest of the hills. Every footstep into the enchanted realm brought me closer to a definitive conclusion. This was a sacred place, and always had been. There was something here, I could feel it. The short hill was so steep I almost had to claw my way up. At the top I reached a plateau. Behind me was a small field scattered with sheep, and at its end was a small cave too narrow to pass through. Looking out over the top of the crest, I was struck by the strange intimacy of my surroundings. It was so foreign, and yet it felt utterly familiar. I felt like if I closed my eyes, I could imagine that this was a noble village—or the site of a *seriously* ancient castle. I looked down as a black feather fluttered against my foot.

Right. Of course.

I sat there quietly, tuning in to the place. As I connected, I began to feel incredible sadness. It was inexplicable to feel a longing for a place that logically I had never been, but that was exactly what I felt. Everything here at Fairy Glen was present, sad, forgotten. But something reached out—something stronger than human memory. This place was special—it felt like a culmination of sorts, a source. I unzipped my pack and let my fingers move without stopping them. Out came some shells from the Aran Islands, a piece of beach glass from the Isle of Man, the rest of what I had left of the Glastonbury Thorn—a few flakes of bark. I slipped the little silver mermaid charm off my key ring and placed it gently on the ground next to the black feather.

All I could feel was loss. Something was lost here. I couldn't control myself.

I began to cry.

"Sig!" Startled, I jerked my head up to spot Eric on a distant hill. "You've got to see this," he shouted. "This place is amazing!"

I brushed away my tears, taking a moment to compose myself. What on earth had come over me? Taking one lingering look at the feather, now standing stiffly upright on the crest of the hill, I went to see what Eric was so thrilled about.

Below him lay a circular labyrinth made of stone. Man-made, clearly, and there was a group of people gathering before it, looking like they were ready to begin a meditation.

"Let's just sit here until they're through," I whispered. "I don't wanna disturb them." They were a group of about eight middle-aged adults, and to my discerning eye, they looked like Glastonbury types, middle-aged and just a little bit woo-woo. These were my people! We sat and waited about twenty minutes, until they picked up their gear and some of them stood, gazing at the labyrinth. Two women in particular caught my eye. I approached them, heart swelling with kinship, hoping to strike up a conversation.

"Hello," I said, giving them my most winning smile. "I couldn't help but notice your group. Were you doing a guided meditation?"

The woman turned and looked at me for a moment, then turned her attention back to the hill in front of her. "Mmm" was her only response. Following her cue, the other woman did the same.

Jesus. I hated snobby pagans. I was here for the faeries, too! It was *exactly* this type of behavior that gives pagan people a bad reputation. I slinked back to Eric and he gave me an encouraging pat.

"You saw that, right?"

"Totally."

"Hey, Eric."

"What?"

"There's something kooky about this place, isn't there?"

"Yeah. I would definitely say so," he said, looking around and scratching his head. "These aren't just hills. It's like there was something *here* before."

"I know exactly what you mean."

We could have stayed there all day. A thought crossed my mind: What would Fairy Glen be like at night? Probably a little scary. A little? Okay, a lot.

"Hey, Eric."

"Yes?"

"Would you sit outside with me tonight and try to get in touch with some Scottish Highland faeries?"

He shrugged. "Sure."

If we hadn't already gotten engaged, I swear in that moment, in that magical glen, I would have gotten down on one knee and proposed.

That evening was our last in Skye, and we went out into the night with all the proper supplies. Warm clothes, a bottle of Scotch (you know, to keep away the chill), two bars of chocolate, and my head lamp. Going up into Fairy Glen at night felt disrespectful, so instead we drove into the countryside until we spotted a sweeping hill littered with tall green ferns and a place to pull over. I doled out my chocolate and Eric beat a path up the hill to explore. It was eight thirty and we figured we only had an hour until the sun set. I sang all the beautiful songs I could think of. I sat quietly. Eric came and went. I gazed out into the ferns, letting my eyes grow soft. There was no one else, just me, waiting. But still it wasn't dark. It was, however, cold. Really cold. I zipped up my fleece and set my jaw. I wasn't going anywhere.

At quarter to midnight, Eric came back up from the car, where he'd been sitting listening to music for the past hour. *Blast these long summer daylight hours!* Only now was it growing dark. We were both exhausted. He held out his hand, a look of sympathy on his face, and enveloped my cold fingers in his warm ones. I'd been at it nearly four hours.

Our last dinner together in Scotland was at an Italian restaurant in Edinburgh. We sprinted there in the pouring rain. We'd rented a hotel room for our last night and Eric was leaving at four a.m. Both rubbing sleep from our eyes, I watched as he gathered his belongings, my heart in my throat. He looked at me sadly for a moment, but when my lower lip began to tremble, he forced a small smile.

"We'll be together again before you know it."

I was trying really, really hard not to cry.

"Just a little less than three weeks," I said, trying to be brave. "Thank you for everything. Thank you for coming here to be with me."

He reached out and touched my cheek. "I wouldn't have missed it for the world."

"I said it to a four-year-old, but now I really mean it. You were the best faery-hunting assistant *ever*."

He chuckled. "You be safe."

"I will. You be safe." He leaned in for a kiss, and then he was gone.

I crawled back into bed despondent and lay there awake. At some point my eyes must have closed and I woke up and loneliness slammed me all over again. With no clear direction as to where to head next, I checked into a hostel and slipped into a three-day funk, just sitting at the computer trying to figure out where to spend my last days in Scotland. There were no signs this time. Apparently, I would have to decide on my own. One night I got drunk with a French girl named Clemance, who was tiny, birdlike, and tan, with a small silver stud piercing her bottom lip.

"It's been really hard," I slurred. "No one believes in faeries anymore."

She looked at me like a kid who dropped her ice-cream cone.

"*Sheet!*" she exclaimed.

"I know," I said. *Sheet* exactly. All of a sudden it hit me.

The signs had been there all along but I had been too afraid—too afraid I was going to be disappointed.

That's when I knew: I was going to Findhorn.

23

The Faery Magic of Findhorn

*The community has developed as a place where spiritual
principles common to all religions, and with no doctrine or
creed, are put into action in everyday life.*
—FINDHORN FOUNDATION & COMMUNITY VISITOR GUIDE

I'D been avoiding Findhorn, an internationally famous experimental-living community, from the very beginning. Even if I hadn't known it, I ignored it more staunchly after running into the unfriendly meditators beside the labyrinth at Fairy Glen: I had a particular intolerance for people who claimed to be spiritual and yet couldn't be bothered to be kind to one another. Growing up in Ithaca I'd experienced my fair share of passive-aggressive spiritualists, too. Because of this—my continued lack of faith in humanity—I didn't think a place like Findhorn could possibly be legit.

The community became famous in the 1960s when Peter and Eileen Caddy, along with their three children and their friend Dorothy Maclean, moved into a rented caravan in the Findhorn Bay Caravan Park in the north of Scotland. It was a depressed area that neighbored a Royal Air Force base, with nothing green to speak of—just nearby ocean and sand. Using compost, they created a garden to subsist on. It was while tending their vegetable garden that Dorothy realized she could communicate with the plants. She soon determined that she was in contact with the overarching intelligence of the plants, known as nature devas, who gave her directions on how to make the most of their tiny garden. (Devas are considered to be a species of being, if you will, within the faery kingdom.) From the sandy soil they began to grow fruits, vegetables, flowers, and legendary forty-pound cabbages. Soon people were flocking to Findhorn to commune with nature. What had been an infertile trailer park at the end of an airfield base began its transformation into the vibrant community it is today, a haven to thousands of visitors each year.

When I was in middle school, I had come across a book about Findhorn in the school library, and couldn't believe it was actually marked nonfiction. A magical place with devas, faeries, and nature spirits and everyone can go there to live for free? Of course, that was the olden days.

On the bus to Inverness I watched the countryside roll by. Fields of barley and wheat, black-and-white cows awaiting their last march, chewing their cud as they gently sniffed the early morning air. There were white horses and rock quarries and sheep, of course, and the wild grasses on the side of the road were bursting with flowers the names of which my father taught me—Queen Anne's lace, purple rocket, and the petals of the lady's slipper that were beginning to wilt at last, scattering to the ground.

I felt a wash of relief to be headed back up into the Highlands. As I sat I reflected back on the pearls I'd collected from my journey. Alison in Hampstead: *Learn to trust*. Brian Froud: *Rediscovering our belief results in a reawakening*. Peter Knight: *Choose love over fear*. Charlotte on the Isle of Man: *Follow your intuition; listen to your knowing*.

But how could I put that all to use? If I was going to achieve what I set out to achieve, Findhorn was my last chance to find a way. I'd booked a room with a woman named Lini who lived in Findhorn Park, as it was called, right on the foundation grounds. Lini drove into town to pick me up, something no other B and B owner in the United Kingdom would ever have done. I liked her instantly. She was smart and sweet-tempered with ginger-colored hair and warm brown eyes. We talked easily as we drove alongside the ocean, finally coming through the gates and into the park. So this was Findhorn. I let my eyes soak it in. Everything was bursting with flowers! We passed the funky and cool-looking Phoenix General Store, driving on a small lane filled with houses, all looked to be eco-friendly and each one was unique. And when we reached the B and B, Lini offered to take me for a tour. "I've got nothing else to do," she said with a smile. "I'd like to take a walk anyway." As we strolled side by side, Lini pointed out the Findhorn meeting center, dubbed Universal Hall, with its tall, wooden doors carved with huge faerylike wings, the organic café, various meditation rooms and sanctuaries, and the barrel houses—little hobbit-looking houses at the edge of the woods, made from recycled whiskey barrels. Everything in Findhorn was sustainable. At last, we stopped for a moment, looking around. "This place was nothing but gorse and sand." Lini shook her head as we looked out over the gardens. "Forty years ago this place was begun by a partnership with the nature devas. Of course, as time goes on, a community is going to grow and evolve. Stretch away from its roots. But you don't have to dig very deep to find that all of that is still here, under the skin of things."

She was right. Everything was done with thought, intention, and care. And the last stop on our tour was my favorite—the Boutique. A small shack with neatly ordered racks and shelves, the Boutique was Findhorn's free store. People brought the items they no longer wanted—clothes, books, jewelry—and could take what they liked. After traveling all summer, it was like paradise. I left a sundress and picked out a beautiful skirt, handmade in Guatemala.

Back in my room, I saw that Lini had set up a table by the window for me to write. Stacked on it were no less than ten books she thought might be helpful in my search for the Findhorn faeries. I didn't have the heart to tell her there was no way I could get through all of them; I was only staying for two days.

So I decided to stay for four.

It was a good thing I did, too, because the day after I had been planning on leaving, there was a talk and group meditation scheduled on trolls and gnomes. I hadn't really given much thought to either trolls or gnomes since the Alux in Mexico—the former were scary, the latter wore pointed hats and lived in trees—but now I would get the chance. I spent the day walking the grounds, observing, and exploring all the way out to the Moray Firth, where a path through the sand led to the beach. The dunes were a fragile area and protected, so aside from the walking paths they were entirely wild. I walked along the beach as far as I could go. On the way back, as I reflected on the lack of faery presence in recent days, I gazed across the landscape. Gorse and prickly bushes grew in almost anything, here, in sand. But there were some pretty areas, too—pines and grassy slopes at the back of the dunes, between the Findhorn property and the beach. I was just about to head back onto the main path when I got a very distinct feeling. More of an order, really. And it was a voice in my head, though hard to explain, I had grown familiar with.

Go over there.

A voice or an impulse—I couldn't really tell. But it was the same impulse that I had been listening to all summer.

Go over there! it insisted. I followed my directions over to a small, circular clearing, inaccessible from the pathway due to a thick hedge of prickly gorse and shrubs that encircled a ring of grass. Feeling silly, I stood there, looking into the hedges.

Okay. Now what? I thought, somewhat sarcastically.

Say hello.

Say hello? Say hello to who? This was crazy. This was what happened when I indulged my imagination. I started giving myself directions to do stupid things out of complete boredom, it must be.

Say hello. Introduce yourself.

Okay. Know what? Fine. I'll do it. Because I am just *that* crazy. I am just a crazy faery lady in the middle of Scotland, and who cares anyway?

Hello, I said in my head, I'm Signe. I'm here because I'm researching a book on faeries. Any experiences that I'm granted I would love to be able to share with my readers. And my friends. And my future husband. And my family. All of whom are beginning to think I am certifiably insane.

It was somewhat heartfelt, somewhat sarcastic, but I thought it anyway, with a smile. Never hurts to be polite when having imaginary conversations. I stood there hopefully, waiting for a few long moments. At times, I thought I saw the bushes move, but it could've been a bird. I was, after all, only a few hundred yards from the ocean. Shrugging my shoulders, I headed back to my room and my cozy stack of reading.

That afternoon the sun was out and it drizzled, creating the most decadent rainbow I'd ever seen. It arched across the park, and people came out from their houses to gaze up at it and say good evening. The people of Findhorn were certainly magical. But were there faeries here? Lini and I'd been spending quite a bit of time together, so I was thrilled when she grabbed an umbrella and walked the puddled path with me to the trolls and gnomes extravaganza. The session that evening was held by a Swedish woman named Marie Soderberg, with the assistance of a man named John Wragg. We made ourselves comfortable and looked around to see it was only a small group of us who'd gathered that night.

"Good evening, everybody," Marie began. "I was walking in the woods of Sweden when I began to have . . . weird experiences. I'd always been interested in esoteric subjects, and growing up in Sweden, gnomes and trolls were actually a big part of our culture. But I'd never truly given them much thought. Until one day, as I was sitting quietly in the woods, I felt energies approaching me. And as I 'tuned in' to them, I realized—these were gnomes!"

I waited, as images of gnomes carved in wood flashed on the projector behind her. "They told me that I was supposed to help them. That I'd been chosen to travel around and be . . . well, like the gnomes' spokeslady, really. And they told me something else. That they actually work in partnership with the trolls."

According to Marie, every house or property had a gnome that looked after it—and if they were lucky, it looked after the human inhabitants as well. They knew what was going on with each plant, each tree, they oversaw everything that flourished on the property. They worked in concert with the nature devas of each plant to ensure that all the flora were growing as designed by the divine spirit that is life. The trolls, Marie explained, were in charge of harnessing and directing the energy. And thus, the two worked hand in hand. Trolls containing and amplifying energy, the gnomes focusing it to achieve the ultimate goal: natural perfection.

The idea of little dudes with pointed hats and gray beards, for me, felt inauthentic. But Marie reminded us that when we "see" the faery kingdom, they're at a disadvantage—they must use our thought forms to communicate with us. So they appear in archetypes, how we want to see them, or perhaps the only way we *can* understand what we were seeing. Since Brian Froud had mentioned this to me, I'd read further that faeries often grow fond of the image they project, and they might stick with the same one for many years—brown hair, green eyes, blue clothing, whatever—perfecting it over their lifetimes, which were rumored to span centuries compared to ours. Human beings, apparently, are just a flash in the pan.

I tuned back in to Marie, who was talking about a man who'd visited the previous week and given a tour of various faery sites around the park, such as he saw them. Two in particular. And both of them were located in the dunes.

Now she had my attention.

"On the tour, we were led to this spot," she said, clicking a slide projector to a photograph of a clearing with bushes surrounding it.

"He called this place the Amphitheater. Our guide said that this was like . . . oh, how can I explain it . . . like the faeries' parliament. Faery creatures of all types come here to discuss issues, or just to generally convene." I squinted at the photo.

Could that be? *No way.*

"If you'd like to go there and check it out, here's where it is on a map that John and I put together." She clicked to a hand-marked drawing. "They're actually two of them. One here, and one here. The faeries use them both." It was exactly where I'd been. This couldn't be real! I shook my head in disbelief.

"Maybe the next time you guys are out walking, you can stop by and say hello!" she suggested cheerfully.

Just say hello. Introduce yourself. I sat in stunned silence. I couldn't be making this stuff up—I'm not freaking . . . psychic! Maybe I really had been standing in front of a parliament of faery creatures. In retrospect, it might've been wise to be less sarcastic. There was a definite pattern that had emerged on my journey. If I was open, and I listened, I'd be given something—a clue, an instruction. If I chose to act on it, there *was* a verification. I was still reeling when Marie requested we get comfortable to prepare for our guided meditation. I closed my eyes, slowed my breathing, and focused on her voice.

"Imagine yourself in a home. It doesn't have to be the home you live in now, just a place you love or have really loved."

The image of our house in Charleston was a cozy one—I'd go with that.

"Now step through the door. Imagine it is winter, and there is a fire crackling in the hearth. There is a spirit that guards and protects every home, and *you.* Pick a place you are most comfortable and sit down there. See if he or she will come to you."

I imagined myself walking past the kitchen toward the sunroom. And in that moment, I was surprised to see a little gray-haired gnome, about three feet high, with a pointed green hat, walk in from the patio. He didn't notice me, just plodded through, with a little bit of a waddle. He was instantly endearing: old, rather innocent-looking, and sweet. I somehow understood without thinking about it that he knew I was there, but he wasn't acknowledging me because *he* was used to not being acknowledged, and it made me so sad. Sensing my gaze, he turned to look at me, and his face grew . . . wise. Hoping to communicate with him, I moved outside and sat cross-legged on the patio where he plopped down across from me. "Now you can ask him anything you want," Marie suggested.

I considered him a moment.

Are you happy that Eric and I live here now? I asked.

He smiled. I didn't hear him speak; instead, I saw scenes flash in my head. Eric and I viewing the house when it was for sale. The backyard with the majestic red pine and the sweet little shed with the black shutters. I saw Eric working in the shed with lawn equipment and me on my hands and knees, gardening. We were happy, smiling. I got the feeling that he had somehow *brought* us there, that he would hold us, and I saw a nest. I understood. He wanted to always make this a good nest for us. Then I felt a surge of love coming from him, and it was for me and Eric. He loved us. It was very fatherly. Like he was proud of us.

"Now, ask him if there's anything that he would like for you to do," Marie instructed. Immediately, before even formally asking, I saw our neighbors' houses, the bits and pieces that we can see from our yard, covered by a fast-growing plant. *I get it,* I thought. *You'd like us to plant more green things, plant more trees.* Then he showed me the shed. And I got the sense that the shed was important to him, and that we should keep it nice, organized, orderly, and give it a use. Right now, it housed empty, ,rusted paint cans and expired fertilizers. It was weird how I felt these things to be true, what he was communicating. It was utterly vivid.

"Now it's time to thank your gnome and say goodbye for now. If you'd like, you can establish a time to meet with him or her again, in an actual place, or through meditation."

I'll see you when I get back to the house, I thought. *I'm so excited to know that you're there.* I sent him warmth, gratitude. He showed me an image of Eric sitting on the couch watching TV, with the cat asleep on the arm of the couch beside him. The gnome was standing there, looking at them, guarding them. It was surprisingly moving.

"Next," Marie's voice came, "we're going to meet some trolls!" I jerked partway out of my meditative trance. No way did I want to meet a troll. But I tried to calm myself. I'd had such a good time using my imagination to meet our friendly house gnome. Maybe I should just relax and give this a shot.

"You find yourself out in the woods," Marie intoned. "They can be woods that you are familiar with, or just a really beautiful grove of trees." I pictured myself walking through Palmetto Islands County Park near our house, surrounded by tall palmettos and southern brush.

"Find a small clearing," Marie said, "and sit down on the ground or on the trunk of a tree."

Ha! Fat chance in Charleston. Unless you're fond of getting swarmed by fire ants. But luckily this was meditation, so I sat, suspending my disbelief. "Now you may become aware of a troll energy." I became aware of a small creature, about a foot and a half tall, who resembled a darker, long-haired orangutan. It was peeking at me from behind a nearby tree. It was so sweet-looking and shy, and it seemed so lonely, I couldn't help but feel a wave of sympathy. It came close to me then, and I wasn't afraid. It sat down next to me, and the next thing I knew, it had leaned its little head against me. It looked up at me with tender little eyes, and then surprised me by reaching out to hold my hand.

"You may find," Marie said then, "that they're shy at first, but are actually quite sweet. They love to cuddle, and they might want to hold your hand, or come into contact with you if you're okay with that." My troll and I were so far ahead of the rest of the class! "Your troll may seem a little sad," she said, "and if you want to, you can give it a hug." I hugged its hairy little body to mine, and I instantly felt it go from sad to bursting with joy. I put it down on the ground and it danced around me, grinning in delight, swinging its arms like a little monkey.

"You might notice a change in the troll's demeanor," Marie said. "Hugs make them really happy." All right. It was a little odd that things were happening in my visualization before Marie said the exact same thing. Perhaps this wasn't going to be convincing for anyone else. Maybe it was just serving a personal need. But it was convincing to me.

On the way back to the house Lini and I swapped stories—she'd met her house gnome as well and, like me, was profoundly touched by the experience. She, too, felt a surprising authenticity, and we confided that we were both looking forward to getting together with these loving beings in meditation again soon. That night as I drifted off to sleep I remembered something else Brian Froud had said. "Within the meditation, you do actually genuinely touch faery land—you're in it, whether you realize it or not." The thought made me smile. Perhaps the faeries were far closer than we thought.

I spent the rest of my time at Findhorn attending regular group meditations or sitting in the nature sanctuary while people around me sang in the early morning hours. Findhorn had somehow cleaned me, put me back together. I'd been eating vegetarian for four days, and my body felt light and clean. I'd been skipping wine at the general store, helping myself instead to Lini's incredible selection of herbal teas.

In Scotland, I think, people remember where they came from. We come from the earth, are composed from its elements. And yet we treat it with such disrespect—the only thing that can truly sustain us. I simply can't understand. Maybe the problem is that most of us live in the places that can make you forget. You can't walk around expecting to feel an organic connection to a high-rise. And I could never quite find peace in a city that never slept. But there was something about Scotland that allowed you to truly feel the land, and the force of it all can bring tears to your eyes.

Findhorn was the last stop on my faery-finding journey. I reflected back as I rode the train from Edinburgh to London. I'd seen what I thought might have been faery lights in Glastonbury. All summer long, I'd had bizarre impulses, which I followed, despite not fully knowing why. I didn't know what I could say I'd accomplished. But I knew one thing. I was different now. And yet I felt more myself than I had ever been. In leaving one life behind to go on a search for the fantastical, I had rediscovered a whole new one. In chasing the beliefs I had as a child, I'd somehow managed to grow up. And I truly liked the woman I'd become.

As my plane lifted off the ground at Heathrow, I wished for a safe journey, smiling at the thought of a thousand little winged creatures supporting the plane's mass. I'd spent so much time with people who were living magical lives—from Brian and Wendy Froud to the entire peaceful and progressive community at Findhorn. And in seeing the way these people chose to live, their values, how they treated one another, the planet, the wonder with which they greeted each day of living, I was able to see the world around me as enchanted once again, too.

Maybe, I mused, it's not us who are helping the faeries by believing in them. Perhaps it's the humans who stand to benefit, if only we could make the faeries believe in us once more.

24

The Truth About Faeries:
Putting the Pieces Together

Life itself is the most wonderful fairy tale.
—HANS CHRISTIAN ANDERSON

Eric met me at the airport; hands in his pockets, he gave me almost a sheepish grin, and his dimple was right where I'd remembered it. Outside Charleston International the palmettos swayed in the evening breeze and the night air felt balmy, humid. My massive pack soon rested just inside the front door, and I looked upon my house in new wonder. Good God! I had a whole huge closetful of clothes I could wear—and a washer and dryer—no more washing my clothes in the sink! Just riding in a car was a luxury—*you mean, no waiting for the bus?* Everything felt new after having been away for three months. After a hot shower I pulled back the sheets and crawled into bed, my feet reaching over to find Eric's. We intertwined our legs and I drifted into a fast and dreamless sleep.

Now that I was back, my focus was on collecting the pieces to the puzzle, trying to understand if there could be hidden connections in any of the clues I'd been given throughout the course of the summer. By digging through history, I hoped to discover what stuck and what led me amok.

Among what I termed loosely as "evidence," I had the photo from the old Fairy Bridge on the Isle of Man of the inexplicable small, glowing light. In addition, Raven had since forwarded me pictures of bizarrely colored orbs from our nighttime climb down Glastonbury Tor. But it was the less concrete occurrences (typical of faery) that I had found the most compelling: In England I'd experienced the inexplicable sparkling in the hedgerow of the Chalice Well Garden. There'd been the robin that seemed to find me at will with various insects in its beak, and the seeming arrival of my faery advocate—after which point I felt guided throughout the rest of my trip through feelings, and even sometimes, uh . . . a distinguishable voice in my head.

On the Isle of Man I'd felt overly sleepy in Castletown, destroyed (or sacrificed?) my iPod when my water opened in my pack, and there was the murder of Betsy Crowe—and the connection, if any, it might have had with my hike that day. I'd had the bizarre encounter with the towering man and his black dog in the fields of Glen Auldyn, and then there was little George's eerie hint that we were getting close to Fairy Bridge . . . when none of us had a clue where we were. After which point I'd met Charlotte, who cropped up to provide me with a "tune-up" as well as the rock I wished for on my birthday after my visit to Fairy Bridge, which I found on Point of Ayre. And let us not forget the bikers: gifts from the faeries if ever there were.

In Ireland, Peter Guy took me to the site of the last battle between the Tuatha Dé Danann and the Fir Bolgs, where I somehow knew the function of the old "cattle well" before asking the museum attendant. There'd been the disappearing and reappearing of the tent poles (and the borrowed pedometer), and the image in my mind of the bearded redheaded man at the fort on Black Head near Doolin. In Crusheen, Eddie Lenihan told me of faeries shape-shifting into human form and their connection to the mysterious black dogs. And there was the strange vision of an ancient line of pagan people climbing and worshipping at Mount Brandon. In Scotland there was my odd confirmation at Findhorn, when I'd been told to "say hello" to the faeries by the beach, and the strange way things seemed to happen in my trolls and gnomes meditation *before* Marie Soderberg suggested they might occur.

Then there were the things I thought of as "the Connectors." Wendy Froud mentioned that the faeries might leave me gifts—things that would mean something only to me, like the black feathers I'd been finding all summer. Another connector could be the strange terracing I'd noticed on both Glastonbury Tor and Fairy Glen on the Isle of Skye. Then there were the bizarre shapes of the hills themselves: Glastonbury Tor, Hango Hill in Castletown on the Isle of Man, Fairy Glen in Uig, and Doon Hill in Aberfoyle.

Most urgently, now that I was back at my desk, I wanted to dig into the backstory of Betsy Crowe. A certainty had settled within me and had haunted me throughout the trip—there was *something* to discover, some hidden connection. I tore through the pages of an obscure British volume called *Manx Murders*. *Please, oh, please.* And there she was. Elizabeth "Betsy" Crowe, murdered in 1888. I held my breath and read on. Her brutal murder, on Old Douglas Road outside Ramsey, rocked the entire island, and it had remained unsolved.

But Betsy's neighbor, twenty-five-year-old John Gelling, had been brought in as the main suspect. The book contained a map of the area, not drawn much to scale, but it gave me an idea of where the Old Douglas Road was—a rough cart track that ran from Ballure Bridge up along the tiny glen, and then along the reservoir until it intersected with the paved road I'd crossed. The field with the ruin was beyond. There was no way of telling whether the stone house I visited belonged to Betsy, John Gelling, or another neighbor. Comparing the map of the murder scene to a modern map of the area and tracing my route, it seemed I was near the murder spot, separated only by a small stream, where I'd seen the blue coat hanging inexplicably in the middle of the dark forest. A coincidence, I was certain. But I kept reading.

There were some suspicious oddities in Gelling's account of his whereabouts that night. But the piece of the story that stopped me in my tracks was yet to come.

Gelling was asked by prosecutors about a jacket, one which he had washed the morning after the murder. He claimed that toffee had melted and stained the pocket of the coat the previous week. The prosecutor challenged that it was blood. The coat was wet from the shoulders down to the tail, quite a thorough cleaning job for a stain in a pocket. I read on, my heart in my throat.

The jacket in question was blue.

A traveler walks to an abandoned cottage and then begins to fear for her life on a trail in the forest, just prior to seeing a blue jacket hanging in the woods. She is perhaps fifty yards away from the place where a woman was murdered 121 years before.

The evidence against Gelling was, after a grueling inquest, found to be circumstantial, and despite the weight of suspicion he was never found guilty of murder.

He never even went to trial.

All I know is the terror I felt and what I saw. I've since spent many nights lying awake, thinking about Betsy Crowe and the blue jacket, struggling for closure. Each time comes the vision of that tree—the old gnarled tree that stands stooped by the ruins—and the feeling that whoever had lived in that house had loved that tree. Who knows? It certainly wouldn't have been uncommon at the time—perhaps Betsy Crowe was a believer in faeries.

As I focused next on the subject of the black feather, pieces began to fall into place, little by little. While crows (ravens, Irish croachs, or whatever you want to call them) were a most common bird in Ireland

and the United Kingdom, they were certainly not the only birds. I've stumbled across many feathers in my lifetime of woods walking—turkey feathers, jay feathers, cardinal feathers, pheasant feathers, osprey feathers—but never so many black feathers, dropped in my path, in a period of three months. I wanted to know why I was continually finding them at faery sites throughout my journey—and why had I been compelled to use them as part of what could only be described as offerings?

In folklore, crows almost always appeared as messengers. Their purpose was to relay a message from the world of the dead, the afterlife, or the divine, to a mortal. To my surprise, I learned that Celtic folklore in particular was filled with them.

In the Celtic pantheon, the crow was sacred to a being called the Morrigan, and I was embarrassed to say I'd overlooked her. When I'd first come across the Morrigan (in Peter Berresford Ellis's myth *The Ever-Living Ones*), she was introduced as the Great Queen of Battles. But when you look at the etymology of the name, it actually translates quite literally to "Great Queen" (*mór*, great; *rígan*, queen). In the eleventh century, when *The Book of Invasions* was finally transcribed on paper, the Morrigan was listed as one of the Tuatha Dé Danann. But as I traced the mythological thread further back, I discovered that the Morrigan was known by another name: Anann. And Anann was known by another name, too.

Danu.

I felt like I'd just opened a set of Russian nesting dolls. Danu was, of course, the bringer of all life, the biggest deal in the Celtic pantheon; she was the Celtic Jesus, Buddha, Mohammed. And, according to myth, Danu was "the mother" of the race we so fondly call "the faeries."

I had unwittingly been honoring the ultimate queen of the faeries at every significant site I visited. And in light of that, I couldn't help but wonder—were my car accident (which cost me money) in Chagford and the death by drowning of my iPod after my trip up Snaefell (which cost me money) literally a form of Celtic votive tribute like that which the old deities were used to receiving? Or was this simply another validation, to prove that their hand was in it all along? More than that, though, I wondered if I hadn't been put to work on a greater purpose. Awakening, connecting something in those places that needed to be brought to the surface once more. Typical to faery, it was illuminating and confusing all at once.

There were so many other links and commonalities I stumbled upon after arriving home.

Regarding the mysterious terracing on Glastonbury Tor, the Glastonbury Abbey website says, "If the maze on the Tor is real, human labor formed it four or five thousand years ago, during the period of the vast ritual works that created Stonehenge." And it bore a striking similarity to the terracing I noticed on the hills of Fairy Glen on Skye. It was an intriguing connection. What *were* these forgotten places, so long ago?

Then there were the shapes of the hills themselves. The Glastonbury Tor, Doon Hill, and Fairy Glen all shared the same surprisingly conical forms. There was something off-putting, too, about the mound shape of Hango Hill on the Isle of Man. When we compared photos of Fairy Glen to those of archeological sites of discovered hill forts in the United Kingdom and Ireland, Eric and I agreed: buried under the layers of earth and sediment that we now know as Fairy Glen was undoubtedly an ancient hill fort. On the Isle of Man a burial mound known as Cronk ny Merriu ("Hill of the Dead") was excavated and found to contain several Bronze Age artifacts. Cronk ny Merriu bore an eerie resemblance to Fairy Glen as well. And Hango Hill, I learned, hadn't been excavated but was rumored to be the site of an ancient burial mound as well. As I did more research, I found many claims that Doon Hill in Aberfoyle looked more like an artificial mound than it did a natural hill. And its name, Doon, was derived from "dún," which I learned is the Gaelic word for a man-made mound (Dún Aengus, for example). If these were in fact ancient pagan places, it would be a short step in local lore as time wore on, and memories faded, to relegate them to the faery kingdom.

Whatever lay beneath, it blew my mind that people assumed these hills were just hills. But then again, would I ever want to see them excavated to uncover their secrets? As Eddie Lenihan said, "That's not my property. That's *theirs*." These places are so deeply ancient, so incredibly sacred. Perhaps sometimes it's best to let secrets lie.

As the shorter days of autumn approached, things were still unfolding. Thumbing through a book I'd skimmed very early on in my search, when places like the Isle of Man were just names without images and memories attached, I came across something that made me smile. "Herbalism is a specialty of Manx faeries," Edain McCoy wrote in *A Witch's Guide to Faery Folk*. "And some of them can be induced to lead humans to cures."

Eat some clover, I'd been instructed in Castletown. Perhaps I should have given more credit to the faeries when I began to feel less disoriented after munching clover on the Isle of Man.

The next day I did some more research on Ireland—in particular, the fort we'd visited on Black Head, outside of Doolin. I'd been searching for its proper name—not an easy task considering there are hundreds of unnamed forts in the Burren alone. So I was actually shocked when I managed to find it. The old fort on Black Head was called Cathair Dhuin Irghuis. The Fort of Irghuis. I dug through my mythology books, all my books on Celtic lore. Nothing. Finally, in *Archaeology of the Burren: Prehistoric Forts and Dolmens in North Clare*, by Thomas Johnson Westropp, something caught my eye. My pulse raced as I scanned the page.

In the depths of Irish prehistoric legend, it was stated that a Fir Bolg chief named Irghus had ruled the Headland of Burren.

All this was my kingdom.

His name had been preserved on that lonely fort tucked into the limestone slabs of Black Head. Did the lost and weary pagan chief still haunt his earthly domain? In my mind's eye, I could still see the redheaded man with the warm brown eyes standing next to me on that hillside in Ireland. Could I really have been communicating with the ancient Fir Bolg chieftain Irghus? If that were so, the Fir Bolgs certainly weren't the monsters that The Book of Invasions had claimed. I read that limestone is often considered by the paranormal community to be a substance that somehow amplifies spiritual activity, and of course, the Burren is almost solely composed of limestone. But what about the shells from the Aran Islands I felt compelled to leave—what was the connection between the two? Perhaps that piece to the puzzle lay amid the massive stones of Dún Aengus on Inishmore.

Aengus was a Celtic god, son of Dagda, and one of the Tuatha Dé Danann. But I was shocked to discover something that I had missed. Prying further I found what I was looking for: Dún Aengus was originally thought to be a Fir Bolg fort. Perhaps the Fir Bolgs were indeed pursued and fled from across Ireland in droves to their stronghold—one of the Fir Bolg's most powerful and significant forts? I then found a small citation in The Book of Invasions that stated the Tuatha had allowed the Fir Bolgs to live on in Connacht—an area of Ireland that includes Doolin and the Aran Islands. Dún Aengus and Cathair Dhuin Irghuis—the link I'd thought was only a product of my imagination—had a basis in fact. Well, in so much as The Book of Invasions could be taken as fact. Nonetheless, it was a mystifying testament to the power of human intuition.

So what are faeries, exactly? Truth be told, I don't know if this is a riddle any mortal can solve—I don't know that we're allowed to. The best we can do is gather the clues we're permitted to glimpse and try to draw a conclusion from there. My personal beliefs, while born from skepticism, had transformed through a learned ability to listen to my intuition—as well as to the world around me. Everything speaks if we can only learn how to listen.

It could be what we call faeries are unseen beings that are connected to the energies of the earth. There may be as many types of "faeries" as there are species of animals on our planet. Through interactions over time, we classify them as best we can: trolls, gnomes, leprechauns, flower faeries, the list goes on and on. But they are all energy, just like we are. Different types of energy. And then we have the lordly race also known as the Gentry, the Hidden People, or the Shining Ones. Far superior to us in knowledge, wisdom, and perhaps even their capacity to love, the faery advocate assigned to me in Glastonbury would have been one such being. They are the "nobility" of the faery world—once revered as gods by the Celts. As far as their physicality, I can only speculate. Ninefh had described faeries as spirits that were partially incarnated on the physical plane but lacking in one element. Could that explain how they were able to shimmer into our physical world and make things disappear and reappear at whim? Like the pedometer, the tent poles? Like a black feather in your path? The Aborigines of Australia believe (today!) that humans possess the ability to shape-shift, and there are those among their tribes who practice shape-shifting at will, or so they say. So would it be such a stretch to reconsider the bird in the gardens of Glastonbury? *You know I'm not the bird,* I'd heard in my head. Or to remember the white-haired man staring off into the distance in the fields of Auldyn Glen?

So who were the Fir Bolgs, the Tuatha Dé Danann? Perhaps we'll never know. But what I do know is that the beings we call faeries can sweep into our lives if we only invite them, to show us how to live better, love better, treat our planet better. They can teach us, perhaps, natural ways to heal, and maybe help us come to a better understanding of what our bodies truly need. Necromancers of the spirit world, they show us how to honor our own magic, myths, and legends: in keeping these things alive, we are all a part of the faery faith.

I should have known the faeries would save the best for last. Now that I could recognize it, their fingerprints could be seen all over their handiwork—like magicians, they prefer to unveil mysteries with a masterful flourish.

Raven had sent me a package of pictures from Glastonbury along with the CD of our nighttime ceremony as promised, but I was on deadline and it had remained unopened. As my deadline approached, I got an early morning phone call.

"Signe," Raven said, "I got the strongest feeling this morning that I needed to call you right away. I'm supposed to tell you this: if you sing, you'll find something that you're missing *right now*, for your book."

So of course I tried to sing.

I felt like Will Farrell in Elf: *I'm singing . . . 'cause the faeries told me, that if I'm singing, I'll find something I am looking for . . .*

Meanwhile the unopened package sat there, staring at me accusingly as I worked at my computer. Finally guilted into action, I put my earphones in and let the recording of the ceremony play. After all, what kind of faery researcher was I, if I didn't even review all my evidence? Frankly, I had been embarrassed to hear myself letting it all hang out for the faeries that night in Glastonbury, but I found that I relished being able to experience that night again. I was typing away as I listened somewhat absentmindedly, smiling here and there, when I heard something I simply could not explain.

Turning up the volume, I played it back. At the fifty-four-minute mark, just after we had finishing singing, just as Raven was looking out into the night with tears in her eyes, saying, "They are *definitely* here," there was flute music playing.

Pan flute music to be exact. It sounded somewhat ethereal, disembodied. But it was unmistakable. There was no one else there, and hadn't been the whole night. We had the garden reserved. We certainly hadn't heard anything with our ears—Raven would have definitely said something like, "Oh my God, Signe! Can you hear that? *Faery music!*" To which I would have rolled my eyes. And we were too far away from the bustling shops of Glastonbury for music to have somehow carried over. Even in that case, we would've heard it in real time.

I immediately called Raven to tell her—she'd listened to the recording and not even picked up on it. She was over the moon. I played it for Eric, for my mother. Everyone agreed—it was certainly pan flute music. The pedometer in Ireland, the tent poles—I knew faeries were notorious for being able to take things from our physical world and then being able to somehow bring them back. Was this why the recording had disappeared from Raven's iPod that night, only to show up at the end of our trip with the bizarre 3/3/09 marked as the recording date? If so, I wondered what *else* we might have captured on that recording, prior to its disappearance. If there was something else, it was something we weren't meant to have. And maybe it didn't matter. They had left this one thing.

Somehow, we had captured the music of the faeries.

When it came to my father, my trip had created the breakthrough I was seeking. Though perhaps typical to the ways in which the faery world worked, it was not in a way I'd expected. There was no magical cure for the pain of death. When you lose someone, the pain never goes away. After a while, though, if you're living your life right, it does begin to lessen, one day at a time. Sometimes I think I'm okay, I'm getting over it. I think, *I'm healing, I can do this.* And then I have a bad day—I get into an argument with a friend, or I maybe think I'm losing my mind writing a book about faeries. Those days or nights, when I'm already laid bare, that's when the grief hits me the hardest. It takes hold of me and soon I am rocking in the mess of it all. He was a complicated, sad, beautiful, angry mess, and one hell of a father. What I realize now is that you can't cure a loss; you can only honor it. And as the rocking ceases, I know that I am honoring my father simply by living my life. By pursuing my dreams.

The faeries, it seems, like to tie up all their endings. Now that this adventure was over, where would they leave their messenger, when all the notes have been passed along? What would life be like, here in Charleston, now that I'd peeked behind the veil of possibility?

Sunday, October 4, was a full moon. I watched twilight fall and the bright globe of it rise from the sunroom. Outside the temperature had been cooling; the nights now brought with them a welcome chill. Through the screen door I could hear the peepers still peeping—louder perhaps, now that they felt the end was near. Autumn was coming. I grabbed some chocolate from a drawer in the kitchen and slid back the patio door, stepping barefoot into the night. The red pine stood tall and thick, sheltering our yard with its towering branches. The broken stone bench by the shed glowed in the moonlight, and at the far end of the yard, the leaves of the river birch rustled in the wind. The thick foliage from our wax myrtles had grown dense over the summer, sheltering the yard from our neighbors. I twisted open the paper and foil on the chocolate, breaking it into chunks between my fingers. I placed some on the bench, some beneath the pine, some at the foot of the shaggy old river birch, singing softly.

I wasn't afraid of the night, though these southern shadows sometimes cast themselves in dark and haunting ways. I was afraid of what might happen to me, to my belief, if I tried this in my own backyard and it failed. But now I knew there were many kinds of magic in life. Like the magic of simply being present. The magic of connecting with an old friend. The magic of laughter, of nature, of curiosity, of adventure.

The enchantment we weave into our lives ripples into the lives of others. No matter how small a change, it can inspire if we can only learn to listen, hear it, catch it, obey it—one day we wake up and life can never be the same again.

In that moment I knew I had a magic all my own here in Charleston. I stepped back onto the patio and sat on the cool stone, letting my gaze soften, watching the wax myrtles ruffle in the breeze. Not expecting, just waiting.

A quote came to mind, something I'd come across this past summer from T. S. Eliot. I smiled in the darkness. Now I knew where to put it.

> *We shall not cease from exploration.*
> *And at the end of all our exploring*
> *Will be to arrive where we started*
> *And know the place for the first time.*

ACKNOWLEDGMENTS

This book wouldn't have been possible without the help of many faery godpeople.

To my mother, Linda Johanson, and father, Alan S. Pike, who always urged me to write. You've given me endless untold beautiful moments, and so much love—thank you. And to Kirsten Pike—for being a best friend *and* an older sister to boot.

To my literary agent, Yfat Reiss Gendell—a dear friend and the quintessential professional, who possesses the quickest wit, most effortless sense of style in everything, and the brightest spirit. The team at Perigee has wowed me with their warmth, drive, and collaborative spirit. I owe endless thanks to my editor, Marian Lizzi, for guiding me with unwavering vision, talent, and belief. Much gratitude goes out to publisher John Duff, marketing director Patrick Nolan, and publicity manager Melissa Broder. To editorial assistant Christina Lundy for her kind and polished professionalism, managing editor Jennifer Eck, and cover designer Andrea Ho. Last but never least, my gratitude goes out to the Penguin sales force, whom I've seen firsthand are simply the best in the business.

Thanks to all who helped me find my footing on the faery path: Brian and Wendy Froud, Robert Gould, Eddie Lenihan, Shelagh Weeden, Lini Seward, Jill Schmitt, Mike and Ali Read, Charlotte MacKenzie, Bob Curran, Peter Guy, Anne and Declan Guy, Karla Gutiérrez, Ed Lenahan (for bookmarks!), Diana McClure, Coleen Shaughnessy, Ellen Whitehurst, Jo and Ed, and always to my big cousin Stan the Man. To Raven Keyes, without whom there would be no book, and who makes each day magical. To Elizabeth Paulson and Stephanie Higgs, for our friendship and many more adventures to come. To John, Wol, Big John, Joe, Paul, Huw, Mark, and Sam—keep the stove on, I'm a-comin'. I am ever grateful to Jon Cuizon, for all the light. And to my gal-pal Lindsey Benoit, a beautiful girl and a Mack truck of energy and enthusiasm, who consulted on publicity for Faery Tale.

Endless thanks to the talented writers who gave Faery Tale an early read: Carolyn Turgeon, Michael Taeckens, Jeanine Cummins, Cathy Alter, Jennifer Finney Boylan, Sharman Apt Russell, Jillian Lauren, David Yeadon, A. J. Jacobs, Lucy Danziger, Rita Goldman Gelman, and Tanis Helliwell.

To all my friends and family for letting me talk as crazy as I damn well wanted to, and loving me all the same: Nancy and Mark Liebetrau, Dick and Grace Leighton, Ben and Cameron Liebetrau, Becky Saletan and Marshall Messer, Rebecca Campbell, Anthony McGowan (and Gabriel and Rose), Elizabeth Butler, Liv Cook, Laura All. And to my little cousin Murielle Johanson—the coolest kid I know.

Most of all, to Eric Liebetrau, my husband, without whom this book would never have been possible: I'll be contemplating over the next few decades how I can thank you enough for your unwavering love and support as I undertook this journey.

You are my happily ever after.

FAERY INTERESTING READING AND EXPLORATION

Janet Bord, *The Traveller's Guide to Fairy Sites*, Gothic Image Publications, 2004

Cassandra Eason, *A Complete Guide to Faeries & Magical Beings*, Weiser Books, 2002

Peter Berresford Ellis, *Celtic Myths and Legends*, Carroll & Graf Publishers, 2002

W. Y. Evans-Wentz, *The Fairy-Faith in Celtic Countries*, Forgotten Books, 2007

Anna Franklin, *Working with Fairies*, New Page Books, 2006

Brian Froud, *Brian Froud's World of Faerie*, Insight Editions, 2007

Wendy Froud, *The Art of Wendy Froud*, Imaginosis, 2006, www.worldoffroud.com

Raven Keyes, www.ravenkeyes.com

Peter Knight, www.stoneseeker.net

Eddie Lenihan and Carolyn Eve Green, *Meeting the Other Crowd*, Tarcher, 2004, www.eddielenihan.com

Charlotte MacKenzie, www.cm-healer.co.uk

John Matthews, *The Sidhe: Wisdom from the Celtic Underworld*, Lorian Press, 2004

Diana McClure, www.etsy.com/shop/FairieHomes

Edain McCoy, *A Witch's Guide to Faery Folk*, Llewellyn, 1994

Stan Munroe, www.toothpickcity.com

Jo Rowe-Leete, dartmoorjoro@gmail.com

Coleen Shaughnessy, www.coleenshaughnessy.com

Otta Swire, *Skye: The Island and Its Legends*, Birlinn Limited, 2006

William Butler Yeats, *The Celtic Twilight*, Dover Publications, 2004

READERS GUIDE

Faery Tale
Signe Pike

1. As *Faery Tale* opens, Pike describes the loss of hopefulness and wonder she experienced as the realities of adult life set in. Have you ever felt this way? How does Pike's perspective shift when she ventures out to investigate the legitimacy of unseen forces in our world?

2. Faith proves to be an integral step on Pike's journey toward belief. In your opinion, what is the relationship between belief and faith? Is it possible to have one without the other, or are they one and the same?

3. Black feathers, sparkling lights, ethereal music caught in a deserted garden—these are only a few of the signs that Pike attributes to faerie activity in the book. How did Pike's encounters with an unseen world strike you?

4. The importance of stories—our personal ones as well as myths passed down over generations—is a major theme in the book. Does a story have to be factually true to hold meaning? Do we lose something when our stories are lost?

5. It was the untimely death of Pike's father that moved her to begin research-ing the unseen. But her relationship with her father was a complicated one. Did her journey teach her anything about the question of life after death? In what ways did researching faeries help her come to terms with her grief and deep sense of loss regarding the death of her father?

6. Brian and Wendy Froud believe that faeries can use our imaginations and thought patterns to project themselves and communicate with us. Do you agree with this sentiment? Why or why not?

7. At the foundation of *Faery Tale* is the hope that we can treat the earth, each other, and all living beings with more consideration and respect. How can searching for faeries help us be more attuned to the world around us?

8. Pike writes, "The enchantment we weave into our lives ripples into the lives of others. No matter how small a change, it can inspire if we can only learn to listen, hear it, catch it, obey it—one day we wake up and life can never be the same again." Did *Faery Tale* inspire you to seek enchantment on your own, and if so, in what ways?

9. In the woods on the Isle of Man, Pike had a terrifying feeling she was being pursued, and later uncovers the story of Betsy Crowe. What connection, if any, do you think the murder of Betsy Crowe had with Pike and her search for faeries?

10. Putting the pieces together: As Pike began to research the existence of faeries, strange linkages and connections began to appear. Were they signs, signals, or instructions? Pike believes that her memoir resulted in a book filled with clues left by the faeries for herself and her readers. But what do these clues amount to? What clues or meaningful events can you find? How do they relate to one another? What might they mean? And which clues or events are most significant to you as a reader?

Scour the text with a keen eye—you may even discover hidden connec-tions that Pike herself has yet to find.

ABOUT THE AUTHOR

Signe Pike lives in Charleston, South Carolina, with her husband, Eric Liebetrau; a fat dog named Lucy; a mischievous black cat named Willoughby; and, of course, their resident faeries. She is currently at work on her next exploration into things unseen. Visit www.signepike.com to write to her, to find information on upcoming workshops and retreats, or to see photos and evidence collected from her journey.